INTERNET
SECURITY
DICTIONARY

Springer

New York
Berlin
Heidelberg
Barcelona
Hong Kong
London
Milan
Paris
Singapore
Tokyo

INTERNET
SECURITY
DICTIONARY

VIR V. PHOHA

Springer

Vir V. Phoha
phoha@acm.org

LIBRARY OF CONGRESS CATALOGING-IN-PUBLICATION DATA

Phoha, Vir V.
Internet security dictionary / Vir V. Phoha.
p.   cm.
Includes bibliographical references and index.
ISBN 0-387-95261-6 (sc : alk. paper)
1. Computer networks—Security measures—Dictionaries.
2. Internet—Security measures—Dictionaries.   I. Titles.
TK5105.59 .P56   2002
005.8′03—dc21   2001053056

Printed on acid-free paper.

Text design by Steven Pisano.
Manufacturing supervised by Jerome Basma.
Typeset by Impressions Book and Journal Services, Inc., Madison, WI.
Printed and bound by Edwards Brothers, Inc., Ann Arbor, MI.
Printed in the United States of America.

9 8 7 6 5 4 3 2 1

ISBN 0-387-95261-6   SPIN 10796881

Springer-Verlag   New York Berlin Heidelberg
A member of BertelsmannSpringer Science + Business Media GmbH

This work is dedicated to my father

KRISHAN LAL PHOHA

for his example and encouragement,

which have put me on the

path of intellectual discovery, and

to my late mother

SHANTI RANI PHOHA

for her spiritual guidance.

CONTENTS

INTERNET SECURITY TERMS *1*

APPENDIXES

PREFACE

Recent years have seen an explosive growth of the Internet. When the Internet passed from government and academic realms to the public sector, it brought along a laissez-faire attitude about security. Its explosive growth, flaws in its basic structure, its facilitation of instant access to information repositories, and its widespread availability has made it increasingly vulnerable. There have been many malicious attempts, or *attacks* to exploit this vulnerability of the Internet from all over the world; the attacks on the Internet have kept pace with the growth of the Internet.

The natural instinct of individuals, organizations, and nations to protect themselves against attacks and operational intrusions or upsets in the flow of information has spawned a high level of interest, research activity, and technological developments in the Internet security field. New security protocols, and new countermeasures against attacks that break, slow, or inconvenience users and organizations are evolving every day. These developments constantly introduce new terms and concepts into the Internet security vocabulary. Although nascent, the field has gained sufficient maturity that its vocabulary can begin to be standardized for common use by professionals. This dictionary is an effort to organize and define these terms precisely and coherently.

PURPOSE AND SCOPE

The purpose of this dictionary is to provide reliable definitions and descriptions of Internet security terms in clear and precise English. Designed as a tool to bring about a common understanding of technical terms to the lay user and the professional, the dictionary will serve as an introduction to Internet security for the nonprofessional user who is looking for the precise meaning(s) of a specific term or for a cursory overview of the field. This dictionary should also serve as a reference for the security professional who is an expert in a specialized area and who may need to refer to precise or commonly accepted meanings of terms.

The terms collected in this dictionary are those used by researchers, designers, developers, manufacturers, vendors, system administrators, and other users of Internet security technology. These terms were taken primarily from the technical literature, including journal articles and magazines, books, and Requests for Comments (RFCs).

This dictionary covers eight main areas: (1) authentication, including biometrics, encryption/public key infrastructure, digital signatures, timestamping, and certificate management; (2) encryption; (3) network-level security, including IP, IPsec, SHTTP, and SSL; (4) firewalls and remote management; (5) Internet security policies, risk analysis, integration across platforms, management and auditing; (6) mobile code security, Java/Active X/scripts, and mobile agent code; (7) virus protection and intrusion detection; and (8) security in Internet commerce. Since the TCP/IP protocol is at the heart of Internet routing, this dictionary contains many terms related to server processes, TCP/IP, and routing as well.

FEATURES

This dictionary addresses all major aspects of Internet security technology, provides detailed definitions and illustrations where required for clarity, gives cross-references for easy backtracking of terms, and lists each acronym as a separate entry with a reference to the full term it identifies. The accompanying CD-ROM version contains a searchable PDF version of the complete dictionary. Viewing the PDF file requires that the Adobe Acrobat Reader be installed on the computer. The Adobe Acrobat Reader can be downloaded free of cost from the Adobe Web site, http://www.adobe.com.

REVIEW PROCESS

Security experts from around the world have been consulted in both the content and the organization of the dictionary to ensure authoritative, comprehensive coverage. A distinguished board of experts drawn from academia, industry, and government has reviewed the selected list of terms for comprehensiveness, and the description of each term for accuracy and usefulness. This board has been carefully chosen to represent eminent researchers and leaders in Internet security, computer science, engineering applications, and a broad spectrum of Internet users for specialized technology developments and everyday activity.

I plan to keep the contents of the dictionary up-to-date. Please send suggestions to include important new Internet security terms or comments for improvement to phoha@acm.org.

ACKNOWLEDGMENTS

A work of this size requires help from many people. First and foremost, I would like to thank the Technical Advisory Board of this dictionary, especially the chair of the board, Shashi Phoha, for taking time out of a busy schedule to support this work. I greatly appreciate her guidance and vision in critical junctures of this project, in particular her help in assembling an outstanding team of experts who resolved differences in interpretations of terms among the board members.

I am thankful for extensive feedback and discussion with many of the board members for making the definitions precise, clear, and useful. Any omissions and errors are mine. Acting on all the suggestions was painful but it has made this work better. Thank you every one, this work is where it is because of your guidance and encouragement. I would like to thank Richard Brooks, Sandi Brown, James Chase, and John Zachry for reviewing the text of the dictionary.

I would like to thank Wayne Yuhasz, executive editor of computer and information science, Springer-Verlag, who saw promise in my initial ideas and had the vision and patience to help develop this work into its present form. I would like to acknowledge his help in improving the structure, grammar, and style of presentation in this work. He is a consistent source of inspiration, ideas, and encouragement. I am fortunate to have his guidance, support, and feedback. Thank you, Wayne. This work would not have been possible without your help.

I would like to thank Wayne Wheeler, assistant editor, for excellent cooperation, encouragement and for answering my questions promptly.

I would like to thank Steven Pisano, senior production editor, and his team for promptly answering my questions, for the hardwork put into copyediting the manuscript, and for production of the book. Thanks also go to Michael Spano and his marketing team.

ORGANIZATION AND USAGE

ORGANIZATION OF THE DICTIONARY

We have tried to make the organization of this dictionary clear and self-explanatory, but a few guidelines may help the reader. This dictionary contains *terms,* arranged in a strict alphabetical word order, ignoring capital letters, hyphens, slashes, and other forms of punctuation in the sequencing. Numbers are ordered before the letters; thus A1 comes before Ab. Each term is followed by a *description.* The descriptive text is written in American English. If a term has more than one meaning, each is indicated by a number in parentheses, the most common meaning being shown first.

Each acronym is listed as a separate entry with a reference(s) to the full term(s) it identifies. Entries or organizations referred to in the description that relate only to the United States are followed in the text by (U.S.).

Some terms contain cross-references. If a cross-referenced term is defined elsewhere in the dictionary, it is italicized. An example follows:

Term	**Beyond A1**
Description	Determines a level of trust defined by the DoD TRUSTED COMPUTER SYSTEM EVALUATION CRITERIA (U.S.) to be beyond the state-of-the-art technology. Includes all the A1-level features plus additional ones not required at the A1-level. *See also* the ORANGE BOOK.

Some terms in the dictionary cross-refer to other terms and parts of the dictionary. A description of the terminology used for cross-references follows.

See also refers to another entry with a related or similar meaning, or to a term that has additional information. Other cross-references point to **figures, appendixes,** and **notes** in the dictionary. Figures explain or add to the description of a term and follow or are contained in the description of a term. Notes contain additional information relevant to the term. Each Note follows the entry for the term it treats. Many entries refer to the RFCs given in an appendix or to citations in the Bibliography.

The following terminology explains the notation used to refer to figures and notes:

See FIGURE A5 refers to the fifth figure in the section of words starting with the letter A. If the figure is referred to from another term, then the name of the term that contains the figure is enclosed in parentheses following the term: *See* FIGURE C3 (TERM).

See NOTE refers to the note corresponding to the term given in the dictionary. If the note is referred to from another term, then the name of the term that contains the note is enclosed in parentheses following the term: *See* NOTE (HACKER).

An example follows.

> **bespoke** A product or service that is custom made or tailored to individual needs. Also called custom-designed software. *See also* COTS.
> NOTE (1) *Bespoke* is pronounced bee-SPOHK and is more commonly used in the United Kingdom. In the U.S. custom-made or custom-designed software is more common. Traditionally *bespoke* is applied to custom-tailored clothing, but the usage has been extended to information technology. Example usage: Dreamware software company offers *bespoke* software. (2) *Bespoke* is a derivation from the word bespeak, which means ordering of goods; this usage of bespeak can be traced back to 1583.

CD-ROM

The accompanying CD-ROM contains a searchable PDF version of the dictionary. In addition, the dictionary has a complete content index with hotlinks to all the sections, headings, and beginning of every letter in the alphabet. The PDF default settings are adjusted such that a user's Adobe Reader will open with a table of contents bar in the left pane of the Adobe Acrobat window. This helps the reader scan through the Contents and go directly to a list of entries.

Adobe Acrobat Reader can be downloaded free of cost from the Adobe web site, http://www.adobe.com.

STARTING THE CD-ROM

Insert the accompanying disk into the CD-ROM drive, click start, and then choose browse and make sure that the CD-ROM drive is selected. Double click InternetSecurityDictionary.pdf and then click on the icons that you want to choose.

ADOBE ACROBAT READER TIPS

The default settings of the PDF version of the dictionary are set to open with the table of contents set on the left side.

- To increase the viewable size of the page use Ctrl+ and to decrease the viewable size press Ctrl-or the use the page icons on the tool bar.

- To go to the next page or the previous page use the arrows < > on the toolbar.

ADVISORY BOARD

tributed to national and European projects in the areas of dependable communications and computing. He is a member of the review board of a *German focal research programme (DFG SPP) on information security,* and coeditor-in-chief of the *International Journal of Information Security* to be published by Springer-Verlag. He has served on the program committees of the major European conferences on computer security and cryptography and of other international conferences in these areas. He has published numerous research papers on topics in cryptography, information security, and mathematics, and is the author of a textbook *Computer Security.* Dr.tech. (1984) from the University of Linz, Austria.

• LI GONG

Distinguished Engineer and Director of Engineering, Peer-to-Peer Networking, at Sun Microsystems, Inc. Sun's Chief Java Security Architect and Manager of the Java Soft Security and Networking Group during JDK 1.1 and 1.2 developments. He is the author of *Inside Java 2 Platform Security* (Addison-Wesley, 1999). Previously worked at the Stanford Research Institute as a research scientist. Editorial board member *of IEEE Internet Computing.* Associate editor of *ACM Transactions on Information and System Security.* Program chair of the *IEEE Symposium on Security and Privacy, the ACM Conference on Computer and Communications Security,* and the *IEEE Computer Security Foundations Workshop.* Ph.D. from the University of Cambridge.

• S. SITHARAMA IYENGAR

Professor and Chair of the Department of Computer Science at Louisiana State University. Fellow of IEEE and Fellow of the American Association of the Advancement of Science. Awarded the 1999 LSU-Prestigious Distinguished Research Master Award and a University Medal. Authored, coauthored, or edited ten books, including one that was on the bestseller list. Series editor of *Neuro Com-*

puting of Complex Systems and Area Editor for the *Journal of Computer Science and Information.* Over 250 research publications.

• STEPHEN KENT

Chief Scientist, Information Security at BBN Networks. He has chaired the Privacy and Security Research Group of the Internet Research Task Force since its inception in 1985. He is also the cochair of the Public Key Infrastructure working group. He is the author or coauthor of numerous publications on network security. S.M. and Ph.D. (MIT).

• JOHN MCLEAN

Director of the Center for High Assurance Computer Systems and Senior Scientist for Information Assurance at the Naval Research Laboratory. Adjunct Professor of Computer Science at the University of Maryland, the National Cryptological School and Troisième Cycle Romand d'Informatique. Senior Research Fellow of the University of Cambridge Centre for Communication Research and Chair and U.S. National Leader of the Technical Cooperation Program (TTCP) C4I Technical Panel on High Assurance Systems and Defensive Information Warfare. Associate editor of *Distributed Computing, Journal of Computer Security,* and *ACM Transactions on Information and System Security.* Ph.D. in Philosophy in 1980 from the University of North Carolina at Chapel Hill.

• ALFRED MENEZES (Canada)

Professor, University of Waterloo and member of the managing board of the Centre for Applied Cryptographic Research. Previously worked at Auburn University, Alabama. He is on the editorial board of *Designs, Codes, and Cryptography* and an accreditation board member of *Computer & Communications Security Reviews.* His primary research interests are in elliptic curve cryptography, key establishment protocols, practice-oriented provable security, and wireless security. He has published numerous research papers in cryptography, and is coauthor of the *Handbook of Applied Cryptography* and author of *Elliptic Curve Public Key Cryptosystems.* Ph.D. (1992) University of Waterloo, Canada.

• FLEMMING NIELSON (Denmark)
Professor at the Technical University of Denmark, previously guest professor at the Max Planck Institute of Computer Science and Associate Professor at the University of Aarhus. Site leader for the project *Secure and Safe Systems based on Static Analysis* funded by the European Union. Author of several books and numerous journal and conference articles. Ph.D. from the University of Edinburgh (1984) and a D.Sc. from the University of Aarhus (1990).

• EIJI OKAMOTO (Japan)
Professor at Department of Information Science, Toho University, Japan. Previously worked at University of Wisconsin, Texas A & M University, Japan Advanced Institute of Science and Technology, and Central Research Laboratories, NEC Corporation. Editor or author of eight books on information security. Editor-in-chief of *International Journal of Information Security,* General Cochair of ISC2001 and many other conferences and symposia in information security. Ph.D. (1978) Tokyo Institute of Technology.

• SHASHI PHOHA
Chair of the Technical Advisory Board. Director of Information Science and Technology Division at the Applied Research Laboratory and Professor of Electrical and Computer Engineering, Pennsylvania State University. Founder and Director of a University/Industry consortium for establishing a National Information Infrastructure Interoperability Testbed, funded by DARPA. Member of the Board of Directors of the International Consortium CERES Global Knowledge Network, along with representatives of thirteen other international universities. On the Board of Directors

of Autonomous Undersea Vehicle Technology Consortium for International Cooperation Between Research, Technology, Industry and Applications. Panelist on the National Information Infrastructure Standards Panel (ANSI). Author of over 150 scholarly articles and book chapters. M.S. (1973) Cornell University, Ph.D. (1976) Michigan State University.

• ASOK RAY
Professor of Mechanical Engineering, Pennsylvania State University. Previously worked at Carnegie Mellon University, Massachusetts Institute of Technology, GTE Strategic Systems, the Charles Stark Draper Laboratory, and MITRE. Fellow of ASME. Editor of *IEEE Transactions on Aerospace and Electronic Systems* and Associate editor of *IEEE Transactions on Control Systems Technology.* Author of a Springer-Verlag book, *Intelligent Seam Tracking for Robotic Welding* (1993), and over 350 research publications.

• JEFFREY SCHILLER
Network Manager at Massachusetts Institute of Technology (MIT). He is a coauthor of *Kerberos* cryptographic authentication system, which is widely used in secure operating environments. He served as the manager and principal designer of the MIT campus computer network since its inception in 1984. He is an area director for security on the Internet Engineering Steering Group (IESG) and oversees security-related working groups of the Internet Engineering Task Force (IETF). He is also a founding member of the Internet Privacy Coalition.

• JOHN YESBERG (Australia)
Senior Research Scientist at Australia's Defence Science and Technology Organization, specializing in high-assurance information security systems. Also a visiting scholar at the University of Queensland's Software Verification Research Centre. Ph.D. from University of Queensland, Australia.

INTERNET
SECURITY
TERMS

A

A1 The NATIONAL COMPUTER SECURITY CENTER (NCSC) of the U.S. Department of Defense has published TRUSTED COMPUTER SYSTEM EVALUATION CRITERIA (DoD 5200.28-STD, also referred to as the ORANGE BOOK. The ORANGE BOOK defines a series of security ratings such as A1, B2, B3, C1, C2, and D. Here is a brief explanation of the ratings: **D:** MINIMAL PROTECTION. This rating is given to systems that do not qualify for higher ratings. **C1:** DISCRETIONARY SECURITY PROTECTION. Requirements correspond roughly to those expected from a classical time-sharing system. **C2:** CONTROLLED ACCESS PROTECTION. Additional requirements for C2 are access control at a per user granularity, clearing of allocated memory, and auditing. **B1:** LABELED SECURITY PROTECTION. Additional requirements over C2 are security labels. **B2:** STRUCTURED PROTECTION. Additional requirements of B2 over B1 include a trusted path to the user, notification of security-level changes to the user when a process started by the user changes its security level. The OS should be structured so that only a minimal portion of it is security sensitive. COVERT CHANNELS must be identified and their bandwidth estimated.

B3: SECURITY DOMAINS. Additional requirements involve the absence of bugs in the operating system that would allow the circumvention of MANDATORY ACCESS CONTROLS. **A1:** VERIFIED DESIGN has the highest level of trust defined in the ORANGE BOOK and contains formal procedures for the analysis of the system's design and rigorous controls on its implementation.

A5 A GSM standard for digital cellular mobile telephones. A5 is a stream cipher with 64-bit keys that is used to ENCRYPT a link from the telephone to the base station. *See also* GSM.

Abstract Syntax Notation 1 An ISO standard for data representation and data structure definitions. More details of ABSTRACT SYNTAX NOTATION 1 (ASN.1) may be obtained from http://www.asn1.org/.

access The opportunity to make use of a resource such as a database, a program, or a module; a part of memory; or any information system (IS) resource.

access control Governs direct access to information resources according to security requirements. Access control consists of (1) high-level access policies and rules that define permitted access and (2) control procedures (security mechanisms) implementing these policies.

access control list (1) A data structure associated with a resource (object) that specifies the users (subjects) and their rights on this resource. ACCESS CONTROL LIST (ACL) is different from a CAPABILITY. (2) In an object-oriented system, an ACL describes how other objects can relate to its objects, whereas CAPABILITY describes how this object can relate to other objects.

access control mechanism A security safeguard that enforces security rules and policies to prevent unauthorized access to system resources while permitting authorized accesses. Requiring a user ID and password to log on to a computer system is an example of an ACCESS CONTROL MECHANISM.

access control set A synonym for ACCESS CONTROL LIST.

access level Used to label the sensitivity of data and resources. Secrecy and integrity levels are combined to form a label (S, I), where S defines the sensitivity level and I the integrity level. For example, SeaView Model uses access level to implement both BLP and Biba security models. The hierarchical portion of the security level is used to identify the sensitivity of IS data and the CLEARANCE or AUTHORIZATION of users. Access level, in conjunction with the nonhierarchical categories, forms the sensitivity label of an object. *See also* CATEGORY.

access list Refers to a compilation of users, programs, or processes and the access levels and types to which each is authorized.

access mode ☞ ACCESS TYPE.

access period A segment of time, generally expressed in days or weeks, during which access rights prevail.

access profile Associates each user with a list of protected objects the user may access.

access type The type of action [operation] that is permitted on an object. Read, write, execute, append, modify, delete, and create are examples of access types.

accessible space The area within which the user is aware of all persons entering and leaving. This area denies the opportunity for concealed TEMPEST surveillance, and delineates the closest point of potential TEMPEST intercept from a vehicle. *See also* INSPECTABLE SPACE.

accountability The process allowing for the auditing of IS activities to be traced to a source that may then be held responsible.

accounting legend code The numeric code used to indicate the minimum accounting controls required for items of accountable COMSEC MATERIAL within the COMSEC MATERIAL CONTROL SYSTEM.

accounting number A number assigned to an item of COMSEC MATERIAL to facilitate its control.

accreditation The formal declaration by a DESIGNATED APPROVING AUTHORITY (DAA) that approval is given for an IS to be operated in a particular security mode using a prescribed set of safeguards. ACCREDITATION is given only when the DAA judges that the associated level of risk is acceptable.

accreditation package A product comprising a SYSTEM SECURITY PLAN (SSP) and a report documenting the basis for the ACCREDITATION decision.

accrediting authority Synonymous with DESIGNATED APPROVING AUTHORITY (DAA).

accuracy A security principle that keeps information from being modified or otherwise corrupted, either maliciously or accidentally. ACCURACY protects against forgery or tampering. *See also* INTEGRITY.

ACL ☞ ACCESS CONTROL LIST.

active Denotes something that requires action on the part of the user as opposed to no action (passive). The use of ACTIVE is common in a security context, for example, a security alarm that requires a user to turn it on is an ACTIVE restraint, whereas an airbag in a car is a PASSIVE restraint.

active attack A type of attack that involves altering a system's status or content, for example, changing the contents of a file or adding additional files, in contrast to a PASSIVE ATTACK like browsing.

active threat A type of threat that involves the alteration—not simply the interception—of information. For example: an active tap is a type of wiretapping that accesses and COMPROMISES data, usually by generating false messages or control signals, or by altering communications between legitimate users. The danger of an ACTIVE THREAT is primarily the authenticity of the information being transmitted. Contrast with PASSIVE THREAT.

add-on security Hardware, software, or firmware mechanisms that can be incorporated into an already operational IS to provide new security benefits. Synonyms include retrofittable security and insertible security.

address mask Also called NETMASK. A bit mask used to select bits from an IPv4 Internet address for subnet addressing. The mask is 32 bits long and selects the network portion of the Internet address and one or more bits of the local portion. Sometimes called a SUBNET MASK. In Figure

A1, the host address 138.47.18.156 is bitwise ANDed with the SUBNET MASK 255.255.255.0 to get the SUBNET ADDRESS 138.47.18.0. Subnetting allows a single network address to be shared among multiple subnets, each of which may be a physically distinct network. The number of subnets depends upon the choice of ADDRESS MASK. All hosts on a subnet are configured with a same mask. *See also* SUBNET MASK.

administrative security The management of rules and procedures that result in the protection of a computer system and its data. Sometimes called PROCEDURAL SECURITY.

address resolution A means for mapping a network layer address onto a media-specific address, for example, mapping an IP address to an Ethernet or token ring address.

Address Resolution Protocol The INTERNET PROTOCOL used to dynamically map INTERNET ADDRESS to physical address on lo-

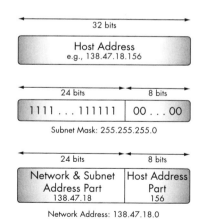

FIGURE A1. Use of an address mask to get a subnet address.

cal area networks. It is limited to networks that support hardware broadcast.

NOTE: *RFC 826 outlines the details to convert network protocol addresses to 48-bit Ethernet addresses for transmission on 10 Mbit ETHERNET hardware. Generalization of this protocol to hardware other than 10 Mbit ETHERNET have also been made.*

Advanced Encryption Standard   A new U.S. government encryption standard that supercedes DES. The ADVANCED ENCRYPTION STANDARD (AES) specifies the Rijndael algorithm with key sizes of 128, 192, and 256 bits and a block size of 128 bits.

Advanced Research Project Agency Currently called DARPA. The U.S. government agency that funded the ARPANET. *See also* DEFENSE ADVANCED RESEARCH PROJECTS AGENCY.

adversary   (1) A person or organization who is an opponent, competitor, or an enemy who may want to destroy or disable an (your) IS and who must be denied ACCESS to information. (2) Someone who is trying to thwart a security system.

advisory   The assessment of significant new trends or developments regarding the threat to the IS of an organization. This assessment may include analytical insights into trends, intentions, technologies, or tactics of adversaries. Examples include CERT advisories. *See also* CERT.

AES ☞   ADVANCED ENCRYPTION STANDARD.

AFIWC ☞   AIR FORCE INFORMATION WARFARE CENTER.

Air Force Information Warfare Center The U.S. AIR FORCE INFORMATION WARFARE CENTER (AFIWC) was activated on September 10, 1993, to meet the need created by the growing importance of information warfare. It was created to be "an informa-

tion superiority center of excellence devoted to offensive and defensive counter-information and information operations." (It has existed under various names since 1953; see note below.) It draws on the technical strength from the former Air Force Electronic Warfare Center, the Air Force Cryptologic Support Center's Securities Directorate, and Air Force Intelligence Command. Its mission is to "explore, apply, and migrate offensive and defensive information warfare capabilities for operations, acquisition and testing, and provide advanced information warfare training for the Air Force." See http://www.aia.af.mil/common/homepages/pa/cyberspokesman/jan/atc3.htm.

NOTE: *The AFWIC has had many name changes. In July 1953 AFIWC was first activated as the 6901st Special Communication Center. In August 1 953 it was renamed the Air Force Special Communication Center and in 1975 it was redesignated the Air Force Electronic Warfare Center.*

ALC ☞   ACCOUNTING LEGEND CODE.

alert   Generally refers to a notification of a computer-based threat or an attack directed at the IS of an organization.

alternative COMSEC custodian   Person or a group designated to perform the duties of the COMSEC CUSTODIAN during his/her temporary absence.

American National Standards Institute One of several U.S. organizations that develop standards including those for computer networking and security.

American Standard Code for Information Interchange   A mapping between text characters and binary numbers. *See also* EBCDIC.

NOTE: *UNIX and DOS-based OPERATING SYSTEMS, except Windows NT, use the AMERICAN STANDARD CODE FOR INFORMATION*

INTERCHANGE (ASCII) for text files. Windows NT uses UNICODE.

ankle-biter   A person with limited knowledge or expertise related to computers or information sciences who wants to hack into systems, for example, those who use programs downloaded from the INTERNET to break into systems. Also known as SCRIPT KIDDIE.

anomaly detection model   A model of intrusion detection characterized by recognizing deviations from the normal behavior (anomalous) of a process or a network. Examples of anomalies include slow response despite light system load, frequent ACCESS to specific files, and unusual combinations of system calls.

anonymous electronic cash   Electronic cash that does not leave a trail to the person who spent it.

ANSI   ☞   AMERICAN NATIONAL STANDARDS INSTITUTE.

antijam   Measures to ensure communications despite deliberate attempts to jam the transmitted information.

antispoof   Measures and techniques to prevent an opponent masquerading as a different identity or machine.

API   ☞   APPLICATION PROGRAM INTERFACE.

applet   A "small application" that is a Java program that runs on a browser. The Java model imposes certain security restrictions on applets, including inability to read or write to the local file system and to open network connections to any system other than the host from which the APPLET was downloaded.

application layer   The topmost layer in the TCP/IP model, providing application protocols for services like electronic mail, file transfer, and remote terminal connection.

application program interface   A set of calling conventions defining how a service is invoked through a software package.

ARP   ☞   ADDRESS RESOLUTION PROTOCOL.

ARPA   ☞   ADVANCED RESEARCH PROJECT AGENCY.

ARPANET   A packet-switched NETWORK developed in the early 1970s that was the primary demonstration of networking computer systems. ARPANET was decommissioned in June 1990. The present INTERNET evolved from ARPANET.

ASCII   ☞   AMERICAN STANDARD CODE FOR INFORMATION INTERCHANGE.

ASN.1   ☞   ABSTRACT SYNTAX NOTATION 1.

assurance   ☞   INFORMATION ASSURANCE.

asymmetric cryptography   A CRYPTOGRAPHIC system where ENCRYPTION and DECRYPTION are performed using different keys. These schemes use two mathematically related keys. The DECRYPTION key is hard to determine from the encryption key. An ENCRYPTION key, or PUBLIC KEY, is made known, but the decryption key, or private key, is kept secret. Encryption and decryption are two mathematical functions that are inverses of each other. Also called PUBLIC KEY CRYPTOGRAPHY. See Figure A2. *See also* SECRET KEY CRYPTOGRAPHY.

Athena   A project conducted at the Massachusetts Institute of Technology that developed a number of interesting technologies, including the KERBEROS cryptographic authentication system.

attack   An unauthorized intentional act on a computer, a NETWORK, or an IS with malicious intent.

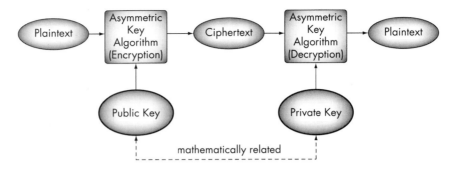

FIGURE A2. Asymmetric key encryption.

attention character In TRUSTED COMPUT-ING BASE (TCB) design, a character entered from a terminal that tells the TCB that the user wants a secure communications path from the terminal to some trusted code to provide a secure service for the user.

audit To examine a record of events that might have some security significance such as when ACCESS to resources occurred.

audit log ☞ AUDIT TRAIL.

audit record ☞ AUDIT TRAIL.

audit trail The chronological record of system activities, used to enable the recon-struction and examination of the sequence of events and/or changes in an event.

authenticate To determine that some-thing is genuine. In the context of INTERNET security, to reliably determine the identity of an individual or communicating party (peer entity authentication) or the source of a message (data origin authentication).

authentication The process of reliably determining the identity of a communicating party or the source of a message.

authentication header A field that pro-vides integrity and AUTHENTICATION checks in an INTERNET PROTOCOL packet format.

authentication system The cryptosys-tem or process used for AUTHENTICATION.

authenticator (1) Used to confirm the identity of a station, originator, or individ-ual. It can be something the user has, e.g., a smart card or DONGLE; something the user knows, e.g., a password or challenge re-sponse; or a physical characteristic of the user, e.g., fingerprint or a retina scan. (2) A field in a message used to establish its source.

authenticity A security principle that en-sures that a message is received in exactly the form in which it was sent. *See also* MES-SAGE AUTHENTICATION CODE.

authorization Permission to ACCESS a resource.

authorized vendor The manufacturer of INFOSEC equipment authorized to pro-duce quantities in excess of contractual re-quirements for direct sale to eligible buy-ers. Eligible buyers are typically U.S. government organizations or U.S. govern-ment contractors. *See also* AUTHORIZED VEN-DOR PROGRAM.

Authorized Vendor Program Program in which a vendor producing an INFOSEC

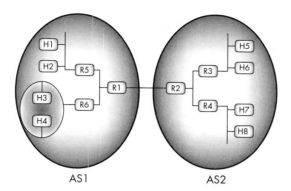

FIGURE A3. An example of a network with two autonomous systems, AS1 and AS2.

product under contract to the NATIONAL SECURITY AGENCY (U.S.) is authorized to produce that product in numbers exceeding the contracted requirements for direct marketing and sale to eligible buyers. Eligible buyers are typically U.S. government organizations or U.S. government contractors. Products approved for marketing and sale through the AUTHORIZED VENDOR PROGRAM are placed on the Endorsed Cryptographic Products List.

auto-manual system Programmable, hand-held CRYPTO-EQUIPMENT used to perform ENCODING and DECODING functions.

automated security monitoring The use of automated procedures to ensure that security controls are not circumvented. Also, the use of these tools to track actions taken by subjects suspected of misusing an IS.

automatic home agent discovery Process by which a mobile node obtains the address of a home agent on its home NETWORK. This process requires the transmission of a registration request to the subnet broadcast address of its home NETWORK.

automatic remote rekeying A procedure to rekey a distant CRYPTO-EQUIPMENT electronically without specific actions by the receiving terminal operator.

autonomous system Internet (TCP/IP) terminology for a collection of gateways (routers) that fall under one administrative entity and cooperate using a common Interior Gateways Protocol. In Figure A3, R denotes a router, for example, R1 is router 1, and H denotes a host, for example, H1 denotes host 1.

availability Timely, reliable ACCESS to data and information services for authorized users.

B

B1 ☞ A1.

B2 ☞ A1.

B3 ☞ A1.

backbone The primary mechanism connecting a hierarchical distributed system. All systems that are connected to an intermediate system on the backbone are assured of being connected to each other. This mechanism does not prevent systems from setting up private arrangements with each other to bypass the backbone for reasons of cost, performance, or security.

back door Synonymous with TRAP DOOR.

background authentication AUTHENTICATION that takes place automatically "in the background" when a user requests a service. The user does not have to do anything explicitly to obtain AUTHENTICATION.

backup Copies of files, data, and programs made to facilitate recovery from failures of primary system.

banner Display on a computer screen, printout, or an IS that shows parameters for system or data use.

baseband Descriptive characteristic of any network technology that uses a single carrier frequency and requires all stations attached to the NETWORK to participate in every transmission. Contrast with BROADBAND.

bastion host A FIREWALL host, which acts as an interface point to an external untrusted network. BASTION HOSTS are critical to an organization's security. Because BASTION HOSTS act as an interface point to the outside world, they are often subject to INTRUSION.

Bell–LaPadula security model An ACCESS CONTROL model that aims to protect information CONFIDENTIALITY. ACCESS CONTROL rules (axioms) are expressed in terms of information (object) CLASSIFICATION, called data sensitivity, and subject authorizations, called subject clearance. Information is allowed to flow from low security level to high security level but not in the opposite direction. *See also* STAR (*) PROPERTY and SIMPLE SECURITY PROPERTY.

benign data Condition of CRYPTOGRAPHIC data that cannot be COMPROMISED by human

ACCESS. Data that, because it has been encrypted, is no longer sensitive, and cannot be COMPROMISED by eavesdropping. It may also be data that does not contain any viruses or other malicious code.

benign environment An environment that is not hostile and may be protected from external hostile elements by physical, personnel, and procedural security COUNTERMEASURES.

bespoke A product or service that is custom made or tailored to individual needs. Also called custom-designed software. *See also* COTS.

NOTE: *(1) BESPOKE is pronounced bee-SPOHK and is more commonly used in the United Kingdom. In the U.S. custom-made or custom-designed software is more common. Traditionally bespoke is applied to custom-tailored clothing, but the usage has been extended to information technology. Example usage: Dreamware software company offers BESPOKE software. (2) BESPOKE is a derivation from the word bespeak, which means ordering of goods; this usage of bespeak can be traced back to 1583.*

beyond A1 Indicates a level of trust defined by the DoD TRUSTED COMPUTER SYSTEM EVALUATION CRITERIA beyond the state-of-the-art technology. Includes all the A1-level features plus additional ones not required at the A1 level. *See also* A1 and the ORANGE BOOK.

Biba model An ACCESS CONTROL model that aims to protect integrity of information resources against unauthorized modifications. ACCESS rights are described in terms of integrity levels of subjects (processes acting in behalf of the users) and objects (information resources). Information is allowed to flow from high integrity object to low integrity object but not in the opposite direction.

binding Used in many senses; two of the most common are (1) associating an IP address with a machine name, (2) association expressed in a CERTIFICATE between a public key and an identity. Binding also refers to a process of associating a specific communications terminal with a specific CRYPTOGRAPHIC key or associating two related elements of information.

biometric device A device that AUTHENTICATES people using BIOMETRICS.

biometrics (1) IDENTIFICATION or AUTHENTICATION mechanisms that rely on the measurement of an anatomical, physiological, or behavioral characteristic of the user, rather than knowledge or possession of information or a key. (2) Method by which a personal characteristic such as a fingerprint, iris print, voiceprint, or face print is used to confirm the user's identity.

Black (1) Refers to information that is not sensitive, or no longer sensitive because it has been encrypted. (2) Designates areas or systems where national security information is not processed. For example, information systems and associated areas, circuits, components, and equipment in which national security information is not processed. *See also* RED.

block encryption Scrambling, in a reversible manner, a fixed-size block of PLAINTEXT to generate a fixed-size block of CIPHERTEXT. If the total PLAINTEXT exceeds the block size, it is first broken into blocks. If the size of total PLAINTEXT or the remainder of the PLAINTEXT after division into blocks is less than the block size, it must be padded.

boot sector virus A virus that overrides the boot sector, therefore making it appear as if there is no pointer to the operating system. The usual message that appears at power up is "Missing Operating System" or "Hard Disk Not Found."

bot A short form of "robot," it refers to a program that performs some services for a user. Two examples of a bot are (1) shopbots that search the Web on behalf of a user to find products, best price for a product, etc., (2) chatterbots that simulate talk with human beings.

On the Web, a first part of a search engine, usually called a spider or crawler, that automatically searches the Web to find pages and updates its database of information about old Web sites.

boundary (1) A boundary is the border that distinguishes a system from its environment. (2) A physical, software, or hardware barrier that limits ACCESS to a system or part of a system.

bridge A node connected to two or more (administratively indistinguishable but physically distinct) subnets that automatically forwards DATAGRAMS when necessary but whose existence is not known to other hosts. See Figure B1. Bridges can usually be made to filter packets, that is, to forward only certain traffic. *See also* REPEATER, ROUTER.

broadband Descriptive of a network that multiplexes multiple, independent network carriers onto a single cable, allowing several networks to coexist on a single cable. This action is usually done using frequency division multiplexing (FDM). Traffic from one network does not interfere with traffic from another, since the communication happens on different frequencies in the medium, a setup that resembles the commercial radio system.

broadcast (1) A packet delivery system in which a copy of a given packet is sent to all hosts attached to the network. (2) A transmission that does not address an individual recipient specifically.

browsing (1) Searching or looking through web sites. (2) An act of searching through IS storage to locate or acquire information, without necessarily knowing the existence or format of the information being sought.

BSD Berkeley Software Distribution. Term used in describing different versions of the Berkeley variety of the UNIX operating system, as in 4.3 BSD UNIX.

bucket brigade attack An ATTACK that is inserted between two legitimate users, relaying their messages to each other, and thereby SPOOFING each of them into thinking they are talking directly to the other.

buffer overflow A very common vulnerability of programs and systems. BUFFER OVERFLOW happens when input or intermediate results exceed the buffer size. Deliberate inputs that result in BUFFER OVERFLOW may result in gaining root-level ACCESS to system or in system crashes. Many programming languages such as C and C++ do not check for the violation of array boundaries into which information is being copied. For example, *gets, strcat,* and *strcpy* do not check the buffer length, so if the input length is greater than the buffer length, a BUFFER OVERFLOW results.

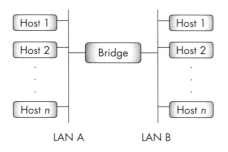

FIGURE B1. An example of a BRIDGE connecting LAN A and LAN B.

bug   A flaw or an unintentional error in the functioning of a program, system, or piece of hardware equipment.

bulk encryption   ENCRYPTION of all channels of a telecommunications link at the same time. This can also be achieved by encrypting the output of a multiplexed communications over a link.

Byzantine fault   A general system fault model inspired by the Byzantine Generals Problem [NL96]. It is a pessimistic model, allowing components (systems) to fail in coordination in the least favorable way. This model allows components to fail in an arbitrary manner. Systems designed to tolerate these faults are robust.

BYZANTINE FAULT models are characterized by systems that can produce erroneous inputs for decisions (control) and are useful in designing systems that are fault tolerant when some components may produce erroneous results.

C

C1 ☞ A1.

C2 ☞ A1.

C2W ☞ COMMAND AND CONTROL WARFARE.

CA ☞ CERTIFICATION AUTHORITY.

CAP ☞ CONTROLLED ACCESS POINT.

call back A security mechanism of redial-in connections to a network whereby users call in, identify, request a connection, and hang up. The computer system then calls the users back at their registered phone numbers, thus preventing ACCESS from attackers at other phone numbers.

call sign cipher A CIPHER system used to ENCIPHER or DECIPHER call signs, address groups, and address-indicating groups.

canister A type of protective package used to contain and dispense keypunched or printed tape forms.

capability (1) A list associated with each subject that defines the system objects and the permissions of the subject on these object. (2) An unforgeable token that gives the holder certain rights to an object.

capability list A list associated with each subject that defines the system objects and the permissions of the subject on these objects. In a capability-based system, ACCESS to protected objects—such as files—is granted if the subject possesses a capability for the object.

CAPI ☞ CRYPTOGRAPHIC APPLICATION PROGRAMMING INTERFACE.

Capstone chip Microprocessor chip that implements the ESCROWED ENCRYPTION STANDARD (EES), a DIFFIE–HELLMAN-based key exchange algorithm, the DIGITAL SIGNATURE ALGORITHM (DSA), the SECURE HASH ALGORITHM 1 (SHA-1), and a random number generator. *See also* CLIPPER CHIP.

captive account An account on a time-sharing system that is allowed to execute only a specific program or a restricted set of programs to control ACCESS to system resources.

Carnivore An Internet surveillance tool introduced by the U.S. Federal Bureau of Investigation to allow law enforcement agents to facilitate electronic surveillance in a packet-mode communications environment. Its purpose is to intercept and collect e-mail and other electronic communications only when authorized by a court order. CARNIVORE has been renamed DCS1000.

NOTE: *There has been a great deal of privacy concern with regard to the use of CARNIVORE, since it may ACCESS and process a large amount of Internet traffic not targeted for surveillance through a court order. Details of an independent technical review of CARNIVORE commissioned by the U.S. Department of Justice and conducted by IIT Research Institute can be found at http://www.usdoj.gov/jmd/publications/carniv_final.pdf. Sample documents about CARNIVORE released under the Freedom of Information Act can be accessed through the Electronic Privacy Information Center (EPIC) Web site at http://www.epic.org/privacy/carnivore/foia_documents.html.*

carrier sense multiple access with collision detect   A LAN technology for communications over a shared wire. Examples include 802.3 and Ethernet.

cascading   (1) The downward flow of information through a range of security levels greater than the ACCREDITATION range of a system network or component. (2) Propagation of controls along a path. For example, cascading revoke follows the path of a grant command to revoke propagated privileges.

category   A restrictive label applied to limit ACCESS to CLASSIFIED or UNCLASSIFIED information.

catenet   A network in which hosts are connected to networks with varying characteristics, and the networks are interconnected by gateways (routers). The Internet is an example of a CATENET.

CAW   ☞   CERTIFICATION AUTHORITY WORKSTATION.

CBC   ☞   CIPHER BLOCK CHAINING.

CBC residue   The last block of CIPHERTEXT when a message is encrypted using CIPHER BLOCK CHAINING. Since it is difficult to find two messages with the same CBC RESIDUE without knowing the key, CBC RESIDUE is often used as an integrity-protecting CHECKSUM for a message.

CCEP   ☞   COMMERCIAL COMSEC ENDORSEMENT PROGRAM.

CCI   ☞   CONTROLLED CRYPTOGRAPHIC ITEM.

CCI assembly   A device embodying a CRYPTOGRAPHIC LOGIC or other COMSEC design that NSA (U.S.) has approved as a CONTROLLED CRYPTOGRAPHIC ITEM (CCI). It performs the entire COMSEC function, but depends upon the host equipment to operate.

CCI component   Part of a CONTROLLED CRYPTOGRAPHIC ITEM (CCI) that does not perform the entire COMSEC function but depends upon the host equipment, or assembly, to complete and operate the COMSEC function.

CCI equipment   Equipment that embodies a CONTROLLED CRYPTOGRAPHIC ITEM (CCI) component or CCI ASSEMBLY and performs the entire COMSEC function without dependence on the host equipment to operate.

CCITT   ☞   COMITÉ CONSULTATIF INTERNATIONAL TÉLÉPHONIQUE ET TÉLÉGRAPHIQUE.

CDC   ☞   CERTIFICATE DISTRIBUTION CENTER.

CDSA   ☞   COMMON DATA SECURITY ARCHITECTURE.

Central Office of Record   A federal office that keeps records of accountable COMSEC MATERIAL held by elements subject to its oversight.

CER   ☞   CRYPTOGRAPHIC EQUIPMENT ROOM.

CERT   ☞   COMPUTER EMERGENCY RESPONSE TEAM.

certificate   A data structure signed with a PUBLIC KEY digital signature stating that a specified PUBLIC KEY belongs to someone or something with a specified identification. See Figure C1. X.509 is a PUBLIC KEY distribution standard.

Certificate Distribution Center The name the DASS system gives to its online system that distributes certificates and user private keys. *See also* DISTRIBUTED AUTHENTICATION SECURITY SERVICE.

certificate management A process to manage certificates, including the generation, storage, protection, transfer, loading, use, and destruction of CERTIFICATES.

Certificate Management Protocols The Internet X.509 PUBLIC KEY INFRASTRUCTURE (PKI) CERTIFICATE MANAGEMENT PROTOCOLS defined in RFC 2510. Protocol messages are defined for all relevant aspects of certificate creation and management.

certificate of action statement Statement attached to a COMSEC audit report that is used by a COMSEC CUSTODIAN to certify that all actions have been completed.

certificate revocation list A digitally signed data structure listing all the certificates issued by a given CA that have not yet expired but have been revoked, and hence are no longer valid.

certification (1) AUTHENTICATION of identity. (2) The practice of indicating, by the issue of a certificate, that a product or system has been evaluated and found to meet a set of specified security requirements.

certification agent (1) A third party (system) that judges AUTHENTICITY. (2) An individual responsible for making a technical judgment of the system's compliance with stated requirements, identifying and assessing the risks associated with operating the system, coordinating the certifica-

| Version |
| Serial Number |
| Algorithm Identifier (Algorithm, Parameter) |
| Issuer |
| Period of Validity (Not Before Date, Not After Date) |
| Subject |
| Subject's Public Key (Algorithm, Parameters, Public Key) |
| Signature |

FIGURE C1. An example of an X.509 certificate.

tion activities, and consolidating the final CERTIFICATION and ACCREDITATION PACKAGES.

certification authority (1) A trusted node that issues CERTIFICATES. A CERTIFICATE is a signed message specifying a name and a corresponding PUBLIC KEY, used with PUBLIC KEY CRYPTOGRAPHY. (2) An agency that issues digital certificates to organizations or individuals. (3) Third level of the PUBLIC KEY INFRASTRUCTURE (PKI) certification management authority, which is responsible for issuing and revoking user certificates and exacting compliance with the PKI (refers to U.S. DoD PKI) policy as defined by the parent POLICY CREATION AUTHORITY (PCA).

certification authority hierarchy A tree structure in which a root CERTIFICATION AUTHORITY issues certificates for other subordinate CERTIFICATION AUTHORITIES, which may issue further certificates.

Large-scale deployment of public key systems must support multiple CAs and the relationship among them. Two common structures for expressing this relationship are top-down CERTIFICATION AUTHORITY HIERARCHY and a collection of top-down hierarchies. A diagrammatic representation of these two structures is given in Figure C2.

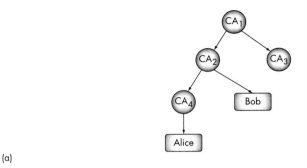

(a)

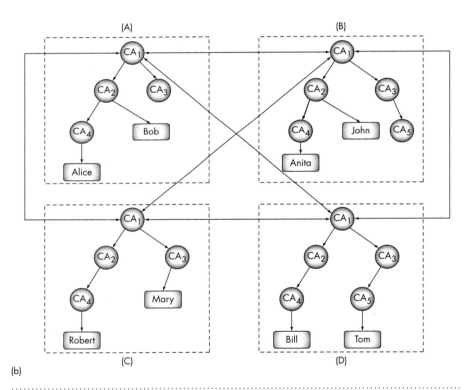

(b)

FIGURE C2. Certificate hierarchy. (a) An example of a certificate hierarchy. In this figure rectangles represent subscribers, and ovals represent CAs. (b) Completely connected islands-of-trust schema connecting four islands of trust (A), (B), (C), and (D).

Following the convention in Internet security, Figure C2 (a) uses the names Alice and Bob to explain the concept of CERTIFICATION AUTHORITY HIERARCHY. Alice and Bob are the users who have been issued CERTIFICATES. In the figure rectangles represent subscribers, and ovals represent CAs. An arrow between two CAs means that the source CA has certified the destination CA to issue certificates (e.g., CA_4 has certified the public key of Alice). The certification path between Alice and Bob goes through CA_4 and CA_2.

To overcome the problem of the entire Internet population trusting one central CA, the Internet trust mechanism is developing as "islands of trust," where each community, based on geographic location and other requirements, trusts a particular CA, so that there is a root CA for each community and these root CAs cross-certify each other. Figure C2 (b) shows a completely connected islands-of-trust schema connecting (A), (B), (C), and (D). This arrangement allows certification paths between pair of subscribers and is applicable to large-scale public-key applications such as secure e-mail and e-commerce.

The root authority that issues certificates is also called the IPRA (INTERNET POLICY REGISTRATION AUTHORITY) and registers certification authorities known as POLICY CREATION AUTHORITY (PCA). IPRA certifies only PCAs and not CAs or users. PCAs have their own policy of issuing certificates.

certification authority workstation

A workstation that is used to issue CERTIFICATES. Usually it is a COMMERCIAL OFF-THE-SHELF (COTS) workstation with a trusted operating system and special-purpose application software that is used to issue certificates.

NOTE: *This terminology is used mainly in the U.S. DoD and is not widely used outside the DoD environment.*

certification package   Product of the CERTIFICATION effort documenting the detailed results of CERTIFICATION activities.

certification test and evaluation   Software and hardware security tests and evaluation conducted during the development of an IS.

certified TEMPEST technical authority An experienced, technically qualified U.S. government employee who has met established certification requirements in accordance with NSTISSC-approved criteria and has been appointed by a U.S. government department or agency to fulfill CTTA responsibilities.

CFB   ☞   CIPHER FEEDBACK.

CGI   ☞   COMMON GATEWAY INTERFACE.

challenge   Information given to an entity so that it can cryptographically process the information—using a secret quantity it knows—and return the result (called the response). This exercise's purpose is to prove knowledge of the secret quantity without revealing it to an eavesdropper. This process is known as CHALLENGE–RESPONSE AUTHENTICATION.

NOTE: *Although CHALLENGE now refers to a CRYPTOGRAPHIC process, it previously referred to a cryptic process by which two people (e.g., spies) would AUTHENTICATE each other.*

challenge and reply authentication   A prearranged procedure in which a subject requests the AUTHENTICATION of another and the latter establishes its validity with a correct reply.

challenge–response   In this type of AUTHENTICATION, a user responds (usually by

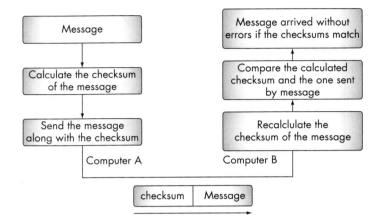

FIGURE C3. An example of the use of CHECKSUM in MESSAGE INTEGRITY.

performing some calculation) to a CHAL-LENGE (usually a numeric, unpredictable one) to AUTHENTICATE his/her identity.

Chaos Computer Club   A loosely knit organization centered in Germany that made news by staging some high-profile break-ins into computer networks.

checksum   A small fixed-length quantity computed as a function of an arbitrary-length message. A CHECKSUM is computed by the sender of a message, recomputed, and checked by the recipient of a message to detect data corruption. Originally, the term CHECKSUM meant the specific integrity check consisting of adding all the numbers together and throwing away carries. Usage has extended the definition to include more complex noncryptographic functions such as CRCs, which detect hardware faults with high probability, and CRYPTOGRAPHIC functions such as MESSAGE DIGESTS, which can withstand attacks from clever attackers. See Figure C3.

check word   CIPHERTEXT generated by CRYPTOGRAPHIC LOGIC to detect failures in CRYPTOGRAPHY.

Chernobyl packet   An IP Ethernet DATA-GRAM that passes through a GATEWAY between two SUBNETS and has the source and the destination addresses as the broadcast addresses. This type of packet results in a broadcast storm. Also called KAMIKAZE PACKET.

CIK ☞   CRYPTO-IGNITION KEY.

CIPE ☞   CRYPTO IP ENCAPSULATION.

cipher   Any CRYPTOGRAPHIC system or CRYPTOSYSTEM in which PLAINTEXT is concealed by transposing the letters or numbers or substituting other letters or numbers according to a key or by rearranging the PLAINTEXT or by all of the above.

cipher block chaining   A method of using a BLOCK ENCRYPTION scheme for encrypting an arbitrary-size message. Figure C4 explains CIPHER BLOCK CHAINING (CBC). In this figure, vector IV is a random number generated and sent along with the message. This vector is used as an INITIALIZATION VEC-TOR for the first PLAINTEXT message block B1

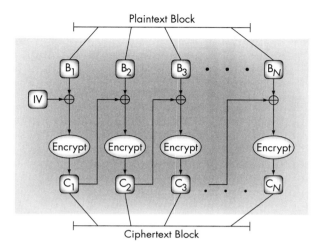

B_i: Plaintext Block

C_i: Ciphertext Block

IV: Initialization Vector

FIGURE C4. An example of cipher block chaining.

(CIPHERTEXT for block 1). A block is 64 bits long. CIPHERTEXT for block i, C_i, is XORed with PLAINTEXT for block $i + 1$, B_i, before being run through an ENCRYPTION ALGORITHM.

cipher feedback   A method of using a BLOCK ENCRYPTION scheme for ENCRYPTING a message of arbitrary size. Figure C5 shows CIPHER FEEDBACK.

ciphertext   Enciphered information. In Figure C6, the encoding algorithm right-shifts the PLAINTEXT by two letters to produce CIPHERTEXT. A becomes D, B becomes E, C becomes G, and so on, Y becomes B, and Z becomes C. In the figure PLAINTEXT HELLO is enciphered to CIPHERTEXT KHOOR.

ciphertext autokey   CRYPTOGRAPHIC LOGIC that uses previous CIPHERTEXT to generate a KEY STREAM.

ciphony   A process of enciphering audio information that results in ENCRYPTED speech.

circuit-level gateway   Ensures the validity of TCP and UDP sessions by creating a handshake between communicating parties and passing packets through until the end of the session. A type of FIREWALL.

CIX   ☞   COMMERCIAL INTERNET EXCHANGE.

Clark–Wilson model   An integrity model for COMPUTER SECURITY policy designed for a commercial environment (see [DC87]). It addresses such concepts such as NONDISCRETIONARY ACCESS CONTROL, privilege separation, and LEAST PRIVILEGE.

classification   The hierarchical portion of a sensitivity label. The CLASSIFICATION is a single level in a stratified set of levels. For example, in a military environment, each of the sensitivity levels Unclassified, Confidential, Secret, and Top Secret is less sensitive than the level above it. When included in a sensitivity label in a system supporting MANDATORY ACCESS CONTROLS, a CLASSIFICATION is used to limit ACCESS to those cleared at that level.

Figure C7 gives an approximate comparison of security CLASSIFICATIONS of various countries. For more details refer to [ISP97].

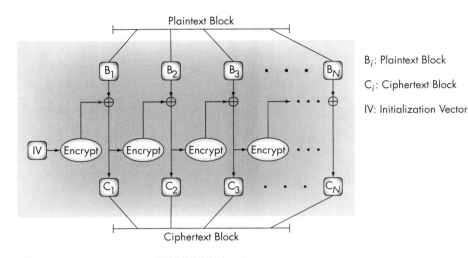

B_i: Plaintext Block

C_i: Ciphertext Block

IV: Initialization Vector

FIGURE C5. An example of cipher feedback.

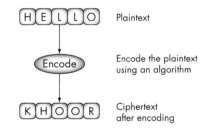

Plaintext

Encode the plaintext
using an algorithm

Ciphertext
after encoding

FIGURE C6. An example illustrating CIPHERTEXT.

classified An adjective describing information that a government does not want divulged for national security reasons. There are various types of CLASSIFICATION, including Confidential, Secret, and Top Secret. *See also* CLASSIFICATION.

classified information Information that has been determined pursuant to Executive Order 12958 (U.S.) or any predecessor order, or by the Atomic Energy Act of 1954 (U.S.), as amended, to require protection against unauthorized disclosure and is marked to indicate its CLASSIFIED status.

clearance (1) Represents an AUTHORIZATION for a user to be granted access to a CLASSIFIED INFORMATION. (2) Represents the sensitivity level (the CLASSIFICATION and the categories) associated with a user in a system supporting MANDATORY ACCESS CONTROLS. A user with a particular CLEARANCE can typically read only information with a sensitivity label equal to or lower than the user's CLEARANCE and write only information with the same sensitivity label.

NOTE: *A person's CLEARANCE is permission to access information CLASSIFIED at that level. It represents reliance placed in that person after background, character, and other checks made by a security authority. In some operating system environments (for example, MLS), a subject (process) with a particular CLEARANCE may only read information with a CLASSIFICATION level equal to or lower than the CLEARANCE, and may only write information at the same CLASSIFICATION of the subject's CLEARANCE. A user with a CLEARANCE of, say, TS is usually able to create a process (subject) with a lower CLEARANCE, say S, to create a file at the S level.*

Country	Security Classification			
U.S.	Top Secret	Secret	Confidential	Other
Australia	Top Secret	Secret	Confidential	Restricted
Canada	Top Secret	Secret	Confidential	Restricted
France	Très Secret	Secret Defense	Confidentiel	Diffusion Restreinte
Germany	Streng Geheim	Geheim	Vs-Vertaulich	—
India	Top Secret	Secret	Confidential	Restricted
Japan	Kimitsu	Gokuhi	Hi	Toriatsukaichui
New Zealand	Top Secret	Secret	Confidential	Restricted
Russia	Cobeoweh-ho	Cekpetho	—	—
United Kingdom	Top Secret	Secret	Confidential	Restricted

FIGURE C7. Approximate comparison of security classifications of various countries.

clearing The removal of data from an IS, its storage devices, and other peripheral devices with storage capacity in such a way that the data may not be reconstructed using common systems capabilities (i.e., keyboard strokes); however, the data may be reconstructed using laboratory methods. Cleared media may be reused at the same CLASSIFICATION level or at a higher level. Overwriting is one method of CLEARING.

cleartext A message that is not EN-CRYPTED. *See also* PLAINTEXT.

client Something (usually a process) that accesses a service (from another process, also referred to as a server) by communicating with it over a computer network.

Clipper Shorthand for CLIPPER CHIP and for the U.S. government's policy regarding the use of this chip.

Clipper chip The hardware implementation of the ESCROWED ENCRYPTION STANDARD. The chip was designed by the U.S. NATIONAL SECURITY AGENCY (NSA) and originally used in a telephone security device manufactured by AT&T. The chip is no longer manufactured.

client–server model A common way to describe network services and the model user process of those services. See Figure C8. Examples include the name-server/name-resolver paradigm of the DOMAIN name system and file-server/file-client relationships such as NETWORK FILE SYSTEM (NFS) and diskless hosts. *See also* NETWORK FILE SYSTEM.

CLNP ☞ CONNECTIONLESS NETWORK PROTOCOL.

closed security environment An environment providing sufficient ASSURANCE that applications and equipment are protected against the introduction of malicious logic during an IS life cycle. Closed security is based upon a system's developers, operators, and maintenance personnel having sufficient CLEARANCES, AUTHORIZATION, and CONFIGURATION CONTROL.

CMCS ☞ COMSEC MATERIAL CONTROL SYSTEM.

CMP ☞ CERTIFICATE MANAGEMENT PROTOCOLS.

CMS ☞ CRYPTOGRAPHIC MESSAGING SYNTAX.

COCOM ☞ COORDINATING COMMITTEE FOR MULTILATERAL EXPORT CONTROLS.

code (1) (COMSEC) System of communication in which arbitrary groups of

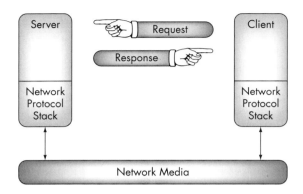

FIGURE C8. A simple client–server model.

words, letters, numbers, or symbols replace other words, phrases, letters, or numbers for concealment or brevity. (2) A system of symbols that make up a CIPHERTEXT. (3) Also refers to a system of instructions that makes up a software source, or executable information.

code book   A document containing PLAINTEXT and code equivalents in a systematic arrangement, or a technique of machine ENCRYPTION using a word substitution technique.

code group   A group of letters, numbers, or both in a code system used to represent a PLAINTEXT word, phrase, or sentence.

code obfuscation   A CODE transformation technique to prevent malicious reverse engineering of CODE. In this technique, original CODE is converted to an equivalent CODE that is functionally identical to the original CODE but is more difficult to decompile and reverse engineer. In general, CODE OBFUSCATION is applied to MOBILE CODE executables because they are isomorphic (similar in form and function) to the source CODE. This ensures platform independence but makes them easy to decom-pile and vulnerable to malicious reverse engineering attacks.

NOTE: *A transformation Γ from a program P to a program Q is an OBFUSCATION transformation [CC98], if (1) both P and Q have same observable behavior except for non-termination and error-termination. Q may have side effects not observable by user such as creating files, sending messages over the Internet and also P and Q may have different performance characteristics; and (2) the transformation Γ makes Q more obscure, complex, or unreadable than P (for metrics of complexity see [SH81], [JM93], [TM76], [WH81]). Colberg [CC98] defines four measures of the quality of an OBFUSCATION transformation, potency, resilience, stealth, and cost. Potency measures how obscure Q is made by Γ, resilience measures ability to withstand attacks from automatic deobfuscators, stealth measures how obfuscated CODE blends with the rest of the program, and cost measures the time and space increase because of obfuscation.*

code signing   CODE SIGNING is used to verify the source of a program. A secure hashing algorithm is used on the code to be executed providing a compact code SIGNATURE. This SIGNATURE is encrypted using the private key of a vendor. CODE is retrieved with the SIGNATURE. The SIGNATURE is decrypted using the vendor's PUBLIC KEY. If the HASH value and decrypted SIGNATURE are identical, the CODE has not been tampered with. This provides CODE accessed via the INTERNET to be treated as "shrink-wrapped" software. Active X from Microsoft uses this technique to verify software INTEGRITY [BS00].

code vocabulary   A set of PLAINTEXT words, numerals, phrases, or sentences for which code equivalents are assigned in a code system.

COI   ☞   COMMUNITY OF INTEREST.

cold start   A procedure for initially keying CRYPTO-EQUIPMENT.

command and control warfare   This term refers to both offensive and defensive operations and is an example of information operations in military settings and information warfare. It involves the use of electronic warfare, military deception, and psychological operations to adversely affect enemy command and control while protecting friendly command and control capabilities.

command authority   An individual who is responsible for the appointment of user representatives for a department, agency, or organization and their key ordering privileges.

Commercial COMSEC Endorsement Program   Relationship between NSA (U.S.) and industry in which NSA provides the COMSEC expertise (i.e., standards, algorithms, evaluations, and guidance) and industry provides design, development, and production capabilities to produce a Type 1 or Type 2 product. Products developed under the CCEP may include modules, subsystems, equipment, systems, and ancillary devices.

Commercial Internet Exchange   An industry organization for Internet service providers.

commercial off-the-shelf   A readily available commercial product (software) that is not developed to particular government or industry specifications or for a particular project. *See also* BESPOKE.

Comité Consultatif International Téléphonique et Télégraphique   It is now called INTERNATIONAL TELECOMMUNICATIONS UNION (ITU), standard organization dominated by European telephone companies known as PTTs, where PTT stands for Postal, Telephone, and Telegraph Authority. Comité Consultatif International Téléphonique et Télégraphique (CCITT) published standards for computer networking, including the X.400 series of documents concerning electronic mail and the X.500 series of documents concerning directory services.

Common Criteria   The COMMON CRITERIA for Information Technology Security Evaluation referred to as COMMON CRITERIA (now it has an equivalent standard ISO/IEC 15408) is a multipart standard to be used as a basis of evaluation of security properties of IT products and services. It is described in three parts. Part 1 provides an introduction and general model. Part 2 provides security and functional requirements. Part 3 contains security ASSURANCE requirements. The COMMON CRITERIA combines ideas from its various predecessors (see NOTE below).

It covers IT security measures and permits comparison of independent security evaluations. The COMMON CRITERIA is designed to serve as a guide for the development of products or systems with IT security functions and for the procurement of commercial products and systems with IT security functions. It also addresses protection of information from unauthorized disclosure, modification, or loss of use.

COMMON CRITERIA defines seven Evaluation Assurance Levels (EAL): EAL1, functionally tested; EAL2, structurally tested; EAL3, methodically tested and checked; EAL4, methodically designed, tested, and reviewed; EAL5, semiformally designed and tested; EAL6, semiformally verified designed and tested; EAL7, formally verified designed and tested. An EAL is a package consisting of ASSURANCE components that represent a point on the COMMON CRITERIA predefined ASSURANCE scale.

More details about COMMON CRITERIA can be obtained from http://csrc.nist.gov/cc/ or http://www.commoncriteria.org.

NOTE: *The origins of the COMMON CRITERIA can be traced to the TRUSTED COMPUTER SYSTEM EVALUATION CRITERIA (TCSEC) developed (1980) in the United States. The COMMON CRITERIA merges ideas from the following predecessors. The INFORMATION TECHNOLOGY SECURITY EVALUATION CRITERIA (ITSEC) version 1.2 published (1991) by the European Commission and based on the joint efforts of France, Germany, the Netherlands, and the United Kingdom. The Canadian Trusted Computer Product Evaluation Criteria (CTCPEC) version 3.0 (1993) combined the ITSEC and TCSEC approaches. The U.S. published the draft Federal Criteria for Information Technology Security version 1.0 (1993) that combined North American and European concepts for evaluation criteria. Building on these efforts, COMMON CRITERIA was developed. COMMON CRITERIA (v1.0) was published in 1996, and COMMON CRITERIA version 2.0 was published in 1998. COMMON CRITERIA version 2.1 is now available for use.*

common data security architecture   A set of specifications of APIs to define a comprehensive approach to security service and security management for computer-based security applications initiated by Intel Corporation.

common fill device   One of a family of devices developed to read in, transfer, or store keys.

common gateway interface   A method or convention to pass a Web user's request between a web server and an application program and to receive data back that is forwarded to the user. Because the gateway is consistent, a programmer may write a COMMON GATEWAY INTERFACE (CGI) program in a number of different languages, such as C, C++, Java, PERL (Practical Extraction and Reporting Language). For example, Microsoft's Active Server Pages (ASP), Java Server Pages, and Servlets are alternatives to CGI.

communications cover   The concealing or altering of characteristic communications patterns to hide information that could be of value to an ADVERSARY.

communications deception   Deliberate transmission, retransmission, or alteration of communications to mislead an ADVERSARY'S interpretation of the communications. *See also* IMITATIVE COMMUNICATIONS DECEPTION and MANIPULATIVE COMMUNICATIONS DECEPTION.

communications profile   An analytic model of communications associated with an organization or activity. The model is prepared from a systematic examination of communications content and patterns, the functions they reflect, and the COMMUNICATIONS SECURITY measures applied.

communications security   COMMUNICATIONS SECURITY (COMSEC). The measures and controls taken to deny unauthorized persons information derived from telecommunications and to ensure the AUTHENTICITY of such telecommunications. COMMUNICATIONS SECURITY includes CRYPTOSECURITY, TRANSMISSION SECURITY, EMISSION SECURITY, and PHYSICAL SECURITY of COMSEC MATERIAL.

community of interest A group of people with a common interest without any regard to geographical boundaries. This term usually refers to groups of people who pursue their meetings or form communities through chat rooms, mailing lists, and discussion servers on the Internet.

compartmentalization A nonhierarchical grouping of sensitive information used to control access to data more finely than with hierarchical security CLASSIFICATION alone.

compartmented mode (1) In COMPARTMENTED MODE, the IS is trusted to prevent a user without formal access to a given compartment from accessing any information in that compartment that is stored within the IS. *See also* MULTILEVEL MODE.

(2) INFOSEC mode of operation wherein each user with direct or indirect access to a system, its peripherals, remote terminals, or remote hosts has all of the following: (a) a valid security CLEARANCE for the most restricted information processed in the system; (b) formal access approval and signed nondisclosure agreements for that information which to a user is to have access; and (c) a valid NEED-TO-KNOW for information that is to be accessed.

compromise (1) Circumvent security measures in order to acquire unauthorized access to information or system resources. (2) A state in which the security objectives of the information system are not maintained.

compromising emanations Unintentional signals that if intercepted and analyzed would disclose the information transmitted, received, handled, or otherwise processed by information systems equipment. *See also* TEMPEST.

computer abuse The intentional or reckless misuse, alteration, disruption, or destruction of information-processing resources.

computer cryptography The use of a CRYPTO-ALGORITHM program by a computer to AUTHENTICATE or encrypt/decrypt information.

Computer Emergency Response Team It plays a major role in awareness, response, and prevention activities related to computer and network security and issues alerts and advisories. COMPUTER EMERGENCY RESPONSE TEAM (CERT) was established in 1988 by the ADVANCED RESEARCH PROJECTS AGENCY (ARPA) in response to the Internet Worm incident (1988). CERT is located at Carnegie Mellon University and has various international centers. *See also* INTERNET WORM.

computer forensics Relates to the collection, preservation, and analysis of computer-related criminal evidence.

Computer Oracle and Password System UNIX security status checker. Checks various files and software configurations to see whether they have been compromised (edited to plant a Trojan horse or back door) and checks to see that files have the appropriate modes and permissions set to maintain the integrity of a security level (makes sure that file permissions do not leave themselves open to ATTACK or access).

computer security Measures and controls that ensure the CONFIDENTIALITY, INTEGRITY, and AVAILABILITY of IS assets including hardware, software, firmware, and information being processed, stored, and communicated.

computer security incident ☞ INCIDENT.

computer security subsystem Hardware or software designed to provide COM-

PUTER SECURITY features in a larger system environment.

COMSEC ☞ COMMUNICATIONS SECURITY.

COMSEC account Administrative entity, identified by an account number, used to maintain ACCOUNTABILITY, custody, and control of COMSEC MATERIAL.

COMSEC account audit Examination of the holdings, records, and procedures of a COMSEC ACCOUNT ensuring that all accountable COMSEC MATERIAL is properly handled and safeguarded.

COMSEC aid COMSEC MATERIAL that assists in securing telecommunications and is required in the production, operation, or maintenance of COMSEC systems and their components. COMSEC keying material, call sign/frequency systems, and supporting documentation, such as operating and maintenance manuals, are examples of COMSEC AIDS.

COMSEC boundary Definable perimeter encompassing all hardware, firmware, and software components performing critical COMSEC functions, such as key generation and key handling and storage.

COMSEC chip set A collection of U.S. NSA-approved microchips.

COMSEC control program Computer instructions or routines controlling or affecting the externally performed functions of key generation, key distribution, message ENCRYPTION/DECRYPTION, or AUTHENTICATION.

COMSEC custodian A person designated by a proper authority to be responsible for the receipt, transfer, accounting, safeguarding, and destruction of COMSEC MATERIAL assigned to a COMSEC ACCOUNT.

COMSEC end-item Equipment or combination of components ready for use in a COMSEC application.

COMSEC equipment Equipment designed to provide security to telecommunications by converting information to a form unintelligible to an unauthorized interceptor and, subsequently, by recovering such information to its original form for authorized recipients; also, equipment designed specifically to aid in, or as an essential element of, the conversion process.

COMSEC facility Space used for generating, storing, repairing, or using COMSEC MATERIAL.

COMSEC incident ☞ INCIDENT.

COMSEC insecurity A COMSEC INCIDENT that has been investigated, evaluated, and determined to have jeopardized the security of COMSEC MATERIAL or the secure transmission of information.

COMSEC manager Person who manages the COMSEC resources of an organization.

COMSEC material Item designed to secure or AUTHENTICATE telecommunications. COMSEC MATERIAL includes, but is not limited to, key, equipment, devices, documents, firmware, or software that embodies or describes CRYPTOGRAPHIC LOGIC and other items that perform COMSEC functions.

COMSEC material control system Logistics and accounting system through which COMSEC MATERIAL marked "CRYPTO" is distributed, controlled, and safeguarded. Included are the COMSEC central offices of record, cryptologic depots, and COMSEC ACCOUNTS. COMSEC MATERIAL other than key may be handled through the COMSEC MATERIAL CONTROL SYSTEM.

COMSEC modification ☞ INFORMATION SYSTEM SECURITY EQUIPMENT MODIFICATION.

COMSEC module Removable component that performs COMSEC functions in telecommunications equipment or systems.

COMSEC monitoring The act of listening to, copying, or recording transmissions of one's own official telecommunications to analyze the degree of security.

COMSEC profile Statement of COMSEC measures and materials used to protect a given operation, system, or organization.

COMSEC survey Organized collection of COMSEC and communications information relative to a given operation, system, or organization.

COMSEC system data Information required by COMSEC EQUIPMENT or system to enable it to properly handle and control KEY.

COMSEC training Teaching of skills relating to COMSEC accounting, use of COMSEC AIDS, or installation, use, maintenance, and repair of COMSEC EQUIPMENT.

concept of operations Document detailing the method, act, process, or effect of using an IS.

confidentiality The property of not being divulged to unauthorized parties. A CONFIDENTIALITY service assists in the prevention of disclosure of information to unauthorized parties.

configuration control The process of controlling modifications to hardware, firmware, software, and documentation to ensure that an IS is protected against improper modifications prior to, during, and after system implementation.

configuration management Management of security features and ASSURANCES through the control of changes made to hardware, software, firmware, documentation, test, test fixtures, and test documentation throughout the life cycle of an IS.

confinement Not allowing information of a certain security CLASSIFICATION to es-

cape from the environment in which it is allowed to reside.

confinement channel ☞ COVERT CHANNEL.

confinement property Synonymous with STAR (*) PROPERTY.

connectionless The model of interconnection in which communication takes place without first establishing a connection. Sometimes called a DATAGRAM. Examples include UDP and ordinary postcards. Figure C9 shows that packets with the same source and destination (A to D) may take different routes.

　　Packets 1 and 3 are routed by switch 1 through link 3, and packet 2 through link 7. Switch 2 then routes packets 1 and 3 to switch 3 through link 5. Switch 3 then diverts packets 3, 1, 2 to destination D in the order of their arrival. Contrast this with a CONNECTION-ORIENTED system where the packets will take the same route for same source and destination.

Connectionless Network Protocol An OSI standard network layer protocol for sending data through a computer network.

connection-oriented The model of interconnection in which communication proceeds though three well-defined phases: connection establishment, data transfer, and connection release. Examples include X.25, Internet TCP, and ordinary telephone calls. In Figure C10 a virtual connection is established from node A to node D through links 1, 3, 5, 6 as highlighted by a thick line in the figure. All data transfer for a particular session is through this link until the connection is released.

CONOP ☞ CONCEPT OF OPERATIONS.

contamination The introduction of data of one security CLASSIFICATION or security

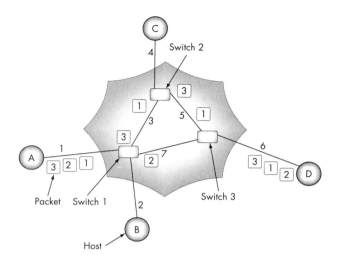

FIGURE C9. A CONNECTIONLESS network.

category into data of a lower security CLAS-SIFICATION or different security category. Typically an undesirable situation. When sensitive information is inadvertently transferred onto an insufficiently secure system, for example secret information copied onto an UNCLASSIFIED computer that might be connected to the Internet, this would contaminate the UNCLASSIFIED computer.

contingency key Key held for use under specific operational conditions or in support of specific CONTINGENCY PLANS.

contingency plan Plan maintained for emergency response, backup operations, and postdisaster recovery for an IS, to ensure the availability of critical resources and to facilitate the continuity of operations in an emergency situation.

controlled access point Provides a network mechanism intended to reduce the risk of password guessing, probing for well-known accounts with default pass-

words, trusted host RLOGIN, and password capture by network snooping. Two local nets—one a secure segment with an AUTHENTICATION service and the other a nonsecure segment—communicate with each other via a CAP. The CAP is essentially a router with additional functionality to detect incoming connection requests, intercept the user AUTHENTICATION process, and invoke the AUTHENTICATION server.

controlled access protection The C2 level of protection described in the TRUSTED COMPUTER SYSTEM EVALUATION CRITERIA (ORANGE BOOK). Its major characteristics are individual ACCOUNTABILITY, AUDIT, ACCESS CONTROL, and OBJECT REUSE.

controlled cryptographic item Secure telecommunications or information-handling equipment, or associated CRYPTOGRAPHIC COMPONENT, that is UNCLASSIFIED but governed by a special set of control requirements. Such items are marked "CONTROLLED CRYPTOGRAPHIC ITEM" or, where space is limited, "CCI."

controlled security mode ☞ MULTILEVEL SECURITY.

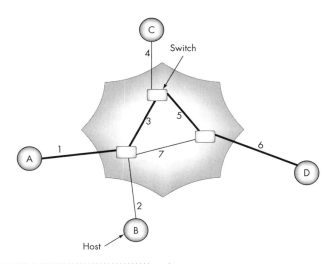

FIGURE C10. A CONNECTION-ORIENTED network.

controlled sharing   A condition existing when ACCESS CONTROL is applied to all users and components of an IS.

controlled space   Three-dimensional space surrounding IS equipment within which unauthorized persons are denied unrestricted access and are either escorted by authorized persons or are under continuous physical or electronic surveillance.

controlling authority   Official responsibility for directing the operation of a CRYPTONET and for managing the operational use and control of keying material assigned to the CRYPTONET.

conversation key   A temporary encryption key issued to communicating entities by an Authentication Service.

cookies   Information about Web site visitors created by Web sites and stored on the visitors' computers.

cooperative key generation   Electronically exchanging functions of locally gener-

ated random components from which both terminals of a secure circuit construct a TRAFFIC ENCRYPTION KEY or a KEY ENCRYPTION KEY for use on that circuit.

cooperative remote rekeying   Synonymous with MANUAL REMOTE REKEYING.

Coordinating Committee for Multilateral Export Controls   International forum for coordinating export control regulations on technology of military significance, including CRYPTOGRAPHY. COORDINATING COMMITTEE FOR MULTILATERAL EXPORT CONTROLS (COCOM) was dissolved in 1994, but the coordination of export regulations has continued under the WASSENAAR ARRANGEMENT, which was established in 1996. *See also* WASSENAAR ARRANGEMENT.

COPS   ☞   COMPUTER ORACLE AND PASSWORD SYSTEM.

COR   ☞   CENTRAL OFFICE OF RECORD.

correctness proof   A mathematical proof of consistency between a specification and its implementation.

cost–benefit analysis   The assessment of the cost of providing protection or security commensurate with the risk and magnitude of asset loss or damage.

COTS ☞ COMMERCIAL OFF-THE-SHELF.

countermeasure A COUNTERMEASURE is the action, device, procedure, technique, or other measure that reduces the vulnerability of an IS.

covert channel A mechanism or a channel not intended for information transfer could be used for that purpose. For example, dynamically creating and deleting files to transmit 0 or 1 bit information. Requires two active agents, one at high and one at low security level, and an encoding schema. *See also* OVERT CHANNEL and EXPLOITABLE CHANNEL.

covert channel analysis Assessment of the degree to which covert channels could be used to contravene the security policy of a system. Typically, this will identify both the channels themselves and the information transfer rates that could be achieved.

covert storage channel The transmission of information by modulating the capacity (or other attribute) of a storage resource. The transmitter creates files on a disk of different sizes or file names. The receiver (who is forbidden from receiving information from the transmitter) is able to determine the amount of free disk space left, or the name of the file, or other attributes, without reading the contents of the file itself. COVERT STORAGE CHANNELS typically involve a finite resource (e.g., sectors on a disk) that is shared by two subjects at different security levels.

covert timing channel COVERT CHANNEL in which one process signals information to another process by modulating its own use of system resources (e.g., central processing unit time) in such a way that this manipulation affects the real response time observed by the second process.

cracker A person who breaks security controls for criminal pursuits. Although not in general use, this term is common among computer professionals and academicians.

CRC ☞ CYCLIC REDUNDANCY CODE.

CRC-32 A particular CRC that produces a 32-bit output.

credentials Secret information used to prove one's identity or AUTHORIZATION in an AUTHENTICATION exchange.

criteria Definitions of properties and constraints to be met by system functionality and ASSURANCE.

critical infrastructures Those physical and information-based systems essential to the minimum operations of the economy and government.

CRL ☞ CERTIFICATE REVOCATION LIST.

cryptanalysis The process of finding weaknesses or flaws in CRYPTOGRAPHIC algorithms.

crypto-alarm Circuit or device that detects failures or aberrations in the logic or operation of CRYPTO-EQUIPMENT. A CRYPTO-ALARM may inhibit transmission or may provide a visible and/or audible alarm.

crypto-algorithm A short form of "cryptographic algorithm." Well-defined procedure or sequence of rules or steps or a series of mathematical equations used to describe CRYPTOGRAPHIC processes such as ENCRYPTION, DECRYPTION, KEY GENERATION, AUTHENTICATION, SIGNATURES, etc.

crypto-ancillary equipment Equipment designed specifically to facilitate efficient or reliable operation of CRYPTO-EQUIP-

MENT, without performing CRYPTOGRAPHIC functions itself.

crypto-equipment   Equipment that embodies CRYPTOGRAPHIC LOGIC.

cryptographic   Pertaining to, or connected with, CRYPTOGRAPHY.

cryptographic application programming interface   CRYPTOGRAPHIC APPLICATION PROGRAMMING INTERFACE (CAPI) specifies an interface to a library of functions for security and CRYPTOGRAPHY services. It separates CRYPTOGRAPHIC routines from applications so if needed software can be exported without any security services implemented, and may later be linked by the user to the local security services. CAPIs can be implemented as CRYPTOGRAPHIC module interfaces, authentication service interfaces, or at a different level of abstraction. Examples of CAPIs include RSA Laboratories' Cryptoki (PKCS #11), NSA's (U.S.) Fortezza, Internet GSS-API (see RFC 1508).

cryptographic checksum   A one-way function that calculates a unique fingerprint of a message (or a file). This provides an integrity check with the property that it is very hard to find a valid CHECKSUM for a message unless the SECRET KEY is known. The data in the message is sent along with the CHECKSUM and at destination the CHECKSUM is recomputed. Any tampering of data is likely to result in a different CHECKSUM. It provides a probabilistic proof that the data was not tampered with.

cryptographic component   Hardware or firmware embodiment of CRYPTOGRAPHIC LOGIC. For example, a modular assembly, printed wiring assembly, or a microcircuit may implement CRYPTOGRAPHIC LOGIC.

cryptographic engine   Hardware or software implementation of CRYPTOGRAPHIC functions. An example of software implementation is RSA's BSAFE, and an example of hardware implementation is the FORTEZZA CARD. *See also* FORTEZZA CARD.

cryptographic equipment room   Controlled-access room in which CRYPTOSYSTEMS are located.

cryptographic initialization   A function used to set the state of CRYPTOGRAPHIC LOGIC prior to KEY GENERATION, ENCRYPTION, or other operating mode.

cryptographic logic   The embodiment of one or more CRYPTO-ALGORITHMS along with alarms, checks, and other processes essential to the effective and secure performance of the CRYPTOGRAPHIC PROCESS(ES).

Cryptographic Messaging Syntax   A general syntax as outlined in RFC 2315 for data that may have CRYPTOGRAPHY applied to it, such as digital signatures and digital envelopes.

cryptographic randomization   Function that randomly determines the transmit state of CRYPTOGRAPHIC LOGIC.

cryptography   (1) Art or science concerning the principles, means, and methods for rendering plain information unintelligible and for restoring encrypted information to intelligible form. (2) The subject area that deals with mathematical techniques related to aspects of information security such as CONFIDENTIALITY, AUTHENTICATION, DATA INTEGRITY, and NONREPUDIATION.

crypto-ignition key   Device or electronic key used to unlock the secure mode of CYPTO-EQUIPMENT.

Crypto IP Encapsulation   A project to build encrypting IP routers that route encrypted UDP packets whose purpose is to securely connect subnets over an insecure transit network. The purpose of IPSEC and

CIPE are the same. However, CIPE is not very flexible in functionality as compared to IPsec. *See also* INTERNET PROTOCOL SECURITY.

cryptology (1) Field encompassing both CRYPTOGRAPHY and CRYPTANALYSIS. (2) The area of making and breaking schemes used for achieving CRYPTOGRAPHIC goals such as CONFIDENTIALITY, AUTHENTICATION, DATA INTEGRITY, and NONREPUDIATION. *See also* CRYPTOGRAPHY and CRYPTANALYSIS.

cryptonet Stations holding a common key.

cryptoperiod Time span during which a key setting remains in effect.

cryptosecurity Component of COMSEC resulting from the provision of technically sound CRYPTOSYSTEMS and their proper use.

cryptosynchronization The process by which a receiving decrypting instance of CRYPTOGRAPHIC LOGIC attains the same internal state as the transmitting encrypting logic.

cryptosystem Associated INFOSEC items interacting to provide a single means of ENCRYPTION or DECRYPTION.

cryptosystem assessment Process of establishing the exploitability of a CRYPTOSYSTEM, normally by reviewing the transmitted traffic protected or secured by the system under study.

cryptosystem evaluation Process of determining vulnerabilities of a CRYPTOSYSTEM.

cryptosystem review Examination of a CRYPTOSYSTEM by the CONTROLLING AUTHORITY, ensuring its adequacy of design and content, continued need, and proper distribution.

cryptosystem survey Management technique in which the actual holders of a CRYPTOSYSTEM express opinions on the system's suitability and provide usage information for technical evaluations.

CSMA/CD ☞ CARRIER SENSE MULTIPLE ACCESS WITH COLLISION DETECT.

CT&E ☞ CERTIFICATION TEST AND EVALUATION.

CTTA ☞ CERTIFIED TEMPEST TECHNICAL AUTHORITY.

cybercrud Mostly useless computer-generated gibberish that people either ignore or are intimidated and annoyed by.

cybersquatting Registering a domain name that is a trademark of another person or company with the hope that the original owner will pay money to retain the domain rights.

cybervandalism The electronic defacing of an existing Web page or site.

cyclic redundancy check Error-checking mechanism that checks data integrity by computing a polynomial-algorithm-based CHECKSUM.

cyclic redundancy code Code produced by CYCLIC REDUNDANCY CHECK. *See also* CYCLIC REDUNDANCY CHECK.

D

D ☞ A1.

DAA ☞ DESIGNATED APPROVING AUTHORITY.

DAC ☞ DISCRETIONARY ACCESS CONTROLS.

daemon process A PROCESS that runs continuously in the background on a computer with no associated user, waiting for some event to occur or some condition to be true. DAEMON PROCESSES can provide services and perform administrative functions. Also called DEMON PROCESS.

dangling threat Set of properties about the external environment for which there is no corresponding vulnerability and therefore no implied risk.

dangling vulnerability Set of properties about the internal environment for which there is no corresponding threat and, therefore, no implied risk.

DARPA ☞ DEFENSE ADVANCED RESEARCH PROJECTS AGENCY.

DASS ☞ DISTRIBUTED AUTHENTICATION SECURITY SERVICE.

data aggregation The compilation of individual data systems and data elements where the resulting aggregate has higher sensitivity to security than the highest sensitivity of the individual component. DATA AGGREGATION is best illustrated by looking at the aggregation of credit card purchases by an individual. Knowing a single purchase by a credit card is not very interesting or useful, but knowing a complete historical pattern about what, how, and when a person buys things could be very valuable.

data-driven attack An ATTACK that is triggered by the presence of a certain (possibly innocuous/inconspicuous) pattern in the data supplied to a program.

Data Encryption Standard CRYPTO-GRAPHIC ALGORITHM designed for the protection of UNCLASSIFIED data and published by the NATIONAL INSTITUTE OF STANDARDS AND TECHNOLOGY (U.S.) in FEDERAL INFORMATION PROCESSING STANDARD (FIPS) Publication 46. The same binary key is used for ENCRYPTION and DECRYPTION. *See also* ADVANCED ENCRYPTION STANDARD.

Figure D1 shows three stages: an initial permutation stage, 16 steps of encryption, and a final permutation stage. Each of the

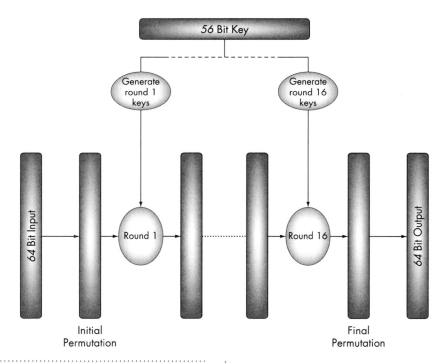

FIGURE D1. An illustration of DES.

16 steps operates on 48 of the 56 bits of the DATA ENCRYPTION STANDARD (DES) key.

NOTE: *FIPS Publication 46-3 (October 1999) specifies two CRYPTOGRAPHIC algorithms, the DATA ENCRYPTION STANDARD (DES) and the Triple Data Encryption Standard (TDEA). Details of FIPS 46-3 and these standards are available at http://csrc.nist.gov/publications/fips/ fips46-3/fips46-3.pdf.*

datagram ☞ INTERNET DATAGRAM.

data integrity Condition when data is unchanged from its source to destination.

data link layer The OSI layer that is responsible for data transfer across a single physical connection, or series of bridged connections, between two network entities. *See also* ISO OSI.

data origin authentication Corroboration that the source of data is as claimed.

data security The protection of data from unauthorized (accidental or intentional) modification, destruction, disclosure, or denial of service.

data transfer device Fill device designed to securely store, transport, and transfer electronically both COMSEC and TRANSEC keys, designed to be backward compatible with the previous generation of COMSEC common fill devices, and programmable to support modern mission systems.

DCE ☞ DISTRIBUTED COMPUTING ENVIRONMENT.

DDoS ☞ DISTRIBUTED DENIAL OF SERVICE.

decertification The revocation of the CERTIFICATION of an IS item or equipment for cause.

decipher To DECRYPT. To transform CI-PHERTEXT to PLAINTEXT. Deciphering is a narrower term than decrypting. ENCIPHERMENT specifically uses a CIPHER, whereas ENCRYPTION can use any means of concealment of data.

decode To convert encoded text to PLAINTEXT.

decryption To undo the ENCRYPTION process.

dedicated mode IS security mode of operation wherein each user with direct or indirect access to the system, its peripherals, remote terminals, or remote hosts has all of the following: (a) valid security CLEARANCE for all information within the system; (b) formal access approval and signed nondisclosure agreements for all the information stored and/or processed (including all compartments, subcompartments, and/or special access programs); and (c) a valid need-to-know for all information contained within the IS. When in dedicated security mode, a system is specifically and exclusively dedicated to and controlled for the processing of one particular type or CLASSIFICATION of information, either for full-time operation or for a specified period of time.

default classification Temporary CLASSIFICATION reflecting the highest CLASSIFICATION being processed in an IS. DEFAULT CLASSIFICATION is included in the caution statement affixed to an object.

Defense Advanced Research Projects Agency A central research and development organization for the Department of Defense (DoD). This U.S. government agency funded ARPANET. More details about DEFENSE ADVANCED RESEARCH PROJECTS AGENCY (DARPA) are available at http://www.darpa.mil.

Defense Information Infrastructure Connects U.S. DoD mission support, command and control, and intelligence computers. It is an interconnected system of computers, communications, data applications, people, training, and other support structures serving the DoD's needs.

degaussing Procedure that reduces the magnetic flux to virtually zero by applying a reversing magnetic field. Also called demagnetizing.

delegated accrediting authority ☞ DESIGNATED APPROVING AUTHORITY.

delegated development program INFOSEC program in which the director of the NATIONAL SECURITY AGENCY delegates, on a case-by-case basis, the development and/or production of an entire telecommunications product, including the INFOSEC portion, to a lead department or agency.

delegation Giving some of your rights to another person or process.

demon dialer A system that can be programmed to repeatedly dial the same phone number or a list of phone numbers.

demon process ☞ DAEMON PROCESS.

denial of service attack An ATTACK made on a computer system that denies a victim's access to a particular service. The victim may be a single server, multiple servers, a router, or a network of computers. Examples of DENIAL OF SERVICE (DoS) ATTACK include e-mail bombing and TCP SYN flooding, where an intruder sends a sequence of connection requests, that are TCP messages with SYN bit set to the target system to overflow the available buffer space.

dependability Defined with respect to some set of properties, a measure of how or whether a system can satisfy those properties.

dependence A subject is said to depend on an object if the subject may not work properly unless the object (possibly another subject) behaves properly. One system may depend on another system.

depot maintenance ☞ FULL MAINTENANCE.

derf Unauthorized and malicious use of a terminal or a console that has been left unattended and a user has not logged off from a terminal or the console.

DES ☞ DATA ENCRYPTION STANDARD.

descriptive top-level specification TOP-LEVEL SPECIFICATION written in a natural language (e.g., English), an informal design notation, or a combination of the two. DESCRIPTIVE TOP-LEVEL SPECIFICATION, required for a class B2 or B3 (as defined in the ORANGE BOOK, DEPARTMENT OF DEFENSE TRUSTED COMPUTER SYSTEM EVALUATION CRITERIA, DoD 5200.28-STD) information system, completely and accurately describes a TRUSTED COMPUTING BASE. *See also* FORMAL TOP-LEVEL SPECIFICATION.

designated accrediting authority ☞ DESIGNATED APPROVING AUTHORITY.

designated approving authority Official with the authority to formally assume responsibility for operating a system at an acceptable level of risk. This term is synonymous with DESIGNATED ACCREDITING AUTHORITY and DELEGATED ACCREDITING AUTHORITY.

design controlled spare part Part or subassembly for COMSEC EQUIPMENT or device with an NSA (U.S.) controlled design.

design documentation Set of documents, required for TRUSTED COMPUTER SYSTEM EVALUATION CRITERIA (TCSEC) classes C1

and above (as defined in the Orange Book, U.S. Department of Defense TRUSTED COMPUTER SYSTEM EVALUATION CRITERIA, DoD 5200.28-STD), whose primary purpose is to define and describe the properties of a system. As it relates to TCSEC, design documentation provides an explanation of how the security policy of a system is translated into a technical solution via the TRUSTED COMPUTING BASE (TCB) hardware, software, and firmware.

dial back Synonymous with CALL BACK.

dictionary attack An attempt to break a system or guess a password or a key by using a dictionary of common keys.

Diffie–Hellman key exchange A method of establishing a shared key over an insecure medium. This public-key algorithm was first published in a seminal paper [WD76b] by W. Diffie and M.E. Hellman. This algorithm depends for its effectiveness on the difficulty of computing discrete logarithms. A typical scenario using DIFFIE–HELLMAN KEY EXCHANGE is given in Figure D2 (a), and an outline of the algorithm is given in Figure D2 (b). Because X_A and X_B are private, a potential attacker has only p, α, Y_A, and Y_B, and the attacker has to take discrete logarithms to find the key.

digest A unique message fingerprint generated using a mathematical hash function. Synonyms are HASH, MESSAGE HASH, and MESSAGE DIGEST.

Digital Millennium Copyright Act DIGITAL MILLENNIUM COPYRIGHT ACT (DMCA) implements the two World Intellectual Property Organizations (WIPO) treaties, the WIPO copyright treaty and the WIPO Performances and Phonograms Treaty. It was signed into law on October 28, 1998. DMCA provides provisions related to the circumvention of copyright protection sys-

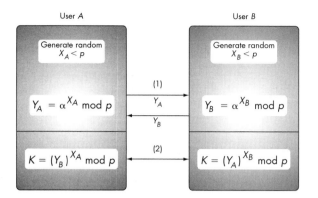

(a)

User A and User B wish to exchange key

Global Public Key

There are two publicly known numbers, a prime number p and an integer α.
$\alpha < p$ and α is a primitive element of p.

User A Key Generation

User A selects a private key X_A	$X_A < p$
Calculate Public key Y_A	$Y_A = \alpha^{X_A} \bmod p$

User B Key Generation

User A selects a private key X_B independent of A	$X_B < p$
Calculate Public key Y_B	$Y_B = \alpha^{X_B} \bmod p$

Each side keeps the X value private and makes the Y value publicly available to the other side. Both A and B now compute key K (see below), and this key K is identical for both users.

Generation of Secret Key by User A and User B

User A Secret Key	User B Secret Key
$K = (Y_B)^{X_A} \bmod p$	$K = (Y_A)^{X_B} \bmod p$

(b)

FIGURE D2. (a) A protocol showing use of Diffie–Hellman key exchange. (b) Diffie–Hellman algorithm.

tems, fair use in a digital environment, and online service provider (OSP) liability. It creates two new prohibitions in Title 17 of the U.S. code related to circumvention of technological measures used by copyright owners to protect their work and on tampering with copyright management information. It adds civil remedies and criminal penalties for violations.

The bill provides exceptions to prohibitions in the bill for law enforcement, intelligence, and other governmental activities, and there are six additional exceptions: nonprofit, library, archive and educational institution exception, reverse engineering, encryption research, protection of minors, personal privacy, and security testing.

NOTE: *The U.S. Copyright Office Summary of the Digital Millennium Copyright Act of 1998 is available from http://lcweb.loc.gov/copyright/legislation/dmca.pdf. This memorandum provides an overview of the law's provisions and briefly summarizes each of the five titles of the DMCA.*

Digital Music Access Technology The DIGITAL MUSIC ACCESS TECHNOLOGY (DMAT) is a trademark for products that were developed with SDMI specifications.

digital signature A block of data that is appended to a message and used to ensure message originator authenticity, integrity, and to provide NONREPUDIATION. Signature creation takes as its input the message and a private signature key and generates a signature. The verification algorithm takes as its input the message (unless a scheme with message recovery is used), the signature, and a public verification key, and returns an accept/reject answer.

NOTE: *The common explanation of signing as "encryption with the private key" is misleading and would at best fit RSA signatures. A convention is emerging whereby digital signatures refer to the mathematical scheme while electronic signatures refer to schemes linking documents to a (legal) person.*

Digital Signature Algorithm A public-key algorithm developed by the National Security Agency (U.S.) and based on the ElGamal signature scheme for producing a digital signature.

Digital Signature Standard A U.S. government standard based on the DSA, RSA, and ECDSA.

DII ☞ DEFENSE INFORMATION INFRASTRUCTURE.

directory service A service provided on a computer network that allows one to look up addresses (and perhaps other information such as CERTIFICATES) based on names or other attributes.

direct shipment Shipment of COMSEC MATERIAL directly from NSA (U.S.) to user COMSEC ACCOUNTS.

disaster recovery plan ☞ CONTINGENCY PLAN.

discrete logarithm problem A discrete logarithm is the inverse arithmetic operation of modular exponentiation, that is, finding x where $a^x = b$ modulo n. Public key CRYPTOSYSTEMS use the fact that modular exponentiation is a computationally easy problem, and finding x (discrete logarithm) is a computationally hard problem. The Diffie–Hellman algorithm uses discrete logarithms to define public and private key pairs.

discretionary access controls ACCESS CONTROL model, where access rights to the system resources are defined for each user of the system. Most commonly used form is ownership based, where the owner of a resource can decide who can access this resource and at what mode. Outside the

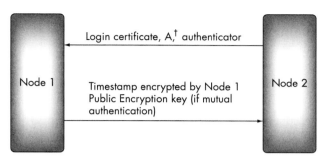

† - A is the encrypted signed Public Key for Node 1

FIGURE D3. Illustration of a DASS
AUTHENTICATION.

military environment, they are usually simply referred to as ACCESS CONTROLS.

distinguished name Globally unique identifier representing an individual's identity.

Distributed Authentication Security Service DISTRIBUTED AUTHENTICATION SECURITY SERVICE (DASS) is a PUBLIC KEY-based AUTHENTICATION protocol developed at Digital Equipment Corporation and documented in RFC 1507. See Figure D3.

DASS is an architecture; the actual product name based on DASS is SPX (pronounced SPHINX). In the DASS architecture, a certification hierarchy follows a naming hierarchy. One CA is responsible for one or more nodes in the naming hierarchy. A CA may sign for parents and children may also cross certify, allowing one CA to sign a certificate for another CA.

DASS uses X.509 syntax for certificates and uses a CERTIFICATE DISTRIBUTION CENTER (CDC) for the distribution of certificates. This system stores certificates and encrypted private keys. To get the encrypted private keys, a password-based AUTHENTICATION exchange is required.

Distributed Computing Environment A group of programs and protocols standardized by the Open Software Foundation built atop a cryptographically protected REMOTE PROCEDURE CALL protocol.

distributed denial of service A DENIAL OF SERVICE ATTACK that is simultaneously activated from many different points on a network. These points of origin may be geographically widespread. The combined effect of these attacks is potentially more devastating than a DENIAL OF SERVICE ATTACK.

DMAT ☞ DIGITAL MUSIC ACCESS TECHNOLOGY.

DMCA ☞ DIGITAL MILLENNIUM COPYRIGHT ACT.

DNS ☞ DOMAIN NAME SYSTEM.

DNSSEC The protocol DNSSEC provides security extensions to the DNS to assure data integrity or AUTHENTICATION. DNSSEC provides data integrity and authentication services to security-aware resolvers or applications through the use of CRYPTOGRAPHIC digital signatures. Security can be provided even through non-security-aware DNS servers in many cases. See RFC 2065 for more details of this protocol.

DNS spoofing Assuming the DNS name of another machine with malicious intent.

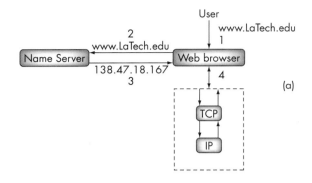

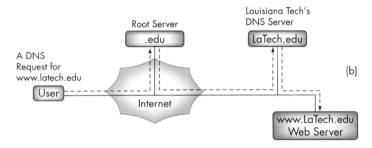

FIGURE D4. An example illustrating DOMAIN NAME SYSTEM.

DNS SPOOFING may be done by either corrupting the cache of a system or by compromising the DNS of a valid DOMAIN.

DoD Trusted Computer System Evaluation Criteria   Document containing the basic requirements and evaluation classes for assessing the degrees of effectiveness of hardware and software security controls built into an IS. This document, DoD 5200.28 STD, is frequently referred to as the ORANGE BOOK.

domain   In the Internet, a part of the naming hierarchy. Syntactically, an internet system domain name consists of names (labels) separated by periods (dots), e.g., tundra.mpk.ca.us.

Domain Name System   The naming convention defined in RFC 1003. DOMAIN NAME SYSTEM names are often referred to as Internet addresses of Internet names. In Figure D4, a user types in a Web site address through a browser. The browser then engages the name server to translate this Web site name into a host address. The numbers 1 through 4 show the sequence of steps before the address goes to the TCP/IP protocol. This procedure is followed for each session of requests, responses, and transfers.

NOTE: *For security extensions to DNS, see DNSSEC.*

dominate   Term used to compare IS security levels. Security level S1 is said to dominate security level S2 if the hierarchical CLASSIFICATION of S1 is greater than or equal to that of S2 and the nonhierarchical categories of S1 include all those of S2 as a subset.

dongle A hardware component that typically attaches to a PC's parallel port (on a Macintosh computer it attaches to the ADB port) to control access to an application on a computer.

DoS ☞ DENIAL OF SERVICE ATTACK.

DOS Disk Operating System (as in MS-DOS for personal computers).

dotted decimal notation The syntactic representation of a 32-bit integer that consists of four 8-bit numbers written in base 10 with periods separating them. Used to represent IP addresses in the Internet, such as 192.67.67.20.

download To transfer information such as a file or data over a network from a remote system to a local device, usually disk.

Transferring in the reverse direction is called uploading. This view assumes the network at the top and the individual component at the bottom.

drop accountability Procedure under which a COMSEC ACCOUNT custodian initially receipts for COMSEC MATERIAL and then provides no further accounting for it to its central office of record. Local ACCOUNTABILITY of the COMSEC MATERIAL may continue to be required. *See also* ACCOUNTING LEGEND CODE.

DSA ☞ DIGITAL SIGNATURE ALGORITHM.

DSS ☞ DIGITAL SIGNATURE STANDARD.

DTD ☞ DATA TRANSFER DEVICE.

dynamic web page Contents in a DYNAMIC WEB PAGE are based on a user's request and can be dynamically generated by a program, for example by a CGI script.

E

eavesdrop Passive attack where the attacker listens in on a conversation without the knowledge or consent of the communicating parties.

EBCDIC ☞ EXTENDED BINARY CODE DECIMAL INTERCHANGE CODE.

ebXML A set of specifications initiated by the United Nations (UN/CEFACT) and OASIS to provide an electronic business framework. These specifications are the forerunner of the EDI (Electronic Data Interchange) standard. These specifications are meant for global use and are based on public standards like HTTP, TCP/IP, MIME, UML, and XML. EBXML is a programming language and is computing-platform-independent.

These specifications are modular, and each specification set can be implemented as stand-alone and individually or may be combined in many ways by businesses and organizations following the EBXML standard.

The technical specifications of EBXML consist of five main areas: (1) business processes and information model, (2) company profile, (3) messaging services, (4) registry and repository, and (5) collaborative partner agreements. For more details, see the information at http://www.ebXML.org.

ECB ☞ ELECTRONIC CODE BOOK.

ECC ☞ ELLIPTIC CURVE CRYPTOGRAPHY.

ECDSA ☞ ELLIPTIC CURVE DIGITAL SIGNATURE ALGORITHM.

ECHELON A commonly used term, very hot in European politics, refers to an automated global interception and relay system supposed to be operated by the intelligence agencies of the United States, the United Kingdom, Canada, Australia, and New Zealand. There is no official confirmation of the existence of **ECHELON**, and the following information is speculative. A secret listening agreement, called UKUSA (UK-USA), assigns parts of the globe to each participating agency. It is suggested that **ECHELON** is capable of intercepting and processing many types of transmissions throughout the globe and may intercept as many as 3 billion communications every day, including phone calls, e-mail messages, Internet downloads, satellite transmissions, and so on (Kevin Poulsen, Echelon Revealed, ZDTV, June 9, 1999). More details are available at http://www.aclu.org/echelonwatch/.

EDE ☞ ENCRYPT/DECRYPT/ENCRYPT.

EES ☞ ESCROW ENCRYPTION STANDARD.

EGP ☞ EXTERIOR GATEWAY PROTOCOL.

EKMS ☞ ELECTRONIC KEY MANAGEMENT SYSTEM.

electronically generated key A key generated by the mechanical or electronic introduction of a seed key into a COMSEC device. The desired key is produced by using the seed key and a software algorithm contained in the device.

electronic code book A method of using a block encryption scheme to encrypt a large message. It is the most straightforward method, consisting of independently ENCRYPTING each PLAINTEXT block.

Electronic Digital Signature Act ☞ E-SIGN ACT.

Electronic Signature Directive A European Union (EU) directive stipulating that electronic signatures should become as legally valid as handwritten signatures. The directive is being implemented in the national laws of EU member states.

Electronic Key Management System The U.S. government's group of systems being developed to automate electronic key generation, distribution, use, destruction, etc., and to manage other COMSEC MATERIAL.

electronic messaging services Interpersonal messaging services meeting specific requirements that make them appropriate for conducting official government business.

electronic signature ☞ DIGITAL SIGNATURE.

electronic wallet Software that processes, stores, and provides access to cardholders' financial information, including credit card data and digital account IDs.

electronic warfare Use and control of electromagnetic spectrum for military purposes to conduct warfare or ATTACK or defend against an ADVERSARY.

ElGamal A PUBLIC KEY CRYPTOGRAPHIC system whose security depends on the difficulty of computing discrete logarithms. It is best known for its method of computing DIGITAL SIGNATURES, though the specification includes a technique for encryption as well. Named after its inventor Taher ElGamal.

elliptic curve cryptography PUBLIC KEY CRYPTOGRAPHY systems whose security is based on the intractability of the ELLIPTIC CURVE DISCRETE LOGARITHM problem.

elliptic curve digital signature algorithm The elliptic curve analogue of DSA that has been standardized by ANSI, IEEE, and NIST.

elliptic curve discrete logarithm A computationally harder variant of the discrete logarithm problem. Systems that use ELLIPTIC CURVE DISCRETE LOGARITHM can use smaller key sizes to provide the same level of computational security as systems based on the discrete logarithm problem.

emanations Electrical and electromagnetic signals emitted from electrical equipment and transmitted through the air or another conductor. Also called EMISSIONS.

embedded computer Computer system, usually a microprocessor-based component, that is part of a larger special-purpose system. For example, airplanes, cars, GPS receivers, and videocassette recorders contain embedded computer systems.

embedded cryptographic system CRYPTOSYSTEM whose task is to perform a function that is a crucial element of a larger system or subsystem.

embedded cryptography   CRYPTOGRAPHY engineered into a system that is not typically CRYPTOGRAPHIC.

emissions   ☞   EMANATIONS.

emissions security   Protection designed to deny unauthorized persons information derived from the interception and analysis of COMPROMISING EMANATIONS from computers, monitors, printers, and other information technologies.

encapsulating security payload   A part of the IPsec virtual private networking protocol used to provide AUTHENTICATION, CONFIDENTIALITY, or integrity in an IP datagram packet. See RFC 2406. *See also* INTERNET PROTOCOL SECURITY.

encapsulation   The technique used by layered protocols in which a layer adds header or trailer information to the data. For example, a packet would contain a header from the physical layer, followed by a header from the network (IP), followed by a header from the transport layer (TCP), followed by the application protocol data.

encipher   To ENCRYPT. To transform PLAINTEXT into CIPHERTEXT using an algorithm and secret key. See Figure C5 (cipher feedback).

encode   To convert PLAINTEXT to CIPHERTEXT.

encrypt   To scramble information so that only someone knowing the appropriate key can obtain the original information (through DECRYPTION).

encrypt/decrypt/encrypt   A method of making a secret key scheme more secure using multiple keys. The technique is to first ENCRYPT the message with one key, then do a DECRYPTION with a different key on the resulting CIPHERTEXT, and finally ENCRYPT the result with either the first key used or a third key. This method has the advantage that it is backward compatible with systems using only one key, by using three copies of the same key.

encryption algorithm   Series of steps that uses a key to transform the data so that the original data is rendered unintelligible to anyone without the appropriate DECRYPTION key.

end-item accounting   Accounting for all the accountable components of a COMSEC EQUIPMENT configuration by a single short title.

endorsed for unclassified cryptographic item   Unclassified CRYPTOGRAPHIC EQUIPMENT that has a U.S. government classified CRYPTOGRAPHIC LOGIC and is endorsed by the NSA (U.S.) for the protection of national security information. *See also* TYPE 2 product.

endorsement   NSA (U.S.) approval of a commercially developed product to safeguard national security information.

end system   A system that contains application processes capable of communicating through all seven layers of TCP/IP protocols. Equivalent to Internet host.

end-to-end encryption   A type of ENCRYPTION in which a message is ENCRYPTED from point of origin to point of destination. See Figure E1.

end-to-end security   Securing information in an IS from point of origin to point of destination.

entity   OSI terminology for a layer protocol machine. An entity within a layer performs the functions of the layer within a single computer system, accessing the layer entity below and providing services to the

FIGURE E1. End-to-end encryption.

layer entity above at local service access points.

entrapment   Deliberate insertion of flaws in an IS for the purpose of detecting sabotage attempts.

environment   Conglomeration of external factors that affect the development, operation, and maintenance of an IS.

EPL   ☞   EVALUATED PRODUCTS LIST.

erasure   Process intended to render stored data irretrievable by normal means.

escrow   To hold something in safekeeping.

Escrow Encryption Standard   U.S. government standard for telephone communications specifying the Skipjack ENCRYPTION algorithm and support for the LAW ENFORCEMENT ACCESS FIELD (LEAF). The LEAF allows DECRYPTION in government-authorized wiretaps.

escrow service   An independent party who keeps something (usually an auction buyer's payment) until the buyer receives the appropriate item from the seller.

E-Sign Act   The U.S. Federal Electronic Signature in Global and National Commerce Act, gives the electronic signature and Internet-conveyed record the same legal standing as a pen-and-paper document. To be legally binding, this act requires consumers to agree to electronically signed contracts and consent to receiving records over the Internet. Some notices, such as evictions, health insurance lapses, etc., must still come in the form of paper. The legislation does not prescribe any particular technology to verify an electronic signature; security protocols can be as simple as a password or may consist of emerging new technologies, such as thumbprint scanners.

This act will advance e-commerce by finalizing sales via computers. For example, consumers who shop online for a new car or a home mortgage can seal the deal over their computers.

ESP   ☞   ENCAPSULATING SECURITY PAYLOAD.

Ethernet   A widely used local area network technology invented at the Xerox Corporation Palo Alto Research Center. The medium is a passive coaxial cable and uses CSMA/CD access technology. Ethernet now refers to the whole family of IEEE 802 standards: thin Ethernet, thick Ethernet, wireless Ethernet, fast Ethernet.

Euclidean algorithm   An algorithm to find the GREATEST COMMON DIVISOR of two numbers. It can also be used to compute multiplicative inverses in modular arithmetic.

Evaluated Products List   Equipment, hardware, software, and/or firmware evaluated by the NATIONAL COMPUTER SECURITY CENTER (NCSC) in accordance with DoD (U.S.) TCSEC and found to be technically acceptable.

NOTE: *Many countries maintain EPLs, for example the latest EPL for Defense Signal Directorate of*

Australia is available at http://www.dsd.gov.au/ infosec/aisep/EPL.html. The U.S. EPL by vendor and by class are available at http://www.radium. ncsc.mil/tpep/epl/. The United Kingdom list of evaluated products is available at http://www.itsec. gov.uk/.

event   An occurrence that might affect the performance of an IS.

EW ☞   ELECTRONIC WARFARE.

executive state   An operational state of an IS in which certain privileged instructions may be executed. Synonymous with SUPERVISOR STATE.

exercise key   Key whose sole function is to safeguard communications transmitted through the air during military or organized civil training exercises.

exploitable channel   Channel in which it is possible to violate the security policy of an IS and that can be used or detected outside of the TRUSTED COMPUTING BASE. *See also* COVERT CHANNEL.

exploder   (1) A system to expand an item (usually many items are combined to form a single item) into its components. (2) Component of an electronic mail system that takes a single message addressed to a distribution list and turns it into many mail messages to the individual recipients.

export   Information transfer from one system to another, usually from a trusted to an untrusted system.

Extended Binary Code Decimal Interchange Code   A code developed by IBM for encoding letters, numerals, and punctuation marks as numbers. Now rendered almost obsolete by ASCII and UNICODE.

Exterior Gateway Protocol   A reachability routing protocol used by gateways in a two-level internet. EXTERIOR GATEWAY PROTOCOL (EGP) is used in the Internet core system. *See also* GATEWAY.

External Data Representation   A standard for machine-independent data structures developed by Sun Microsystems. Similar to ASN.1.

extraction resistance   Capability of CRYPTO-EQUIPMENT or secure telecommunications equipment to resist efforts to extract a key.

F

fail safe Property of a system in which any failure will leave the system in a safe state. The system may not operate, but it will not be in an unsafe state. When hardware or software failure is detected, programs and processing systems are automatically protected.

fail secure Property of a system in which any failure will leave the system in a secure state. The system may not operate, but it will not be in an insecure state.

fail soft Selective termination of affected unnecessary processing when it has been determined that hardware or software is about to fail.

failure access Unauthorized access to data after the failure of hardware or software.

failure control Method of detecting when hardware or software is about to fail and providing FAIL SAFE or FAIL SOFT recovery.

false negative (1) In INTRUSION DETECTION, when a system does not issue an ALERT on intrusion because based on the internal monitoring procedures, the intrusion action appears to be nonintrusive. (2) The term

also applies to biometric AUTHENTICATION and other measurement processes. In AUTHENTICATION, a FALSE NEGATIVE means that a legitimate user is not AUTHENTICATED correctly.

false positive (1) In INTRUSION DETECTION, when a system falsely issues an ALERT, treating a legitimate action as a system intrusion. (2) In BIOMETRIC authentication, when a user is wrongly accepted as legitimate.

NOTE: *In BIOMETRIC authentication, a false positive is worse than a false negative because it means that a person has been positively AUTHENTICATED who should not have been.*

Federal Information Processing Standard One of a series of U.S. government documents developed by NIST specifying a standard of various aspects of data processing, including the DATA ENCRYPTION STANDARD (DES) and the ADVANCED ENCRYPTION STANDARD (AES).

Federal Internet Exchange Points FEDERAL INTERNET EXCHANGE POINT (FIX) is a BGP peering point between federal (U.S.) and commercial networks. Used by the U.S. government to exchange data primarily from the military network and NASA Science net to the Internet.

fetch protection   Restriction provided by IS hardware to prevent one user's program from gaining access to data in another user's segment of storage.

file protection   Collection of processes and procedures that prohibit unauthorized access, CONTAMINATION, elimination, modification, or destruction of a file or any of its contents.

file security   Method of limiting access to computer files to authorized users only.

File Transfer Protocol   The Internet protocol used to transfer files between hosts. FILE TRANSFER PROTOCOL (FTP) is an application-level protocol, which uses two parallel TCP connections: (1) control connection and (2) data connection, for file transfer. Control connection is used to send control information between the two hosts. A data connection is established only when the user requests a file transfer to and from the server. See Figure F1.

fill device   COMSEC device that transfers or stores a key in electronic form or that inserts a key into CRYPTO-EQUIPMENT.

filter   (1) To sift through messages or data. For example, filters are applied at the IP layer to block any kind of traffic from or to an IP address. (2) Software that automatically blocks e-mail messages sent from preset addresses or about certain subjects.

fingerprint system   A BIOMETRIC system in which a fingerprint pattern is matched with a stored pattern or a template for AUTHENTICATION.

FIPS   ☞   FEDERAL INFORMATION PROCESSING STANDARD.

FIREFLY   Protocol of key management based on PUBLIC KEY CRYPTOGRAPHY.

firewall   Systems that act as a GATEWAY between two networks to enforce an access policy. This may be hardware or software to enforce a boundary between networks. The purpose of a firewall is to prevent unauthorized access to networks and computer systems.

firmware   A program recorded in permanent or semipermanent computer memory.

FIRST   ☞   FORUM OF INCIDENT RESPONSE AND SECURITY TEAMS.

fishbowl   A monitoring technique in which a user under surveillance is contained and isolated in a system to gain information about the user. *See also* HONEY POT.

FIX   ☞   FEDERAL INTERNET EXCHANGE POINTS.

fixed COMSEC facility   COMSEC FACILITY in an immobile structure or on a ship.

flaming   Sending a nasty message across the Internet.

flaw   Error in an IS that may allow a breach of security.

flaw hypothesis methodology   System analysis and penetration technique in which a list of hypothetical flaws is created based on the analysis of the specification and documentation for an IS. This list is prioritized on the basis of the estimated probability that a flaw exists, on the ease of removing the flaw, and on the amount of control or compromise the removal would provide. This list is used to perform penetration testing of a system.

flooding   Insertion of a large quantity of data that may result in a denial of service. In Figure F2, node A sends packets to all lines that it is connected to (node B and node D) in an uncontrolled fashion. The excess packets result in a DENIAL OF SERVICE

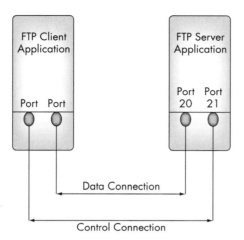

FIGURE F1. An example of an FTP session.

ATTACK by clogging the lines and draining the resources of nodes B and D.

fork bomb   A piece of code that recursively spawns ("forks") copies of itself. It very quickly proliferates to so many copies that all the system resources are consumed.

formal   (1) Having a strict mathematical or logical basis. (2) Following a specific set of rules.

formal access approval   Documented approval by a data owner, which allows others access to a particular category of information.

formal development methodology
Development (of software) strategy that meets design specifications.

formal proof   A mathematical argument that logically justifies each proof step and proves a theorem or set of theorems. These formal proofs provide A1 and beyond A1 assurance under the DoD TRUSTED COMPUTER SYSTEM EVALUATION CRITERIA (ORANGE BOOK).

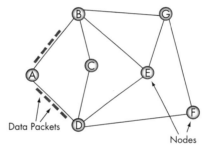

FIGURE F2. A is flooding both B and D with packets.

formal security policy model   A statement of a security policy that is mathematically precise. Typically, a formal security model defines what it means to be secure, the initial state of the system, and how the system changes state. In order for a system to be shown to be secure, the initial state and all possible subsequent states must be proven to remain secure.

formal top-level specification   Top-level specification written in a FORMAL mathematical language so that theorems can be hypothesized and formally proven.

8	16			16	8
Beginning Sequence	Header	Body	//	CRC	Ending Sequence

FIGURE F3. An example of an HDLC frame.

formal verification Using FORMAL PROOFS to show how the formal specification of a system and a formal policy model (design verification) or the formal specification and its high-level program implementation (implementation verification) are compliant.

form factor The outward appearance of a function, for instance the number and size of the input and the number and size of the outputs. In computing, this frequently refers to the shape and size of a piece of hardware; e.g., the form factor of a CD-ROM drive may be "5.25 inch drive bay compatible."

FORTEZZA card A low-cost CRYPTOGRAPHIC hardware implementation for digital signature and encryption services for the desktop. The FORTEZZA crypto card was developed by the U.S. NATIONAL SECURITY AGENCY (NSA) and implements the "key escrow" mechanism outlined in Federal Information Processing Standard (FIPS)-185. The NSA will no longer implement the FIPS and will implement the transition to key recovery. The FORTEZZA technology provides CONFIDENTIALITY, AUTHENTICATION, message integrity, and NONREPUDIATION. Many commercial implementations of the FORTEZZA card are now available.

Forum of Incident Response and Security Teams This is a group of security practioners from government, commercial, and academic organizations who respond to COMPUTER SECURITY INCIDENTS. Its aim is to "foster cooperation and coordination in incident prevention, to prompt rapid reaction to incidents, and to promote information sharing among members and the community at large." More information is available at http://www.first.org.

fragmentation The process in which an IP DATAGRAM is broken into smaller pieces to fit the requirements of a given physical network. The reverse process is termed reassembly. *See also* MAXIMUM TRANSMISSION UNIT.

frame The unit of transmission in a data link layer protocol. It consists of a data link layer header followed by a packet. Figure F3 gives an example of an HDLC (High-Level Data Link Control) frame.

frequency hopping Repeated switching of frequencies to prevent unauthorized interception or jamming during radio transmission.

front-end security filter Security filter kept separate from the rest of an IS to protect system integrity. Synonymous with FIREWALL.

FTP ☞ FILE TRANSFER PROTOCOL.

full maintenance Complete diagnostic repair, modification, replacement and overhaul of INFOSEC equipment, also known as DEPOT MAINTENANCE (U.S.). *See also* LIMITED MAINTENANCE.

functional proponent ☞ NETWORK SPONSOR.

functional testing A segment of security testing in which it is shown whether advertised security mechanisms of an IS will work under operational conditions.

gateway   A node connected to two or more administratively distinct networks and/or SUBNETS to which hosts send DATAGRAMS to be forwarded. The original Internet term for what is now called ROUTER, or, more precisely, IP ROUTER. In modern usage, the terms "gateways" and "application gateways" refer to systems that translate from some native format to another. Examples include X.400 to/from RFC 822 electronic mail gateways. *See also* ROUTER.

GCD   ☞   GREATEST COMMON DIVISOR.

Generic Security Service Application Programming Interface   GENERIC SECURITY SERVICE APPLICATION PROGRAMMING INTERFACE (GSS-API) is a CRYPTOGRAPHIC APPLICATION PROGRAMMING INTERFACE that specifies how applications, for example, communication protocols can securely handle session communication, including AUTHENTICATION, data integrity, and data CONFIDENTIALITY. The GSS-API insulates applications from the specifics of underlying mechanisms making them portable. For example, GSS-API implementations are built on varied secret-key and public-key technologies. More information of the current

(Version 2) GSS-API definition is available in RFC 2078.

GSS-API is also a part of the Open Group Common Environment Specification. Complementary API, such as GSS-IDUP specifies store-and-forward messaging, negotiation facility for selection of a common mechanism shared between peers, and of individual underlying GSS-API mechanisms. More details of GSS-IDUP are available in RFC 2479.

Global System for Mobile Communications   GLOBAL SYSTEM FOR MOBILE COMMUNICATIONS (GSM) is an open, non-proprietary mobile telephone system that uses digital technology and time division multiple access transmission methods to provide international roaming capability. The same phone number can be contacted seamlessly in more than 170 countries using GSM. Addition of GSM satellite roaming provides service access to areas where terrestrial coverage is not available.

NOTE: *In 1982 the Conference of European Posts and Telegraphs (CEPT) formed a study group called the Groupe Spécial Mobile (GSM) to study and de-*

velop a panEuropean public land mobile system. In 1989, the European Telecommunication Standards Institute (ETSI) took up the responsibilities of GSM and published (1990) the phase I of the GSM specifications. Commercial service was started in mid-1991 and its use expanded. In addition to Europe, the standard is common to South Africa, Australia, and many Middle and Far East countries have chosen GSM. The acronym GSM now stands for Global System for Mobile telecommunications. More information about GSM in North America can be found at http://www.gsm-pcs.org/. Other information about GSM can be found at GSM association site at http://www.gsmworld.com.

granularity   The smallest level of clarity. The granularity of an ACCESS CONTROL MECHANISM refers to the smallest unit for which individual ACCESS CONTROLS can be set. In a database system, the ACCESS CONTROL granularity may be at the record level, or for a more richly featured database, the GRANULARITY may be at the individual field level.

greatest common divisor   The largest integer that evenly divides each of a set of integers.

group   A set of users in a system, each of which might be given certain access rights by a security system.

GSM   ☞   GLOBAL SYSTEM FOR MOBILE COMMUNICATIONS.

GSS-API   ☞   GENERIC SECURITY SERVICE APPLICATION PROGRAMMING INTERFACE.

guard   Limits information exchange between systems. A guard can be a specialized type of firewall, typically designed to connect between two SYSTEM HIGH networks operating at different CLASSIFICATIONS or compartments. For example, a guard between a secret network and a confidential network will ensure that no secret information is transmitted to the confidential network.

hacker (1) Someone who plays with computers for the intellectual CHALLENGE. (2) Somebody who enjoys learning the details of systems and to stretch the capabilities of systems as opposed to people who prefer to learn the necessary minimum to work on a system. (3) Someone who penetrates security controls or explores computers and networks with malicious intent.

> NOTE: *Some writers ascribe definition (3) to the term CRACKER, so that the term HACKER applies only to people with no malicious intent, although now hacker and cracker are used interchangeably.*

hacking Unauthorized, possibly malicious attempts to bypass the security mechanisms of computer systems and networks. See note (HACKER).

hacking run HACKING that continues for more than a 12-hour period. It usually continues outside normal working hours.

handprint system A security system that requires a handprint pattern to be matched with a stored pattern.

handshaking procedures The dialogue that allows two ISs to synchronize, identify, and AUTHENTICATE each other.

hard copy key Printed key lists, punched or printed key tapes, programmable read-only memories (PROM), or other physical material for keying.

hardwired key A key that is permanently installed.

hash A one-way function that takes an arbitrary-sized input and yields a fixed-size output. A HASH function is one-way if it is computationally infeasible to find an input that yields a given output. A HASH function is collision-free if no two inputs have the same output. A HASH function is collision-resistant if it is computationally infeasible, given one input, to find a second input such that both have the same output. Hash functions generally need to be collision-resistant. Synonym DIGEST. See Figure H1.

Figure H1 explains the operations of a HASH function. An input message M is broken into separate predetermined fixed-sized blocks $M_1, M_2, \ldots, M_N$. The HASH of M is the result of the application of a transformation, usually a compression function Φ on each block of M. An initial value H_0 is concatenated with M_1, and the function Φ is applied to produce H_1. The process

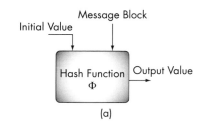

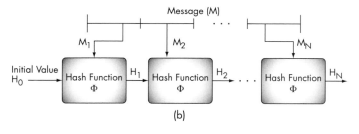

(b)

FIGURE H1. Illustration of hashing.

$H_i = \Phi (M_i \| H_{i-1})$ is repeated on all the blocks H_i. *See also* DIGEST.

NOTE: *Hash functions are usually not keyed, where as MACs based on hash functions are usually keyed, e.g., HMAC.*

hashing Computing a HASH TOTAL.

hash total The value computed on data for finding errors or evidence of manipulation. *See also* CHECKSUM.

hashword The memory address where HASH TOTAL is contained.

high-risk environment Location or geographic area where an information system's security equipment is not secure.

header Control information at the beginning of a message, segment, datagram, packet, or block of data.

high-threat environment ☞ HIGH-RISK ENVIRONMENT.

high water mark An IS's highest security level.

hoax virus Warnings for viruses that do not exist. These warnings are usually transmitted through e-mail messages that are forwarded many times and contain pleas for the receiver to forward the warning to others.

honey pot An IS environment specifically constructed to lure hackers or crackers into attacking it, for the purpose of identifying them and observing them in action. This environment is generally isolated from the rest of the network (or system) to prevent accidental damage. This term was introduced in Cheswick and Bellovin's book FIREWALL AND INTERNET SECURITY [WRC94].

hop A direct communication channel between two computers. In a complex computer network a message might take many hops between its source and destination.

host (1) A computer in an internetwork environment that has access to other computers on the Internet. Hosts are the primary computers connected to the network, which besides contributing to the network load perform operations like running user programs, compilers, and text editors. (2) In a mainframe environment a host is a mainframe computer to which terminals and workstations may be connected, and the host is used as a provider of services.

human safety   A necessary feature of a system to preserve personal and collective safety.

IA ☞ INFORMATION ASSURANCE.

IAB ☞ INTERNET ARCHITECTURE BOARD.

IANA ☞ INTERNET ASSIGNED NUMBER AUTHORITY.

ICMP ☞ INTERNET CONTROL MESSAGE PROTOCOL.

IDEA ☞ INTERNATIONAL DATA ENCRYPTION ALGORITHM.

identification An IS's method of recognizing an entity.

identity token A physical object, such as a smart card or metal key, that AUTHENTICATES identity.

identity validation Tests that an information system uses to identify users or resources.

IDIOT ☞ INTRUSION DETECTION IN OUR TIME.

IEEE ☞ INSTITUTE OF ELECTRICAL AND ELECTRONICS ENGINEERS.

IEEE 1363 standard for public-key cryptography This standard aims to provide a common framework and interoperability for public-key technology. It covers such areas as key agreements, encryption, and signatures.

IEEE 1363 defines three categories of public-key cryptographic algorithms: discrete logarithm, elliptic curves, and integer factorization. It also covers keys and parameters in hybrid systems.

NOTE: *IEEE 1363 became a standard in the year 2000. For more information about this standard, see: http://grouper.ieee.org/groups/1363/index.html.*

IESG ☞ INTERNET ENGINEERING STEERING GROUP.

IETF ☞ INTERNET ENGINEERING TASK FORCE.

IFCC ☞ INTERNET FRAUD COMPLAINT CENTER.

IGP ☞ INTERIOR GATEWAY PROTOCOL.

IKE ☞ INTERNET KEY EXCHANGE.

IMAP vulnerability A buffer overflow vulnerability that exists in some implementations of IMAP (Internet Message Access Protocol) that allows an attacker to execute arbitrary code.

imitative communications deception
Deception effected by an ADVERSARY's tele-communications signals being injected with deceptive messages or signals. *See also* COMMUNICATIONS DECEPTION and MANIPULATIVE COMMUNICATIONS DECEPTION.

impersonation (1) A form of SPOOFING. (2) Pretending to be an authorized user to gain access to a system. Synonymous with MASQUERADING.

implant An electronic device or the modification of electronic equipment in order to intercept information-bearing emissions.

implementation A mechanism (in software, hardware, or both) for correctly realizing a specified design.

import The transfer of information from one system to another; usually refers to information transfer from an untrusted system to a trusted system.

inadvertent disclosure When an unauthorized person unintentionally is granted access to information.

Ina Jo The System Development Corporation's specification and verification methodology, based on a nonprocedural state-transition specification language, Ina Jo, which incorporates user-supplied invariants to formally demonstrate that security properties are met.

incident An assessed event that could or does adversely affect an IS.

incomplete parameter checking A system flaw caused by the failure of the operating system to completely check all parameters for ACCURACY and consistency, and which makes the system vulnerable to penetration.

indicator An expected action taken by an ADVERSARY to prepare for an ATTACK.

individual accountability (1) The positive association of a user's identity with the time, method, and degree of access to an IS. (2) An association of a user's identity with certain actions performed on an IS. For example, there may be individual accountability for an e-mail sent, even if not for the actual login.

inference channel Indirect information flow channel by which CLASSIFIED INFORMATION can be inferred from UNCLASSIFIED data and metadata, e.g., database dependencies, statistical correlation, etc.

information assurance Ensuring the availability, integrity, AUTHENTICATION, CONFIDENTIALITY, and NONREPUDIATION of information and information systems by incorporating protection, detection, and reaction capabilities to restore information systems.

information assurance red team A team that acts like an ADVERSARY to expose and exploit an IS's vulnerabilities to see how the security posture can be improved.

information environment Individuals, organizations, or systems that collect, process, or disseminate information, along with the information itself.

information flow chart A diagram that indicates the flow of information within a system. Frequently used to access the potential for covert channels within a system. INFORMATION FLOW CHARTS are helpful in ensuring that IS information transfers are made only from a lower security level object to an object of a higher security level.

information label Label used in compartmented mode workstations for describing a particular item (subject or object), for example, a file, a window, or a process. An INFORMATION LABEL is similar to a SENSITIVITY LABEL, except that INFORMATION LABEL: 1. Provide additional information of how the item may be managed, for example, it may be labeled "Eyes Only", "Company Proprietary", or "Public"; 2. Represent the sensitivity of the information whereas SENSITIVITY LABEL provides access marking, such as read or read-and-write; 3. Automatically change as the content of the items changes, whereas SENSITIVITY LABEL do not automatically change with change in content.

information level   The security level implied by the CLASSIFICATION and categories on an information label.

information operations   (1) Operations that exploit or adversely affect an ADVERSARY'S information content and systems while protecting one's own. (2) Defending one's own information and ISs, while attempting to affect the information and ISs of adversaries.

information system   The entire infrastructure, organization, personnel, and components for the collection, processing, storage, transmission, display, dissemination, and disposition of information.

information system security   The protection of information systems against unauthorized access to or modification of information, whether in storage, processing, or transit, and against the denial of service to authorized users, including those measures necessary to detect, document, and counter such threats.

information system security equipment modification   The modification of any fielded hardware, firmware, software, or portion thereof, under NSA (U.S.) CONFIGURATION CONTROL. There are three classes of modifications: mandatory (to include human safety); optional/special mission modifications; and repair actions. These classes apply to elements, subassemblies, equipment, systems, and software packages performing functions such as key generation, key distribution, message encryption, DECRYPTION, AUTHENTICATION, or those mechanisms necessary to satisfy security policy, labeling, identification, or ACCOUNTABILITY.

information system security manager   Head of COMPUTER SECURITY matters.

information system security officer   The person responsible for ensuring the security of an information system from design through disposal. Synonymous with SYSTEM SECURITY OFFICER.

information system security product   A security-related item, technique, or service of an information system.

Information Technology Security Evaluation Criteria   Harmonized criteria developed jointly by European nations to specify 6 levels of ASSURANCE. Becoming obsolete due to the adoption of the COMMON CRITERIA.

information warfare   Information operations in times of conflict and war to promote specific actions to deny, exploit, corrupt, or destroy an enemy's information and its functions.

INFOSEC   ☞   INFORMATION SYSTEM SECURITY.

initialization vector   A number used by the CBC, OFB, and CFB ENCRYPTION techniques to initialize the first round. Subsequent rounds use the results of earlier rounds.

initialize   (1) To set the state of a system to its initial configuration. (2) To set the state of a CRYPTOGRAPHIC LOGIC process before key generation, encryption, or any other operating mode.

inspectable space   The three-dimensional space surrounding equipment that processes CLASSIFIED and/or sensitive information within which TEMPEST exploitation is not considered practical or where the legal authority to identify and/or remove a potential TEMPEST exploitation exists. Synonymous with ZONE OF CONTROL.

Institute of Electrical and Electronics Engineers

The INSTITUTE OF ELECTRICAL AND ELECTRONICS ENGINEERS (IEEE) is a professional society for the advancement of electrical and information technology and sciences. It also develops standards including those for networks and security. More information about IEEE is available at http://www.ieee.org

integrated services digital network

INTEGRATED SERVICES DIGITAL NETWORKS (ISDN) combine voice and digital network services in a single medium, making it possible to offer customers digital data services as well as voice connections through a single "wire." The standards that define ISDN are specified by CCITT/ITU.

In Figure I1, the circuit switched, packet switched, dedicated point-to-point, and call services are brought together at an ISDN switch and accessed by a user through a common terminal. ISDN includes two levels of services: the basic rate interface and primary rate interface. Basic rate interface is meant for home and small businesses, and primary rate interface is meant for large-volume users. Both of these services include a number of B and D channels. Each B-channel (B stands for bearer) carries data, voice, and other services, and D-channel (D stands for delta) carries control and signaling information.

integrity

A condition in which data (or a system itself) has not been modified or corrupted without AUTHORIZATION. A system protects the integrity of data if it prevents unauthorized modification, as opposed to protecting the CONFIDENTIALITY of data, which prevents unauthorized disclosure.

integrity check value

A value such as a CHECKSUM, DIGEST, or DIGITAL SIGNATURE that can be used to detect (unauthorized) modifications made to an IS that might breach its INTEGRITY.

interface

(1) Common boundary where interactions occur between independent systems. (2) A part of the boundary around a system through which it interacts with its environment, which may include other systems.

interface control document

Technical design document that species an interface and identifies the authorities and responsibilities for ensuring its correct operation.

interim approval

A temporary AUTHORIZATION to process information in an IS on the basis of a preliminary security evaluation.

Interior Gateway Protocol

The protocol used to exchange ROUTING information between collaboration routers in the Internet. RIP and OSPF are examples of INTERIOR GATEWAY PROTOCOL (IGP).

intermediary

Something that facilitates communication between parties that wish to communicate.

intermediate system

A system that is not an end system but that serves instead to relay communications between end systems. *See also* REPEATER, BRIDGE, and ROUTER.

International Data Encryption Algorithm

A secret-key CRYPTOGRAPHIC scheme developed at the Institute for Signal and Information Processing of the Swiss Federal Institute of Technology, Zurich, by James Massey and Xuejia Lai. See Figure I2. IDEA encrypts a 64-bit block of PLAINTEXT into a 64-bit block of CIPHERTEXT using a 128-bit key. The 128-bit key is expanded into 52 16-bit keys, $K_1, K_2, \ldots, K_{52}$ by chopping off 16 bits from left of

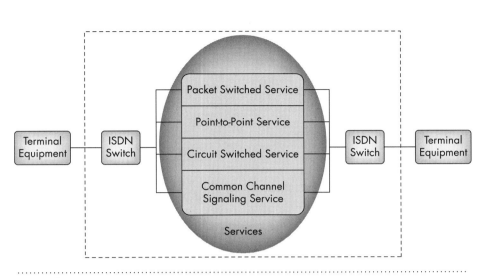

FIGURE 11. ISDN architecture.

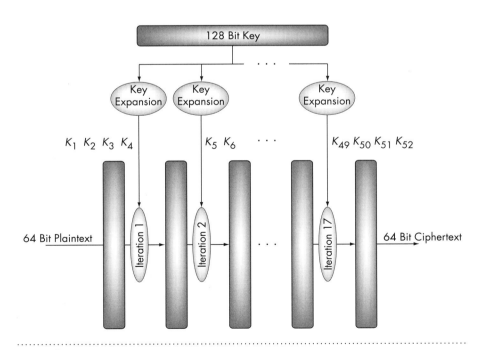

FIGURE 12. Illustration of International Data Encryption Algorithm.

the 128 bit key. The INTERNATIONAL DATA ENCRYPTION ALGORITHM (IDEA) is performed in 17 iterations: Odd-numbered iterations use four keys, while even-numbered iterations use two keys. The procedure generates the ENCRYPTED text over 17 iterations.

International Organization for Standardization   INTERNATIONAL ORGANIZATION FOR STANDARDIZATION (ISO) is a federation of national standards organizations from countries around the world. Established in 1947, ISO is located in Geneva, Switzerland, and is a nongovernmental organization with a mission to promote the development of worldwide standards and related activities. ISO develops and publishes international standards. More details about ISO can be found at http://www.iso.ch.

NOTE: *There is a lack of correspondence between the name International Organization for Standards and its short form ISO (not IOS). The word "ISO" is derived from Greek "isos," which means equal. "Isos" is the root of terms such as "isometric" and "isonomy." The line of thinking from "equal" to "standard" led to the choice of "ISO" as the name of the organization.*

ISO is used around the world and thus avoids many acronyms resulting from the translation of "International Organization for Standardization" into different international languages, such as IOS in English and OIN (Organisation Internationale de Normalisation) in French.

International Telecommunications Union   An international organization that deals with standardization activities related to global communications networks. It was earlier called COMITÉ CONSULTATIF INTERNATIONAL TÉLÉPHONIQUE ET TÉLÉGRAPHIQUE (CCITT). *See also* CCITT.

International Traffic in Arms Regulations   The collection of laws in the United States that regulate the export of defense services and defense technologies. Designations of defense articles and defense services are based primarily on whether an article or service is deemed to be inherently military in character. There has been some controversy about applicability of INTERNATIONAL TRAFFIC IN ARMS REGULATIONS (ITAR) to sending encryption programs outside the U.S. Encryption programs are treated as defense technology, and so their export in electronic form (for example, through e-mail or through the Web) may violate ITAR.

Details of ITAR can be found at http://www.epic.org/crypto/export_ controls/itar.html.

Archives related to ITAR and export of encryption technology can be found at the Electronic Frontier Foundation Web site at http://www.eff.org/pub/Privacy/ITAR_ export.

internet   An internet is a collection of networks tied into a network using an internet protocol. In general "internet" refers to any internet, and "Internet" (with a capital I) to the global Internet (see Figure I3(a)).

The Internet is a conglomeration of autonomous systems (AS), each of which is under the control of a single administrative unit and whose structure is transparent from the outside. As an example, a large corporation's network may be organized as an AS. Figure I3(b) shows a typical routing structure between two ASs within the Internet.

Internet Activities Board   ☞   INTERNET ARCHITECTURE BOARD.

Internet address   In IPv4, a 32-bit address assigned to hosts using TCP/IP. See DOTTED DECIMAL NOTATION.

NOTE: *IPv6 provides 128-bit addresses. Whereas IPv4 which is currently the most used protocol uses*

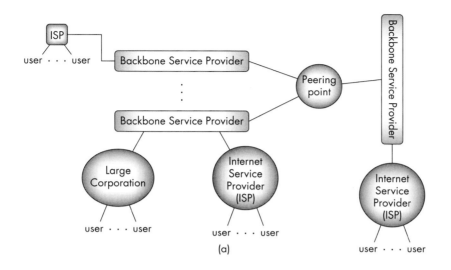

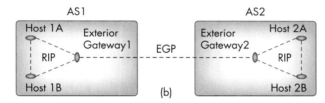

FIGURE 13. Conceptual idea of the Internet.

Activities Board. Earlier history of Internet Activities Board is not traceable from public records. A snapshot of the IAB in 1990, and a short history, are given in RFC 1160.

32 bit addresses. IPv6 provides mechanisms for smooth transition for hosts and routers to dynamically tunnel IPv6 packets over IPv4 routing infrastructure.

Internet Architecture Board The technical body that oversees the development of the Internet suite of protocols and management. It has two subcommittees: IETF (INTERNET ENGINEERING TASK FORCE) and IRTF (INTERNET RESEARCH TASK FORCE). INTERNET ARCHITECTURE BOARD's (IAB) charter is given in RFC 2850. More information is available at http://www.iab.org.

NOTE: *The IAB was set up in 1983 when the Internet was still in its infancy as a U.S. government research project; at that time it was called the Internet*

Internet Assigned Number Authority
A group organized through the Internet Society for maintaining assigned numbers relating to the Internet Protocol suite. Details of INTERNET ASSIGNED NUMBER AUTHORITY (IANA) are available at http://www.iana.org.

Internet Control Message Protocol
The protocol used to handle errors and control messages at the IP layer. INTERNET CONTROL MESSAGE PROTOCOL (ICMP) is used from GATEWAYS to host, and between hosts to report errors and make routing suggestions. ICMP is actually part of the IP proto-

col. Details of the protocol are given in RFC 792.

NOTE: *RFC 1885 gives the specifications of Internet Control Message Protocol (ICMPv6) for the Internet Protocol Version 6 (IPv6).*

internet datagram   The unit of data exchange between a pair of internet modules.

Internet Engineering Steering Group
The executive committee of the INTERNET ENGINEERING TASK FORCE (IETF). A steering committee that oversees the activities of the IETF. More information about INTERNET ENGINEERING STEERING GROUP (IESG) is available at http://www.ietf.org/iesg.html

Internet Engineering Task Force   A standards body whose focus is protocols for use in the Internet. Its publications are called Internet RFCs (REQUEST FOR COMMENTS). More information about INTERNET ENGINEERING TASK FORCE (IETF) is available at http://www.ietf.org

internet fragment   A portion of the data exchanged between a pair of Internet nodes.

This ensures that IP DATAGRAMS can fit inside one packet on any network topology and that packets are fragmented when they are too big to go over a given network. Ethernet can accept packets up to 1,500 bytes long, while FDDI can accept those up to 4,500 bytes long.

In Figure 14, H1 sends a 1,400-byte packet to H2. If we assume that the maximum transmission of the physical network of H1, which may be a point-to-point network, is 512 bytes (where R1 is located), the packet is fragmented into three packets of sizes 512, 512, and 376. Routers R2 and R3 (for example, they may be a part of an Ethernet or an FDDI physical network) do not fragment the packets any further. The three packets are assembled at H2.

Internet Fraud Complaint Center   The INTERNET FRAUD COMPLAINT CENTER (IFCC) (of U.S.) is a joint operation of the U.S. Federal Bureau of Investigation (FBI) and the U.S. National White Collar Crime Center (NW3C) with a purpose to address fraudulent activities over the Internet. IFCC offers a central repository for complaints related to Internet fraud; collects and maintains fraud complaint information to help in preventive and investigative efforts; provides mechanisms for reporting fraud on the Internet; and directs Internet fraud complaints to the appropriate law enforcement and regulatory agencies. For law enforcement and regulatory agencies it provides services and statistical data of current fraud trends and other information. This Web site (see below) contains recent trends and analytical reports and can be used to file a fraud complaint. For more details see http://www.ifccfbi.gov.

internet key exchange   A part of the IPSEC virtual private networking protocol for CRYPTOGRAPHIC key exchange and management, described in RFC 2409.

Internet Network Information Center
Authority that administers and assigns Internet domains and network addresses. More information about INTERNET NETWORK INFORMATION CENTER (INTERNIC) is available at http://www.internic.net/index.html.

Internet Policy Registration Authority
Internet authority that registers policies for CAs. INTERNET POLICY REGISTRATION AUTHORITY (IPRA) certifies only PCAs and not CAs or users. PCAs have their own policy of issuing certificates. *See also* POLICY CREATION AUTHORITY and CERTIFICATION AUTHORITY HIERARCHY.

internetwork private line interface
Interface that provides secure connections between a host and a predetermined set of

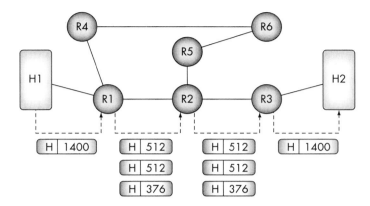

FIGURE 14. Illustration of Internet fragmentation.

corresponding hosts through a network CRYPTOGRAPHIC unit.

Internet Protocol   Standard protocol for the transmission of data in packet-switched communications networks and their interconnected systems. INTERNET PROTOCOL is given in RFC 791.

Internet Protocol Next Generation
INTERNET PROTOCOL NEXT GENERATION (IPNG) is a new version of the Internet Protocol designed by IETF as a successor to IPv4. It is assigned IP version number 6 and is called IPv6. Implementations of IPv6 are available for many operating systems. The overall goal of IPv6 is to create an architectural framework that enables the Internet to grow to a system with millions of interconnections to IPv6 from IPv4 and minimal disruption to existing systems.

In addition to various new features, IPv6 increases the size of Internet addresses from 32 bits to 128 bits, thus increasing the number of available network and host IP addresses.

IPng-compliant systems must imple-

ment IPsec. Details of IPv6 are available at http://www.ipv6.org.

internet protocol security   A VIRTUAL PRIVATE NETWORKING (VPN) protocol standard that can be used to provide NONREPUDIATION, data integrity and privacy, AUTHENTICATION, and replay protection over public IP networks such as the Internet.

> NOTE: *The security architecture for IP is defined in IPsec, the security architecture for IP. Details of IPsec are given in RFC 2401. IPsec provides two security mechanisms (1) The IP AUTHENTICATION HEADER (AH) described in RFC 2402 and (2) The IP encapsulating security payload (ESP) described in RFC 2406.*

Internet Relay Chat   An Internet service that allows real-time text-based communication with other users in Internet locations called chat rooms.

Internet Research Task Force   One of the task forces of the IAB, the group responsible for the research and development of the INTERNET PROTOCOL suite. More information is available at http://www.irtf.org

Internet Security Association and Key Management Protocol   Provides a generic framework for key management. INTERNET SECURITY ASSOCIATION AND KEY

MANAGEMENT PROTOCOL (ISAKMP) is extensible in that it is not limited to specific CRYPTOGRAPHIC algorithms or protocols and hence offers more flexibility with regard to use than Photuris or SKIP protocols. Details of ISAKMP are given in RFC 2408.

Internet worm A program written by Robert Morris Jr. that replicated itself from machine to machine on the Internet in 1988 and clogged the network.

InterNIC ☞ INTERNET NETWORK INFORMATION CENTER. INTERNIC administers and assigns Internet domains and network addresses.

intruder ☞ CRACKER.

intrusion (1) An act in which an ADVERSARY gains access to a system in violation of its security objectives. (2) Acts that COMPROMISE the integrity, CONFIDENTIALITY, or availability of networks and systems.

intrusion detection The science or art dealing with the detection of intrusion into networks or computer systems, and of mechanisms that perform such services.

Intrusion Detection in Our Time A system of intrusion detection that uses pattern-matching techniques.

IO ☞ INFORMATION OPERATIONS.

IP ☞ INTERNET PROTOCOL.

IP datagram The fundamental unit of information passed across the Internet and the unit of end-to-end transmission in IP protocol that contains the source and destination address, along with data and a number of fields that define such things as the length of the DATAGRAM, the header CHECKSUM, and a flag to say whether the DATAGRAM can be fragmented.

IPng ☞ INTERNET PROTOCOL NEXT GENERATION.

IPRA ☞ INTERNET POLICY REGISTRATION AUTHORITY.

IPsec ☞ INTERNET PROTOCOL SECURITY.

IP splicing A method for attacking or intercepting an established TCP/IP connection. Usually, this type of ATTACK occurs after AUTHENTICATION of the users is complete and the attacker assumes the role of a legitimate user.

IP spoofing One machine on the Internet masquerading as another machine by using the latter's IP address.

IPv6 ☞ INTERNET PROTOCOL NEXT GENERATION.

IRC ☞ INTERNET RELAY CHAT.

iron box A setup to trap hackers and keep them on the system (or network) long enough to trace their origin. The setup usually provides bait files to keep the intruder's interest.

IRTF ☞ INTERNET RESEARCH TASK FORCE.

IS ☞ INFORMATION SYSTEM.

ISAKMP ☞ INTERNET SECURITY ASSOCIATION AND KEY MANAGEMENT PROTOCOL.

ISDN ☞ INTEGRATED SERVICES DIGITAL NETWORK.

ISO ☞ INTERNATIONAL ORGANIZATION FOR STANDARDIZATION.

ISO OSI The seven-layer OSI (OPEN SYSTEMS INTERCONNECT) model proposed by ISO has provided a conceptual framework for understanding networks. See Figure I5.

NOTE: *ISO 7498 describes the ISO OSI model. ISO 7498 part 2 defines security architecture but is superseded by ISO/IEC 10745 and ITU-T X.803 "Upper Layers Security Model," ISO/IEC 13594 and ITU-T X.802 "Lower Layers Security*

ISO-OSI Model	TCP/IP Model	Protocols Used
Application	Application	Telnet, FTP, DNS, SMTP, TFTP, HTTP
Presentation		
Session		
Transport	Transmission	TCP, UDP
Network	Internet	IP
Data link	Host to Network	Ethernet, X.25, SLIP, PPP, IEEE 802.3, IEEE 802.5
Physical		

FIGURE 15. Comparison of the ISO model and the TCP/IP model.

Model," and ISO/IEC 10181–1 and ITU-T X.810 "Security Frameworks, Part 1: Overview."

ISS ☞ INFORMATION SYSTEM SECURITY.

ISSM ☞ INFORMATION SYSTEM SECURITY MANAGER.

ISSO ☞ INFORMATION SYSTEM SECURITY OFFICER.

ITAR ☞ INTERNATIONAL TRAFFIC IN ARMS REGULATIONS.

ITSEC ☞ INFORMATION TECHNOLOGY SECURITY EVALUATION CRITERIA.

ITU ☞ INTERNATIONAL TELECOMMUNICATIONS UNION.

IV ☞ INITIALIZATION VECTOR.

J

Java sandbox   A mechanism that confines the scope of Java APPLET actions according to rules defined in a security model.

Java Virtual Machine   Software that provides a virtual machine on which Java software can be executed. See Figure J1.

JIVA   ☞   JOINT INTELLIGENCE VIRTUAL ARCHITECTURE.

Joint Intelligence Virtual Architecture
A system designed by the U.S. government with a purpose to provide modernization of intelligence analytical processes and methodologies. The goal of JOINT INTELLIGENCE VIRTUAL ARCHITECTURE (JIVA) is to provide a single database of knowledge by combining inputs from various agencies to create an intelligence tool to create "virtual intelligence" by using full-motion video

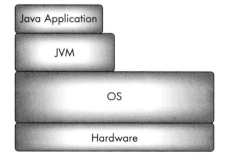

FIGURE J1. Conceptual Representation of the Java Virtual Machine (JVM).

and 3-D representations. For details of JIVA see http://www.fas.org/irp/program/core/jiva.htm.

JVM   ☞   JAVA VIRTUAL MACHINE.

K

kamikaze packet ☞ CHERNOBYL PACKET.

KDC ☞ KEY DISTRIBUTION CENTER.

KEK ☞ KEY ENCRYPTION KEY.

Kerberize To enhance an application to use KERBEROS for AUTHENTICATION and/or ENCRYPTION.

Kerberos A DES-based AUTHENTICATION system developed at Massachusetts Institute of Technology (U.S.) as part of Project ATHENA and subsequently incorporated into a growing collection of commercial products. Detailed specifications of KERBEROS are given in Internet RFC 1510. See Figure K1.

key A quantity used in CRYPTOGRAPHY to ENCRYPT or DECRYPT information. This may be a set of symbols, letters, numbers, or characters that are used to encrypt or decrypt a text or a message.

key archive ☞ KEY ESCROW.

key-auto-key A form of CRYPTOGRAPHIC LOGIC that uses a previous key to create a new key.

key backup ☞ KEY ESCROW.

keyboard attack ☞ ATTACK.

key card A paper card consisting of a pattern of punched holes that establishes a key for a specific CRYPTONET at a specific time.

key distribution center An online trusted intermediary that has a master key for all principals and that generates CONVERSATION KEYS between principals when requested.

Key distribution can be implemented in various ways. In the following illustration we use a scenario based on [GP79] and depicted in Figure K2. Suppose user A wants to start a communication session with user B. We assume that user A shares a secret key K_A and user B shares a secret key K_B with the KEY DISTRIBUTION CENTER (KDC). The following steps take place:

(1) A sends a message *Message_of_A_to_KDC = (ID(A), ID(B), N1)* to KDC that contains identification of A (for example, IP address), identification of B, and a NONCE N_1.

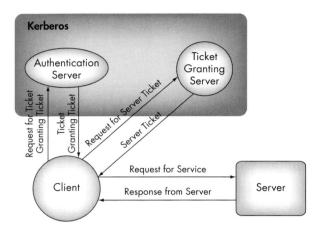

FIGURE K1. Kerberos authentication menchanism.

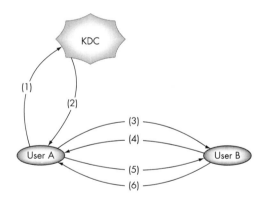

FIGURE K2. Figure explaining key distribution center.

(2) KDC responds with a message that is encrypted using the key of A. The message contains items for both A and B. For A, it has a session key K_S and the original message, and for B it has a session key and identity of A. Both of these are en-crypted using K_B. So, the message from KDC to A is

Message_from_KDC_to_A = Encrypt_ using_KA [(K_S, Message_of_A_to_KDC), Encrypt_using_KB(Ks, ID(A))].

(3) User A then forwards the item intended for B *(Encrypt_using_KB[(K_S, ID(A))])* to B. So, user B now decrypts the message using its own key K_B and knows the session key K_S.

Now both user A and user B have a session key and can start communicating.

To ensure against a replay attack and to AUTHENTICATE, the next two steps are performed.

(4) Using the session key K_S user B sends a nonce N_2 to A.

(5) User A performs a function, for example, adding 1, and sends it to B.

(6) Now users A and user B can start communicating.

key encryption key   Key for encryption or decryption of another key, which is used for secure transmission or storage.

key escrow   A system that provides backups of encryption keys so that data can be decrypted if the primary copy of the key used to encrypt the data is not available. KEY ESCROW can be used for schemes that give access (under court order) to law enforcement agencies and KEY RECOVERY for schemes that give access to owners who have lost their key. Other terms are KEY ARCHIVE, KEY BACKUP, and data recovery system.

keying material   A physical or magnetic key, code, or piece of AUTHENTICATION information. Also known as key material or keymat.

key list   A printed list, pad, or printed tape of a series of key settings for a specific CRYPTONET.

key management   The supervision and control of the generation, storage, use, de-struction, distribution, and revocation of a key.

key pair   A public key and its corresponding private key for use in PUBLIC KEY CRYPTOGRAPHY.

key production key   A key that activates a key-stream generator to produce other electronically generated keys.

key stream   A sequence of symbols produced in a machine or auto-manual CRYPTO-SYSTEM that combine with PLAINTEXT to produce CIPHERTEXT, control transmission security processes, or produce keys.

keystroke monitoring   Recording every keystroke of the user (and usually every character of response). A form of AUDIT TRAIL software or a specialized device usually does this monitoring.

keystroke system   A system that compares a pattern of keystrokes with a stored pattern to determine whether there is a match.

key recovery   ☞   KEY ESCROW

key tag   Information for the identification of certain types of electronic keys.

key tape   A punched or magnetic tape containing a key. A printed key in tape form is referred to as a KEY LIST.

key updating   A CRYPTOGRAPHIC process for modifying a key; it cannot be reversed.

L

label ☞ SECURITY LABEL.

labeled security protections Mechanisms of a TRUSTED COMPUTING BASE (TCB) in which access control decisions are made on the basis of SENSITIVITY LABELS and CLEARANCES.

laboratory attack An ATTACK by which information from data storage media is obtained by using advanced signal recovery equipment in a laboratory setting.

Law Enforcement Access Field The field that must be transmitted by one CLIPPER CHIP to the CLIPPER CHIP at the other end of the conversation. Without it, the receiving CLIPPER will refuse to DECRYPT the conversation. The LAW ENFORCEMENT ACCESS FIELD (LEAF) enables law enforcement to decrypt the conversation, after a court order to obtain the sending CLIPPER'S unique key. The LEAF field was also used in capstone chips.

LEAF ☞ LAW ENFORCEMENT ACCESS FIELD

leapfrog attack Using one system to get a user ID and password to get to another system. This also includes the use of multiple TELNET sessions to log on to a system to avoid a trace. See Figure L1.

least privilege A property of an IS by which users or subjects are given only the minimum access (or privileges) necessary to perform particular authorized tasks. This limits the potential for damage resulting from accidental, erroneous, or malicious unauthorized use of an IS.

letter bomb Malicious software, usually a LOGIC BOMB, distributed via electronic mail. Typically such software is not executed until the mail message is read, or when an attachment is opened.

level of protection The extent to which ISs and networks must be protected based on risk, threat, vulnerability, system interconnectivity considerations, and INFORMATION ASSURANCE needs. Typically the levels of protection are 1. Basic: IS and networks requiring the implementation of standard minimum-security COUNTERMEASURES. 2. Medium: IS and networks requiring the layering of additional safeguards above the standard minimum-security COUNTERMEASURES. 3. High: IS and networks

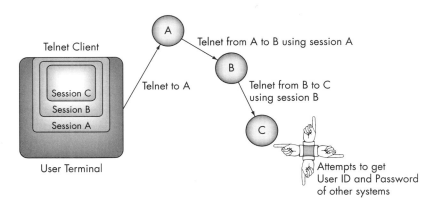

FIGURE L1. Use of multiple telnet sessions for a leapfrog attack.

requiring the most stringent protection and rigorous security COUNTERMEASURES.

life-cycle assurance   The ASSURANCE that a trusted system is designed, developed, and maintained based on controlled standards. In the ORANGE BOOK, these ASSURANCES include security testing, design specification and verification, CONFIGURATION MANAGEMENT, and trusted distribution.

limited maintenance   Maintenance consisting only of fault isolation, removal, and the replacement of plug-in assemblies in INFOSEC equipment. In LIMITED MAINTENANCE, soldering or unsoldering is usually prohibited. *See also* FULL MAINTENANCE.

line conditioning   The elimination of inadvertent signals or noise produced or transported on a telecommunications or information system signal, power, control, indicator, or other external interface line.

line conduction   Inadvertent signals or noise produced or transported on a telecommunications or information system signal, power, control, indicator, or other external interface line.

link encryption   In a communications system, the encryption of information between NODES. Contrast with END-TO-END ENCRYPTION.

list-oriented   A type of computer protection where every protected object has a list of all subjects with AUTHORIZATION to access it. *See also* TICKET-ORIENTED.

LMD/KP ☞ LOCAL MANAGEMENT DEVICE/KEY PROCESSOR.

local address   The address of a host within a network. The actual mapping of an Internet local address onto the host addresses in a network is quite general, allowing for many-to-one mappings.

local authority   An organization that generates and signs user certificates.

Local Management Device/Key Processor   An EKMS platform that generates a key for authorized users and provides automated management of COMSEC MATERIAL.

lock and key protection system   Protection system in which a key or password must be matched with a specific access requirement.

logical completeness measure   A way of determining how effectively and to what extent a set of security and access control mechanisms meets security specifications.

logic bomb Resident computer program that causes an unauthorized act to occur when certain states of an IS are reached.

login A method of being identified and AUTHENTICATED by a computer system.

long title The descriptive title of a COMSEC item.

low probability of detection The result of efforts to hide or disguise intentional electromagnetic transmissions.

low probability of intercept The result of efforts to prevent the interception of intentional electromagnetic transmissions.

MAC ☞ MANDATORY ACCESS CONTROL; MESSAGE AUTHENTICATION CODE; MEDIA ACCESS CONTROL LAYER.

magnetic remanence After a magnetic medium has been cleared, the magnetic representation of residual information left on the medium. *See also* CLEARING.

mail bomb An ATTACK in which many messages are sent to a particular address in order to exceed the mail recipient's mail limit, thereby causing the system to crash or malfunction.

mail gateway A machine that connects two or more electronic mail systems and transfers messages between them. Sometimes the mapping and translation can be quite complex, and generally it requires a store-and-forward scheme whereby the message is received from the system completely before it is transmitted to the next system after suitable translation.

maintenance hook Special instructions (TRAP DOORS) in software that are designed for easy maintenance and additional feature development, but which can be serious se-

curity risks if they are not removed before live implementation.

maintenance key A key intended for in-shop use.

malicious applets Small application programs that are downloaded and executed automatically to perform an unauthorized function on an IS.

malicious code Software or firmware that has the ability to perform an unauthorized function on an IS. This software may be intentionally left in a system for malicious purposes. Examples include VIRUSES, TROJAN HORSES, LOGIC BOMBS, and TRAP DOORS.

malicious host For some mobile agent applications, an agent may contain sensitive information. In which case, it may be necessary to protect the agent from its execution environment. In these situations, the host computer is referred to as a MALICIOUS HOST [WJ00].

malicious logic Hardware, software, or firmware that has the ability to perform an unauthorized function on an IS.

mandatory access control A method of restricting access to objects containing sensitive information. Also the formal AUTHORIZATION of subjects to access this sensitive information. *See also* DISCRETIONARY ACCESS CONTROLS.

mandatory modification An NSA (U.S.) required change to a COMSEC END-ITEM that must be completed and reported by a specific date. *See also* OPTIONAL MODIFICATION.

manipulative communications deception The deceptive alteration or simulation of friendly telecommunications. *See also* COMMUNICATIONS DECEPTION and IMITATIVE COMMUNICATIONS DECEPTION.

manual cryptosystem CRYPTOSYSTEM in which no CRYPTO-EQUIPMENT or auto-manual devices are used to perform the CRYPTOGRAPHIC processes.

manual remote rekeying The electrical rekeying of distant CRYPTO-EQUIPMENT, requiring specific actions by the receiving terminal operator.

masquerader An unauthorized user who exploits a legitimate users account by impersonating an authorized user with means such as guessing a password, intercepting communications, or using malicious code.

masquerading Form of SPOOFING.

master crypto-ignition key A key device with electronic logic and circuits that enables the addition of more operational CIKs to a keyset (maximum of seven) any time after the completion of the fill procedure. The master CIK can be made only as the first CIK during the fill procedure.

material symbol A communications circuit identifier used for supplying more key cards.

maximum transmission unit The largest possible unit of data that can be sent on a given PHYSICAL MEDIUM. For example, the MTU of the Ethernet is 1,500 bytes. *See also* FRAGMENTATION.

MD2 Message digest algorithm documented in RFC 1319. *See also* HASH and MESSAGE DIGEST.

MD4 Message digest algorithm documented in RFC 1320. *See also* HASH and MESSAGE DIGEST.

MD5 Message digest algorithm documented in RFC 1321. *See also* HASH and MESSAGE DIGEST.

media access control layer A sublayer of the OSI data link control layer, defined in IEEE 802.

mediation The interposition of an ACCESS CONTROL MECHANISM between a subject and an object. An arbiter positioned in the middle determines whether or not to allow a subject to perform a given operation on a specified object.

memory scavenging The collection of residual information from data storage.

Menezes–Qu–Vanstone key agreement scheme The Menezes–Qu–Vanstone scheme (1995) is a variant of the Diffie–Hellman algorithm; here, instead of one public–private key pair, each party contributes two public–private key pairs and uses its own two key pairs, the other party's two public keys, and some agreed-upon parameters to decide on a shared secret key.

message The unit of transmission in a transport layer protocol. In particular, a TCP segment of a message. A message consists of a transport protocol header followed by the application protocol data. To be transmitted end-to-end through the In-

FIGURE M1. Message digest.

ternet, a message must be encapsulated inside a datagram.

NOTE: *The above is a specific definition. The term MESSAGE is also used in SMTP and other messaging contexts.*

message authentication code Data that allows a receiver to verify an AUTHENTICATED message. The received message matches the sent message.

message digest The result of applying an irreversible function that takes an arbitarary-sized input and produces a fixed-size output. Also called hash value. See Figure M1. *See also* DIGEST.

message externals Information external to the text of a message, such as the header or trailer.

message hash ☞ DIGEST.

message indicator The sequence of bits transmitted over a communications system whose purpose is to synchronize CRYPTO-EQUIPMENT. Some OFF-LINE CRYPTOSYSTEMS, such as the KL-51 and one-time pad systems, establish DECRYPTION starting points by using message indicators.

Milnet The U.S. Department of Defense spinoff of the ARPAnet.

MIME ☞ MULTIPURPOSE INTERNET MAIL EXTENSIONS.

mimicking Form of SPOOFING, also synonymous with IMPERSONATION or MASQUERADING.

MLI ☞ MULTILEVEL INTEGRITY.

MLS ☞ MULTILEVEL SECURITY.

MNCRS ☞ MOBILE NETWORK COMPUTER REFERENCE SPECIFICATIONS.

mobile code Program that can execute on remote locations without any modification in the code. A MOBILE CODE may travel and execute from one machine to anther on a network during its lifetime. Some systems that create and execute MOBILE CODE are ActiveX, Java, JavaScript, VBScript, Microsoft Word macros, and PostScript. Mobile code can run on multiple platforms such as UNIX and Microsoft Windows. The mobile code interpreter (or the virtual machine) is now a part of Web browsers. Because of security concerns, many forms of mobile code platforms run an untrusted code in a secure fashion. *See also* JAVA SANDBOX and JAVA VIRTUAL MACHINE.

Mobile Network Computer Reference Specifications These specifications extend the concept a NETWORK COMPUTER to define a mobile network computer (MNC).

mobile node A NODE that changes its point of attachment to the Internet as part of its normal use.

In mobile IP, a ROUTER named as a home agent is located on the home network of the mobile host (node). The mobile host has a permanent IP address, with the same network address as the network address of the home network. Other hosts on the Internet use this permanent address. A foreign agent is located on the network to which the mobile host attaches.

Both the home and foreign agent advertise their presence on the networks to which they are attached. The mobile host registers itself with the foreign agent of the network to which it attaches. This foreign agent in turn contacts the home

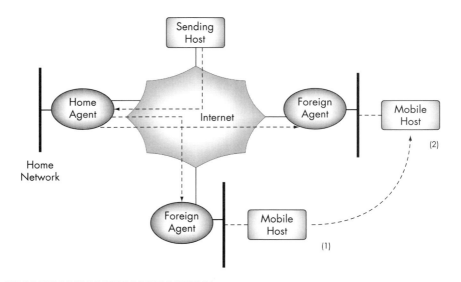

FIGURE M2. Mobile node.

agent of the mobile host and provides the home agent a care-of address. Now the hosts on the Internet can contact the mobile host through its home agent (which has the same network number) and has a care-of address. When the mobile host attaches itself to a new network, the whole process is repeated. Thus, for long-lived applications, the mobility of the host has no effect. Figure M2 shows this scenario, with one sending host, and the mobile host goes first from its home network to a new network (identified as step (1)). It then moves to a new network, and the whole process is repeated (identified as step (2)).

mockingbird   A program that mimics the behavior of legitimate user(s) or a system but can perform malicious activities at the instigation of a user or a process.

model   A representation of a policy or a system design that can be used for analysis or other reasoning about the policy or the system.

modem   Short for modulator/ demodulator. It converts digital signals from a computer to an analog form to transmit over a communication medium that may connect to a network or the Internet (usually a phone line; see NOTE below) and converts an analog signal that has come over a communication medium to digital form so that it can be processed by a computer. See Figure M3.

NOTE: *In addition to modems that connect a computer to a phone network there are other types of modems such as cable TV modems and fiber modems.*

mode of operation   (1) The conditions under which an IS operates based on the sensitivity of information processed and the CLEARANCE levels, formal access approvals, and the need-to-know of its users. There are four authorized modes of operation for processing or transmitting information: dedicated mode, system-high mode, compartmented/partitioned mode, and multilevel mode. (2) There are also

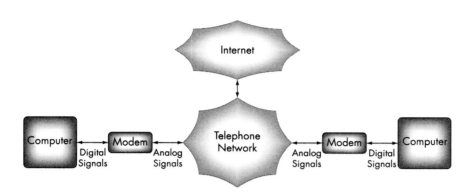

FIGURE M3. Modem.

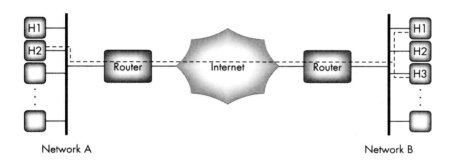

Network A   Network B

FIGURE M4. Multicast.

modes of operation for encryption: ECB, CBC, CFB, and OFB.

monitoring   The recording of relevant information about each operation performed on an object by a subject. It is retained in an AUDIT TRAIL for further analysis.

MQV ☞ MENEZES–QU–VANSTONE KEY AGREEMENT SCHEME.

MTU ☞ MAXIMUM TRANSMISSION UNIT.

multicast   A special form of broadcast where copies of a packet are delivered to only a subset of all possible destinations. It identifies a group of interfaces such that a packet sent to a multicast address is delivered to all of the interfaces in the group. In Figure M4, host H2 on network A is multicasting to hosts H1 and H3 on network B. *See also* BROADCAST.

multihomed host   A computer connected to more than one physical data link. The data links may or may not be attached to the same network. A host is said to be multihomed if it has multiple IP addresses.

multihost-based auditing   The auditing or detecting of intrusion that includes data from multiple hosts.

multilevel device   A device that maintains and separates data of different security levels.

multilevel integrity   An integrity policy whose use depends on the order of multilevel integrity labels.

multilevel mode   An INFOSEC mode of operation wherein all the following statements are true about the users who have direct or indirect access to the system, its peripherals, remote terminals, or remote hosts: (a) Not all users have a valid security CLEARANCE for all the information processed in the IS; (b) all users have the proper security CLEARANCE and appropriate formal access approval for that information to which they have access; and (c) all users are on a need-to-know basis for the information to which they have access.

multilevel security   Information is CLASSIFIED at different levels of security. Information access is permitted according to ACCESS CONTROL policies.

Multipurpose Internet Mail Extensions
A set of specifications to link and transfer nontext files with Internet e-mail and other IP applications including Usenet news.

mutual suspicion   A condition where two ISs must rely upon each other to perform a service, but neither IS trusts the other to properly protect the data they are sharing.

N

Nak attack ☞ NEGATIVE ACKNOWLEDG-MENT ATTACK.

name resolution   The process of mapping a name to the corresponding address. *See also* DNS.

National Computing Security Center
Founded in 1981 as DoD's Computer Security Center, it is now a part of the U.S. NATIONAL SECURITY AGENCY (NSA). It was renamed NATIONAL COMPUTER SECURITY CENTER (NCSC) in 1985. NCSC evaluates computing equipment to ensure that establishments processing CLASSIFIED or other sensitive material are using trusted computer systems and components. This agency developed the TRUSTED COMPUTER SYSTEM EVALUATION CRITERIA (TCSEC) and the TRUSTED NETWORK INTERPRETATION ENVIRONMENT GUIDELINE (TNIEG).

National Institute for Standards and Technology   The U.S. government organization that develops standards for U.S. federal government use. More information about the NATIONAL INSTITUTE FOR STANDARDS AND TECHNOLOGY (NIST) is available at http://www.nist.gov.

National Security Agency   The U.S. government agency responsible for protecting U.S. communications and producing foreign intelligence information. Established by a presidential directive in 1952 as a separately organized agency within the Department of Defense.

National Security Information   Information that in accordance with Executive Order 12958 or any predecessor order requires protection against unauthorized disclosure.

National Security System   Any telecommunications or information system operated by the U.S. government that (1) involves intelligence activities; (2) involves CRYPTOLOGIC activities related to national security; (3) involves command and control of military forces; (4) involves equipment that is an integral part of a weapon or weapons system; or (5) is critical to the direct fulfillment of military or intelligence missions and does not include a system that is to be used for routine administrative and business applications (including payroll, finance, logistics, and personnel management applications). (Title 40

U.S.C. Section 1452, Information Technology Management Reform Act of 1996.)

NC ☞ NETWORK COMPUTER.

NCRP ☞ NETWORK COMPUTER REFERENCE SPECIFICATION.

NCSC ☞ NATIONAL COMPUTING SECURITY CENTER.

need-to-know The need to access, know of, or possess specific information essential to the completion of official duties. A person or an object is provided as much information as is essential to perform a given task precisely.

negative acknowledgment attack A type of ATTACK that exploits the vulnerability of those operating systems that do not handle asynchronous interrupts well and leave the system unprotected during such a time.

NetBIOS ☞ NETWORK BASIC INPUT OUTPUT SYSTEM.

netiquette A combination of the words net and etiquette. A general code of conduct for sending and receiving e-mail and for general use of the Internet.

netmask Also known as SUBNET MASK, ADDRESS MASK. *See also* ADDRESS MASK.

network A collection of two or more interconnected computers. IS combined with a group of interconnected network nodes. See Figure N1.

Typically, a network consists of hosts that are interconnected via a communication subnet. Hosts are the primary computers connected to the network; they contribute to the network load and may perform functions not directly related to networking, such as running users' programs. Typically, hosts are identified at the highest level of the protocol hierarchy by a human user. The communications subnet consists of nodes interconnected via channels; the nodes implement the functionality of the subnet by interfacing the hosts to the network and providing a means of passing messages between them.

Network Basic Input Output System The standard interface to networks on IBM PC and compatible systems.

network computer A lightweight, ubiquitous, extensible, secure, and easy to administer system that ensures universality by using technologies like HTTP, HTML, and Java.

network computer reference specification Specifications that address requirements of new mobile computing devices.

NOTE: *At the time of writing this dictionary these specifications are still being worked on by a consortium of leading industry members in computing.*

Network File System A distributed file system developed by Sun Microsystems that allows a set of computers to cooperatively access each other's files in a transparent manner.

network front end A device that enables a computer system to attach to a network.

network information center A NETWORK INFORMATION CENTER (NIC) provides network information and support to end users and administrators. Originally, there was only one NIC, located at SRI International (U.S.) and tasked to serve the ARPANET community. Many regional and midlevel networks have established such centers to serve the local networking community. There are NICs of local, regional, and national networks all over the world. Such centers provide user assistance, document service, training, and much more.

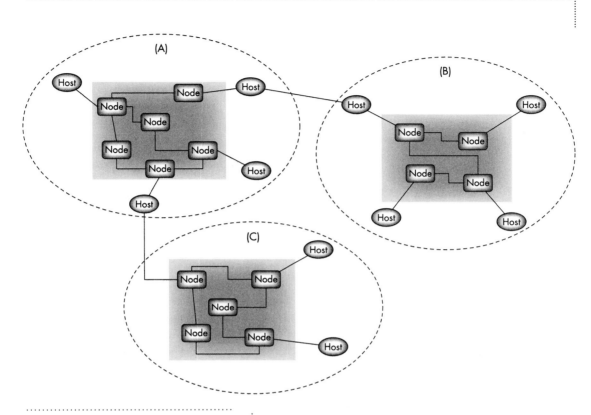

FIGURE N1. Network. Here ovals (A), (B), and (C) individually represent a network, and all three combined are also a network.

NOTE: *SRI International is located at Menlo Park, California (U.S.). In May 1997, Stanford Research Institute officially became SRI International. Details about SRI International are available at http:// www.sri.com.*

network layer The OSI layer that is responsible for routing, switching, and subnetwork access across the entire OSI environment.

network level firewall In this type of FIREWALL, protection is provided by examining packets at the INTERNET PROTOCOL layer.

network reference monitor A method of ACCESS CONTROL in which all access to objects within a network by subjects within the network is mediated by an abstract machine. *See also* REFERENCE MONITOR.

network security The protection of networks and their services that ensure that the network performs its critical functions correctly and without harmful side effects. It prohibits unauthorized modification, destruction, or disclosure.

network security architecture The subset of network architecture concerned with security-relevant issues.

network security officer The individual in charge of network security. *See also* INFORMATION SYSTEM SECURITY OFFICER.

network sponsor   The individual or organization that must state the network's security policy, design the necessary network security architecture, and ensure that the policy is enforced. The vendor is usually the sponsor for COMMERCIAL OFF-THE-SHELF systems (COTS). The project manager or system administrator is usually the sponsor for a fielded network system.

network system   A system based on a clear security architecture and design. It is made up of many interconnected components.

network trusted computing base partition   All of the protection mechanisms within a network, including hardware, firmware, and software, which combine to enforce a security policy. See TRUSTED COMPUTING BASE.

network weaving   Different unauthorized communication networks linked together to avoid detection and trace-back while accessing an IS.

NFS   ☞   NETWORK FILE SYSTEM.

NIC   (1)   ☞   NETWORK INFORMATION CENTER. (2) Many people use NIC as an acronym for Network Interface Card.

NIST   ☞   NATIONAL INSTITUTE FOR STANDARDS AND TECHNOLOGY.

node   A computer in the Internet work environment on which internet protocol services are available.

no-lone zone   Area, room, or space that when staffed must contain two or more appropriately cleared individuals who must remain within each other's sight. *See also* TWO-PERSON INTEGRITY.

nonce   A quantity that any user of a protocol uses only once, for example, a timestamp, a sequence number, or a large random number. It is possible to introduce security weaknesses by using a nonce with the wrong properties.

noncompromisability   A system's ability to withstand COMPROMISE.

noncooperative remote rekeying   ☞   AUTOMATIC REMOTE REKEYING.

nondiscretionary access controls   Same as MANDATORY ACCESS CONTROLS.

nondiscretionary security   A set of U.S. DoD policies restricting access to an item of information based on a CLEARANCE level equal to or greater than the CLASSIFICATION associated with the item that should satisfy the access category's set restrictions.

nonrepudiation   The property of a scheme achieved through CRYPTOGRAPHIC methods in which the recipient is able to prove to a third party that data has been sent by the sender or received by the receiver. This property protects against the sender denying having sent the message and the receiver denying having received the message. The sender is provided with a proof of delivery and receiver is assured of sender's identity. Nonrepudiation as a CRYPTOGRAPHIC property must not be confused with a legal guarantee.

   NONREPUDIATION of origin provides proof of data (message) being sent by the sender; NONREPUDIATION of transmission provides proof of data (message) transmission, and NONREPUDIATION of delivery provides proof of receipt of the data (message) by the recipient. See ISO 7498–2.

nonsecret encryption   ☞   PUBLIC KEY CRYPTOGRAPHY.

nontamperability   A system's ability to withstand tampering.

NSA ☞ NATIONAL SECURITY AGENCY.

NSI ☞ NATIONAL SECURITY INFORMATION.

NTCB ☞ NETWORK TRUSTED COMPUTING BASE PARTITION.

null Meaningless letter, letter symbol, or CODE GROUP within an encrypted message that delays or prevents its DECRYPTION or completes encrypted groups for transmission or transmission security purposes.

OASIS ☞ ORGANIZATION FOR THE ADVANCEMENT OF STRUCTURED INFORMATION STANDARDS.

obfuscation ☞ CODE OBFUSCATION.

obfuscator A tool to do automatic CODE OBFUSCATION.

object An active or passive entity that stores or receives information. Gaining access to an object means also gaining access to the information it contains.

object reuse The reassignment and reuse of a storage medium that contains one or more objects after it has been made certain that the storage medium is free of residual data.

OFB ☞ OUTPUT FEEDBACK MODE.

off-line cryptosystem CRYPTOSYSTEM in which ENCRYPTION and DECRYPTION are separate from the transmission and reception functions.

one-part code A systematically ordered code of PLAINTEXT elements and their accompanying CODE GROUPS in which one listing serves for both encoding and decoding. These codes are normally small and used to pass small volumes of low-sensitivity information.

one-time cryptosystem A CRYPTOSYSTEM employing a key used only once.

one-time pad An encryption method where a long string known only to the sender and the receiver is used as the key for ENCRYPTION and DECRYPTION. This extremely simple encryption method is secure for keeping a message confidential if the string used is truly random, known only to the communicating parties, at least as long as the PLAINTEXT, and never reused.

NOTE: *Some have referred to a one-time pad as a key distribution mechanism rather than an encryption method, because many different algorithms can be used, as long as the conditions above are met.*

one-time tape Punched paper tape that provides key streams on a one-time basis in certain machine CRYPTOSYSTEMS.

one-to-one mapping A function that assigns an output value to each input value in such a way that each input maps to exactly one output.

online cryptosystem A CRYPTOSYSTEM in which ENCRYPTION and DECRYPTION are performed in conjunction with the transmitting and receiving functions.

online server Something that provides a service and is generally available on the network.

open A system, specification, or an item developed with details available to the public. For example, an open Internet working protocol will allow independent Internet working implementations based on documentation alone, and there are no patent, copyright, or trade secret impediments to its deployment. Examples of open systems include OSI seven-layer architecture for interconnection of computer systems.

open security environment An environment that does not provide adequate protection against the loss of CONFIDENTIALITY, INTEGRITY, or AVAILABILITY.

Open Shortest Path First A "protocol standard" IGP for the Internet. *See also* IGP.

Open Software Foundation An organization founded as an industry consortium to develop and license open software. It is best known for OSF/1, a UNIX variant, and DCE, a family of protocols centered on a secure RPC and distributed file system.

open storage The storage of CLASSIFIED INFORMATION in a container that is not approved by the General Services Administration, in an unoccupied accredited facility.

Open System Interconnect The name of computer networking standards approved by ISO. *See also* ISO OSI.

operating system A group of programs that directly control the hardware of a computer and on which all of the computer's other running programs are dependent.

operational code A code mainly consisting of words and phrases appropriate for general communications use.

operational data security The protection of data from either unintentional, unauthorized, or intentional modification, destruction, or disclosure during input, processing, storage, transmission, or output operations.

operational key A key used for over-the-air protection of operational information or for the production or secure electrical transmission of key streams.

operational waiver The authority for the continued use of unchanged COMSEC END-ITEMS until a required change is completed.

operations security The process of controlling and protecting UNCLASSIFIED generic activities to deny unauthorized persons information about capabilities and/or intentions.

OPSEC ☞ OPERATIONS SECURITY.

optional modification An NSA (U.S.) approved change not necessary for universal implementation by all holders of a COMSEC END-ITEM. This class of modification requires all of the engineering/doctrinal control of required change but is usually separate from security, safety, TEMPEST, or reliability.

ORA ☞ ORGANIZATIONAL REGISTRATION AUTHORITY.

Orange Book ☞ TRUSTED COMPUTER SYSTEM EVALUATION CRITERIA (TCSEC).

organizational maintenance Limited maintenance that a user organization completes.

Organizational Registration Authority Branch of the PKI that AUTHENTICATES users' identities and organizational affiliations.

Organization for the Advancement of Structured Information Standards

ORGANIZATION FOR THE ADVANCEMENT OF STRUCTURED INFORMATION STANDARDS (OASIS) uses public standards such as XML and SGML to develop industry specifications that are interoperable. OASIS is a nonprofit, international consortium and its members include organizations and individuals who use these standards. For more details, see the information at http://www.oasis-open.org.

OSF ☞ OPEN SOFTWARE FOUNDATION.

OSI ☞ OPEN SYSTEM INTERCONNECT.

OSPF ☞ OPEN SHORTEST PATH FIRST.

OTAR ☞ OVER-THE AIR REKEYING.

out of band Mechanism different from the regular transmission of data. An out-of-band mechanism for key distribution would be something other than sending messages across the network, for example, by having people talk on the phone to each other or to give each other pieces of paper or floppies that contain keys.

output feedback mode A method of turning a secret key block CIPHER into a stream CIPHER. OUTPUT FEEDBACK (OFB) effectively generates a pseudo-random one-time pad by iteratively encrypting the previous block, staring with an IV.

overrun In the security community, the term OVERRUN means that security is COMPROMISED. A common goal is to minimize the damage done if a single node in a system is overrun and secrets are revealed.

overt channel Communications path designed for the authorized transfer of data in a computer system or network. *See also* COVERT CHANNEL.

over-the-air key distribution The distribution of electronic keys by way of OVER-THE-AIR REKEYING, OVER-THE-AIR KEY TRANSFER, or COOPERATIVE KEY GENERATION.

over-the-air key transfer The electronic distribution of keys without altering the traffic encryption key used on the secured communications path over which the transfer is completed.

over-the-air rekeying The alteration of a traffic encryption key or a transmission security key in remote CRYPTO-EQUIPMENT by sending the new key directly to the remote CRYPTO-EQUIPMENT over the secured communications path.

overwrite procedure Writing patterns of data over data stored on a magnetic medium.

P2P ☞ PEER-TO-PEER.

P3P ☞ PLATFORM FOR PRIVACY PREFER-
ENCES PROJECTS.

PAA ☞ POLICY APPROVING AUTHORITY.

packet A packet is the unit of data
passed across the interface between the Internet layer and the link layer. It includes
an IP header and data. A packet may be a
complete IP datagram or a fragment of an
IP datagram.

packet filter A type of FIREWALL in which
each packet is examined based on local security policy and is accepted or rejected.
See Figure P1.

packet filtering A technique generally
incorporated into ROUTERS to control and
divert the flow of PACKETS based on predetermined characteristics such as origin or
destination of packets, or by the type of
service being offered by a network. This
technique may limit protocol-specific packets to one segment of the network.

packet sniffer A program or a process
that captures and displays the contents of
IP packets on a network.

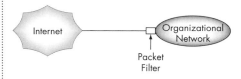

FIGURE P1. Packet filter.

pad Additional bits added to a message
to make it a desired length, for instance, an
integral number of bytes. This meaning of
pad is not related to the word pad as in
the phrase "one-time pad."

parity Bit(s) that can identify any alteration of a block of data.

partitioned security mode An IS security mode of operation in which all personnel have the CLEARANCE for all information
handled by an IS, but not all personnel have
formal access approval and NEED-TO-KNOW.

passive Does not require action on the
part of a user.

passive attack This type of ATTACK does
not result in any system state change or a

change in data; it only monitors or records system state or data.

passive threat A threat in which information is intercepted but not altered. Passive threats can be dangerous because the information may be secret. Contrast with ACTIVE THREAT.

passphrase Sequence of characters that is too long to be a password and is thus turned into a shorter virtual password by the password system.

passwd Password checker that replaces /bin/passwd on a UNIX system, offers enhanced logging, and keeps users from selecting passwords that can be easily guessed.

password A supposedly secret string used to prove one's identity,

password sniffing Eavesdropping to capture passwords, which can then be used to masquerade as a legitimate user.

path The sequence of gateways that at a given moment all the IP datagrams going from a particular source host to a particular destination host will traverse. A path is unidirectional; it is not unusual to have different paths in the two directions between a given host pair.

PCA ☞ POLICY CREATION AUTHORITY.

PCT ☞ PRIVATE COMMUNICATION TECHNOLOGY.

PDS ☞ PROTECTED DISTRIBUTION SYSTEM.

PDU ☞ PROTOCOL DATA UNIT.

peer entity authentication Corroborating the identity of the entity one is connected to.

peer-to-peer A network with typically geographically distributed nodes, temporarily built on the Internet through the IP ad-

dresses of the connected computers. Users use the same program on each machine to connect to each other's machines and share each other's resources and files. A typical application program with these features is Napster, which allows people to share music, usually via MP3 files through P2P networks over the Internet.

PEM ☞ PRIVACY ENHANCED MAIL.

penetration The deceptive bypassing of a system's security mechanisms.

penetration testing Security testing in which authorized evaluators who are familiar with a system's design and implementation try to bypass its security features.

per-call key Unique traffic encryption key generated automatically by certain secure telecommunications systems to access single voice or data transmissions. *See also* COOPERATIVE KEY GENERATION.

perimeter-based security Protecting a network by providing security at all entry and exit points to the network.

periods processing Processing in which different levels of CLASSIFIED and UNCLASSIFIED information cannot be processed at the same time. All information from one processing period must be cleared before another processing period begins.

permission One type of subject—object interaction. Also referred to as consent, typically consent for a particular user to access a particular object in some well-defined way.

permutation A method of encryption where parts of the message are rearranged. Encryption by permutation is not very secure by itself, but it can be used in combination with substitution to build powerful ciphers like DES.

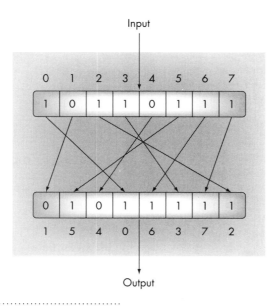

Input

0	1	2	3	4	5	6	7
1	0	1	1	0	1	1	1

0	1	0	1	1	1	1	1
1	5	4	0	6	3	7	2

Output

FIGURE P2. Permuter.

permuter   CRYPTO-EQUIPMENT device that changes the order in which the contents of a shift register are used in various nonlinear combining circuits. Figure P2 shows a permutation of 10110111 to 01011111.

personal identification number   Short sequence of digits used as a pass phrase.

pest program   A program with harmful and generally unexpected side effects. Examples are Trojan horses, logic bombs, viruses, and malicious worms.

PGP   ☞   PRETTY GOOD PRIVACY.

phage   A program that maliciously modifies another program or data by propagating a virus or a Trojan horse.

PHF   A CGI script that came as a part of earlier versions of Apache Web server and NCSA HTTPD. The original version of PHF accepted newline characters (%0a) and

allowed execution of subsequent commands with privileges of the user running the Web server.

Lack of proper parsing and validation of input data could trick this program into executing arbitrary code. For example, in UNIX, including meta characters, e.g., \ / < > ! etc. in the input could result in escaping out to a shell and allowing execution of arbitrary code.

PHF attacks were common in 1996 and 1997.

phf vulnerability   Named after an example cgi-bin script often distributed with earlier versions of several Web servers and commonly used to display the /etc/passwd file. This vulnerability lets an intruder execute arbitrary commands with the privileges of the Web server.

photuris   A key exchange protocol that uses long-term keys to AUTHENTICATE session keys.

phreaker   A person who manipulates a system to make telephone calls at others' expense without their knowledge or consent.

physical layer The OSI layer that provides the means to activate and use physical connection for bit transmission. In plain terms, the physical layer provides the procedures for transferring a single bit across a PHYSICAL MEDIUM.

physical medium Any means in the physical world for transferring signals between OSI systems. Considered to be outside the OSI Reference Model, and therefore sometimes referred to as "Layer 0." The physical connector to the medium can be considered as defining the physical layer, i.e., the bottom of the OSI Reference Model.

physical network interface A physical interface to a connected network having a link-layer address. Multiple physical networks on a single host may share the same link-layer address, but the address must be unique for different hosts on the same physical network.

physical security The protection of computer systems, related buildings, and equipment from intrusion and natural and environmental hazards. Also the ACCESS CONTROL of computer systems and facilities through the use of locks, keys, and administrative measures.

PICS ☞ PLATFORM FOR INTERNET CONTROL SELECTION.

piggyback Using somebody else's legitimate connection to obtain unauthorized connection to a system.

PIN ☞ PERSONAL IDENTIFICATION NUMBER.

ping Package Internet groper. A program used to test the reachability of destinations by sending them an ICMP echo request and waiting for a reply. The term is used as a verb: "ping host X to see if it is up!" and also as a noun: "I sent it a ping but it didn't respond."

ping of death A large ICMP packet sent to overflow the remote host's buffer, causing the remote host to reboot or hang.

PKCS ☞ PUBLIC-KEY CRYPTOGRAPHY STANDARD.

PKI ☞ PUBLIC KEY INFRASTRUCTURE.

PKZIP Software package for data compression and backup from PKware, Inc.

plaintext Unencrypted information.

Platform for Internet Control Selection These are specifications to mark the Internet content with labels (metadata) that define and categorize the content. Filtering software can use these labels to block access to certain data. This also facilitates CODE SIGNING privacy and parents' and teachers' control over the display of and access to Internet content.

Platform for Privacy Preferences Projects This is an emerging standard defined by W3C that covers Web sites' privacy policies. These policies, which are also available in a machine-readable form (on the Web site), include how a Web site handles personal information of its users. P3P-enabled Web browsers can compare users' privacy preferences with a Web site's P3P, thereby giving choice and information to a user. P3P1.0 specifications are now available from the World Wide Web Consortium (W3C) web site at http://www.w3c.org.

plausible deniability A situation in which events are structured such that someone can claim not to have known or done something, and no proof exists to the contrary. The term is usually used by a person or persons who arrange the structure of events for this purpose. *See also* NONREPUDIATION.

playback   Unauthorized resending of a legitimate recorded message.

Point-to-Point Protocol   The successor to SLIP, POINT-TO-POINT PROTOCOL (PPP) provides router-to-router and host-to-network connections over both synchronous and asynchronous circuits. *See also* SLIP.

policy   An expression of the intent of a system's owner or operator within which the system should operate. For example, a security policy describes the owner's intent for the AUTHENTICATION, ACCESS CONTROLS, etc., for a system. There are also specific types of policies for CONFIDENTIALITY, safety, INTEGRITY, etc.

Policy Approving Authority   The primary level of the U.S. DoD PKI Certification Management Authority. It is responsible for the approval of the security policy of each PCA.

> NOTE: *POLICY APPROVING AUTHORITY (PAA) and POLICY CREATION AUTHORITY (PCA) are PKI terms used within a restricted context, e.g., some U.S. and Canadian government PKIs.*

Policy Creation Authority   The second level of the US DoD PKI Certification Management Authority. It is responsible for the formulation of the security policy under which it and its subordinate CAs will issue public key certificates. Also known as a Policy Certification Authority. See note (POLICY APPROVING AUTHORITY).

port   A logical transport protocol endpoint on a host. A single host may transmit or receive information on a number of different ports. Different applications may be associated with different ports. Sometimes an application may use the same "well-known" port number. Other

applications use dynamically assigned port numbers.

port scan   A procedure to probe target computers by sending data packets to ports to see the network services offered.

positive control material   A collective term that refers to a sealed AUTHENTICATOR system, permissive action link, coded switch system, positive enable system, or nuclear command and control documents, material, or devices.

PostScript   A write-only programming language created by Adobe Systems, Inc. to describe printed pages.

PPP   ☞   POINT-TO-POINT PROTOCOL.

preauthentication   A method requiring a user to prove knowledge of a password before access is given to sensitive information that is encrypted with that password. This makes it more difficult for an ADVERSARY to use an off-line password guessing ATTACK.

preproduction model   A version of INFOSEC equipment that uses standard parts and whose form, design, and performance may not be completely evaluated. Also called BETA MODELS.

presentation layer   The OSI layer that determines how application information is represented while in transit between two systems.

Pretty Good Privacy   A strong encryption system for e-mail and file security that uses a combination of public key and secret key encryption. Created by Philip Zimmerman [PRZ95], a computer scientist from Boulder, Colorado. The operation of PRETTY GOOD PRIVACY (PGP) consists of five functions: digital signatures, message encryption, compression, e-mail compatibility, and segmentation. PGP now uses

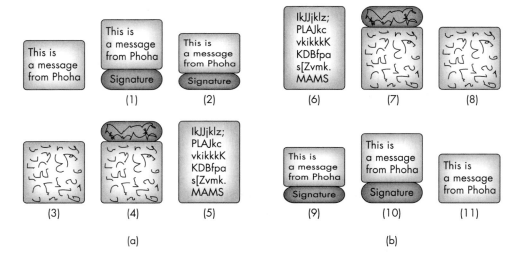

FIGURE P3. PGP.

Diffie–Hellman and DSA as well as or instead of RSA.

Figure P3 shows an example of how PGP works. Part (a) of the figure shows the process before the message is transmitted, and part (b) shows the process after the message is received.

Part (a): In (1) a digital signature (MD5/RSA) using sender's private key is appended to the file containing plaintext message "This is a message from Phoha." In (2) this file is compressed; in (3) this compressed file is encrypted with one-time session key using IDEA; in (4) using receiver's public key, an encrypted copy of session key is added; in (5) this file is converted to ASCII armor format. This converted file is then sent over the network.

Part (b): In (6) the ASCII file is received; in (7) ASCII armor is removed; in (8) one-time IDEA session key is recovered using receiver's private key; in (9) the file is decrypted using one-time IDEA session key; in (10) this file is decompressed and has both the signature and plaintext message. In (11) signature is verified using sender's RSA public key.

principal   A user or the collection of processes in a computer working on that user's behalf. Similar to subject; PRINCIPAL is a generic term used by the security community to include both people and computer systems.

print suppression   Hides characters to ensure PRIVACY. Typically used while a user types in a password.

privacy   Protection from the unauthorized disclosure of data. Security purists use CONFIDENTIALITY for this and use privacy to refer to the protection of personal information; privacy legislation consists of laws requiring government and business to justify which data they keep about people, and to tell people what information those organizations are storing about them.

NOTE: *The usage has not standardized; sometimes, privacy refers to a lower grade of CONFIDENTIALITY, used merely to protect personal information,*

rather than national security CLASSIFIED INFOR-
MATION.

Privacy Enhanced Mail IETF's specifications for secure electronic mail. PRIVACY
ENHANCED MAIL (PEM) provides mechanisms to support encryption, AUTHENTICA-
TION and integrity of e-mail messages in
the Internet. The IETF specification for
PEM cover (1) the format of messages that
use PEM, (2) a hierarchy of certification
authorities, (3) a set of CRYPTOGRAPHIC algorithms, (4) message formats for re-
questing and revoking certificates. PEM
specifies a tree structure hierarchy of CAs
for key distribution and uses RSA public
key technology for encryption and AU-
THENTICATION. More details are available in
RFC 1421, RFC 1422, RFC 1423, and
RFC 1424.

privacy system A commercial encryption system that can protect against a ca-
sual listener, but does not provide protection from a technically competent
cryptanalytic ATTACK.

Private Communication Technology A
protocol that provides session-level security
and is very similar to the SECURE SOCKET
LAYER PROTOCOL of Netscape.

private key The quantity in PUBLIC KEY
CRYPTOGRAPHY that must be kept secure.

> NOTE: *A private key is generally associated with a
> user, and this user is responsible for maintaining its*
> CONFIDENTIALITY.

privileged access A specific user, process, or computer's AUTHORIZATION to access
a computer's resource(s).

privileged user A user of a computer
who has been given more privileges than
normal users, usually to perform system
management functions. A privileged user
may be authorized to bypass the normal
access control mechanism.

probe An attempt to obtain information
about an IS or its users.

process Generally, a sequential locus of
control, as in the execution of a virtual
processor. It may take place on different
processors or on a single processor, but
with only a single execution point at any
one time.

production model The final mechanical
and electrical form of INFOSEC equipment.

promiscuous mail server A server that
sends e-mail over the Internet without con-
firming information on either the sender or
recipient.

promiscuous mode Refers to a setting
of an Ethernet interface that allows it to accept all information regardless of whether it
is addressed to its address. In contrast, in
normal mode, such an interface accepts only
information that is specifically addressed to
that interface or that is broadcast.

proof-carrying code CODE that has
built-in methods to statically check and ensure that code conforms with security policies. This is an active area of research and
the term is generally used in the context of
MOBILE CODE.

proprietary information Material and
information developed by a company pertaining to the company's products, business, or activities. Examples are financial
information; data or statements; trade secrets, product research and development;
existing and future product designs and
performance specifications; marketing plans
or techniques; schematics; client lists; computer programs; processes; and know-how
that have been clearly identified and properly marked by the company as proprietary
information, trade secrets, or company
confidential information.

protected communications   Telecommunications protected by TYPE 2 products or data encryption standard equipment. *See also* TYPE 2 product.

protected distribution system   A wire line or fiber-optic distribution system that transmits CLASSIFIED national security information that is unencrypted through an area of lesser CLASSIFICATION or control.

protected subsystem   A program that can run at a higher level of privilege than the user of the program is entitled to, because it has very structured interfaces that will not allow for anything but security-safe operations.

protection philosophy   The overall design of an IS that describes each of the IS's protection mechanisms. A combination of formal and informal techniques that prove that the security mechanisms can sufficiently enforce the security policy.

protection ring   One of a hierarchy of an IS's select modes that provides certain access rights to authorized user programs and processes for a given mode.

protective packaging   Packaging techniques for COMSEC MATERIAL that protect against penetration, show whether penetration has occurred or was attempted, and prevent premature viewing or copying of KEYING MATERIAL.

protective technologies   Special tamper-evident features and materials for detecting tampering and preventing attempts to COMPROMISE, modify, penetrate, extract, or substitute information-processing equipment and keying material.

protective technology/package incident   Any penetration, such as a crack or cut, of INFOSEC protective technology or packaging.

protocol   A system of rules governing the syntax, transmission, and sequencing of different messages that allow systems to exchange information.

protocol data unit   This is OSI terminology for "packet." A PROTOCOL DATA UNIT (PDU) is a data object exchanged by protocol machines within a given layer. PDUs consist of both protocol control information (PCI) and user data.

protocol layer   Within an overall communications process, a set of component processes each of which provides specific functions and communicates with adjacent layers.

protocol model   A conceptual model that describes how to communicate within a network.

prowler   A program to periodically clean up system resources. It may erase core files and other temporary files that are left behind by users and take up space.

proxy   The mechanism whereby one system "fronts for" another system in responding to protocol requests. PROXY systems are used in network management to avoid having to implement full protocol stacks in simple devices such as modems. In Figure P4 the dotted line indicates a virtual connection between an external client and a server. The connection between the external client and the proxy is called the external connection, and the connection between the proxy and the server is called an internal connection.

Proxy servers also act as go-betweens for unknown protocols. For example, an FTP proxy server may accept requests from a Web browser that does not have FTP implemented and transfer FTP requests to an FTP server.

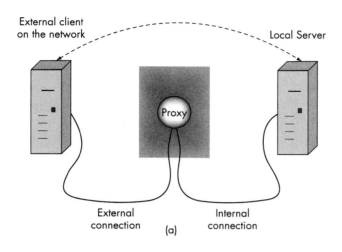

External client on the network

Local Server

Proxy

External connection

(a)

Internal connection

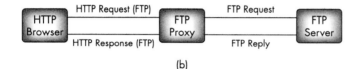

HTTP Browser — HTTP Request (FTP) → FTP Proxy — FTP Request → FTP Server

HTTP Response (FTP) — FTP Reply

(b)

FIGURE P4. Proxy.

proxy ARP A technique by which one machine, usually a ROUTER, answers ARP requests intended for another machine. By "faking" its identity, the ROUTER accepts responsibility for routing PACKETS to the "real" destination. PROXY ARP allows a site to use a single IO address with two physical networks. Subnetting would normally be a better solution.

public cryptography Knowledge of CRYPTOGRAPHY within the public domain, in contrast to CRYPTOGRAPHY that is CLASSIFIED.

public key The quantity in PUBLIC KEY CRYPTOGRAPHY that may be safely divulged.

public key certificate A digitally signed message that binds an identifier (for exam-

ple a person's identity) to a public key or some other attribute.

public key cryptography ☞ ASYMMETRIC CRYPTOGRAPHY.

Public Key Cryptography Standard A series of documents produced and distributed by RSA Data Security, Inc., proposing techniques for using public key CRYPTOGRAPHIC algorithms in a safe and interoperable manner. PKCS provides standards for RSA encryption, Diffie–Hellman key agreement, extended certificate syntax, CRYPTOGRAPHIC message syntax, private key information syntax, certification request syntax, selected attributes, CRYPTOGRAPHIC token interface, and personal information exchange syntax.

PKCS is a collection of 12 documents, PKCS#1 through PKCS#12, and PKCS also provides two supplementary documents: (1) An Overview of the PKCS

Standards and (2) A Layman's Guide to a Subset of ASN.1, BER, and DER.

Public Key Infrastructure (1) A set of standards for user AUTHENTICATION and data transfer. It is emerging as a de facto standard to integrate security for e-business digital content and processes as well as for files and documents. It is based on ASYMMETRIC CRYPTOGRAPHY and uses public and private digital keys and digital signatures for the secure transmission of data and user AUTHENTICATION. (2) The framework responsible for issuing, maintaining, and revoking PUBLIC KEY CERTIFICATES. (3) A set of policies, procedures, hardware, and software that enable various applications to make use of PUBLIC KEY CRYPTOGRAPHY for securing information. Typically, a PKI needs to include at least one CERTIFICATE AUTHORITY, a certificate practice statement, a directory, a means for storing private keys, policies on the use of keys (for signature and/or encryption), policy on the AUTHENTICATION of subjects (prior to issuing a certificate), and a CERTIFICATE REVOCATION LIST. A representative usage of PKI in this context may be "we need to build a PKI."

purging (1) An erasure technique that makes it difficult for an ADVERSARY to recover stored information. (2) The use of a LABORATORY ATTACK to make it impossible to recover stored information.

QoS ☞ QUALITY OF SERVICE.

quality of service A data prioritization at the network layer of the OSI model, bandwidth reservation, control of jitter, latency, error rates, or other attributes that results in guaranteed throughput rates.

quadrant Technology that provides reliable protection of CRYPTO-EQUIPMENT from tamper attacks, by ensuring that as soon as any tampering is detected, all sensitive data and logic are destroyed.

quantum cryptography Originally started in the 1970s by Stephen Wiesner [SW83], it builds on the premise that any ATTACK on a quantum communication channel causes an unavoidable disturbance. This premise is based on the principle that measuring a quantum system in general disturbs it and yields incomplete information about its state before the measurement (Heisenberg's uncertainty principle). This principle is used to build a CRYPTOGRAPHIC system for the distribution of a secret random CRYPTOGRAPHIC key between two parties initially sharing no secret information. The system can be combined with classical CRYPTOGRAPHIC techniques such as the one-time-pad to allow the parties to communicate securely. An introduction and more details about QUANTUM CRYPTOGRAPHY are available in [PW89], [BBE92].

R

Rainbow Series A set of publications produced by the NCSC containing interpretations of ORANGE BOOK requirements for trusted systems. Documents contained in Rainbow Series are available at http://www.radium.ncsc.mil/tpep/library/rainbow/.

randomizer Analog or digital producer of random, unbiased, and usually independent bits. Used for key generation, to provide a starting state for a key generator, and many other functions.

RARP ☞ REVERSE ADDRESS RESOLUTION PROTOCOL.

RAT ☞ REMOTE ACCESS TROJAN.

RBAC ☞ ROLE-BASED ACCESS CONTROL.

RC2 A proprietary secret key encryption scheme marketed by RSA Security. It is a block encryption scheme with 64-bit blocks and a varying length key.

RC4 A proprietary secret key encryption scheme marketed by RSA Security. It is a stream encryption algorithm that effectively produces an unbounded length pseudo-random stream from a varying length key.

RCP A UNIX command for copying a file across a network.

read A fundamental operation in an IS, the only result of which is information flow from an object to a subject.

read access An AUTHORIZATION to read information in an IS.

realm A KERBEROS term for all of the principals served by a particular KDC.

real-time reaction An immediate response to the detection and diagnosis of an attempted penetration, resulting in the prevention of unauthorized access.

recovery procedures The procedures needed for the restoration of an IS's data files and computational capability after a system failure.

Red Descriptive term for information systems and associated areas, circuits, components, and equipment that are processing (unencrypted) national security information.

Red/Black concept Electrical and electronic circuits, components, equipment, and systems that handle national security information (RED) in electrical form, and those that handle non-national-security information (BLACK) in the same form.

Red Book ☞ TRUSTED NETWORK INTERPRETATION ENVIRONMENTAL GUIDELINE (TNIEG).

Red Queen principle A basic premise of information warfare, it states that a system must continue to evolve (be developed) to maintain its competitive advantage relative to the evolution of its enemies. The term is due to L. van Valen (1973) and is drawn from Lewis Carroll's Red Queen in THROUGH THE LOOKING GLASS, who observed, "Now, here, you see, it takes all the running you can do, to keep in the same place."

Red signal Any electronic emission (e.g., PLAINTEXT, KEY, key stream, subkey stream, initial fill, or control signal) whose recovery would reveal national security information.

red team ☞ INFORMATION ASSURANCE RED TEAM; TIGER TEAM.

reference monitor A system component responsible for the mediation of all access to objects by subjects. All data accesses are performed through the reference monitor, which cannot be bypassed. See Figure R1.

reference validation mechanism Part of a TRUSTED COMPUTER SYSTEM that controls access between subjects and objects and whose correct operation is crucial to the protection of the system's data.

reflection attack An ATTACK where messages received from a source are replayed back to it.

release prefix A prefix added to the short title of U.S.–produced keying material to show that it has foreign releasability. Material with the prefix "A" can be released to specific allied nations, and mate-

rial with the prefix "U.S." is intended for U.S. use only.

remanence (1) Residual information left on a storage medium after it has been cleared. (2) A physical property of materials relating to the amount of magnetism left in the material after a magnetizing field is removed. *See also* MAGNETIC REMANENCE and CLEARING.

NOTE: *The Rainbow Series has a book on "Data Remanence," which defines remanence as "the residual physical representation of data which has in some way been erased" (http://www.radium.ncsc.mil/tpep/library/rainbow/NCSC-TG-025.2.html).*

remote access Trojan A Trojan horse that remotely accesses other computer systems over a network or over the Internet.

Remote File System A distributed file system, similar to NFS, developed by AT&T and distributed with their UNIX System V operating system. *See also* NFS.

remote procedure call A paradigm for distributed program execution. Software is executed on a client machine until the program makes a call to a procedure that is to be executed on a remote server. Parameters for that procedure are transmitted across the network to the server, which executes the procedure and returns the results to the client. The client is then able to continue its execution.

remote rekeying A method of rekeying a distant piece of CRYPTO-EQUIPMENT. *See also* AUTOMATIC REMOTE REKEYING and MANUAL REMOTE REKEYING.

repair action An NSA (U.S.) approved change to a COMSEC END-ITEM that does not affect the original characteristics of the end-item and is provided for optional application by holders. Repair actions are limited to minor electrical and/or mechan-

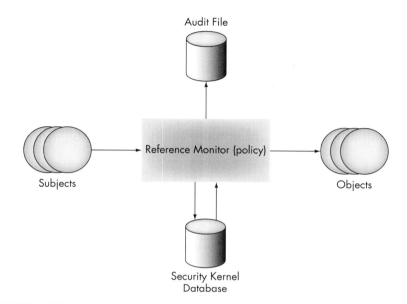

Audit File

Reference Monitor (policy)

Subjects

Objects

Security Kernel
Database

FIGURE R1. Reference monitor.

ical improvements to enhance operation, maintenance, or reliability. They do not require an identification label, marking, or control but must be fully documented by changes to the maintenance manual.

repeater   A device that propagates electrical signals from one cable to another without making routing decisions or providing packet filtering. See Figure R2. In OSI terminology, a repeater is a physical layer intermediate system. *See also* BRIDGE and ROUTER.

replay attacks   Attacks that use previously recorded transactions between two valid protocol entities to initiate a new transaction.

replaying   Storing and retransmitting messages. The word is usually used to imply that the entity doing the replay of mes-

sages is mounting some sort of security ATTACK.

repudiation   Denial of a transmission or receipt of a message.

Requests for Comments   The document series, begun in 1969, that describes the Internet suite of protocols and related experiments. Not all REQUESTS FOR COMMENTS (RFC) describe Internet standards, but all Internet standards are written up as RFCs.

NOTE: *RFCs are available from http://www.ietf.org.*

reserve keying material   A key kept in reserve to meet unforeseen needs. *See also* CONTINGENCY KEY.

residual risk   Risks remaining after the application of security measures.

residue   Data left in storage after the completion of information processing operations but before there has been any DEGAUSSING or OVERWRITING.

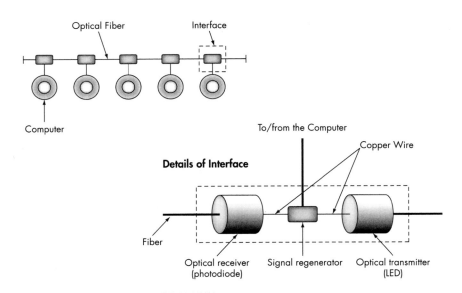

Optical Fiber   Interface

Computer

To/from the Computer

Copper Wire

Details of Interface

Fiber

Optical receiver   Signal regenerator   Optical transmitter
(photodiode)   (LED)

FIGURE R2. A repeater connected to a computer through fiber cable.

resource encapsulation   The reference monitor's mediation of access to an IS resource that is protected and that a subject cannot directly access. Satisfies the requirement for accurate auditing or resource usage.

retina system   A biometric system in which a retina blood vessel pattern must be matched with a stored pattern to gain access.

retrovirus   A type of virus that maintains internal bookkeeping to stay dormant until the backup and other auxiliary storage are also infected, making recovery difficult.

Reverse Address Resolution Protocol
The Internet protocol that a diskless host uses to find its Internet address at startup. REVERSE ADDRESS RESOLUTION PROTOCOL (RARP) maps a physical address to an Internet address. *See also* ADDRESS RESOLUTION PROTOCOL.

revocation   Taking back privileges, either from a person or an entity such as a process that is no longer trusted.

RFC ☞ REQUESTS FOR COMMENTS.

RFS ☞ REMOTE FILE SYSTEM.

Rijndael   The Rijndael (pronounced "rhine-dahl") algorithm is a secret key algorithm created by Belgian cryptographers Joan Daemon and Vincent Rijmen. It uses keys of size 128, 192, and 256 bits. This algorithm will serve as the ADVANCED ENCRYPTION STANDARD (AES) for all U.S. federal agencies.

NOTE: *Details of the technical reference of RIJNDAEL are given in [JD00] and [JD01]. For many downloads and more details about RIJNDAEL, visit the web site http://www.esat.kuleuven.ac.be/ ~rijmen/rijndael.*

RIP ☞ ROUTING INFORMATION PROTOCOL.

RIPE-MD-160   A MESSAGE digest algorithm. This is a 160-bit CRYPTOGRAPHIC hash function, designed by Hans Dobbertin, Antoon Bosselaers, and Bart Preneel. This hash function is intended as a secure replacement for the 128-bit hash functions MD4, MD5, and RIPEMD. RIPE-MD-160 is a strengthened version of RIPEMD and is tuned for 32 bit processors. RIPEMD was developed in the framework of the EU project RIPE (RACE Integrity Primitives Evaluation, 1988–1992). *See also* HASH, MESSAGE DIGEST, MD4, and MD5.

risk The probability that a particular security system vulnerability will be exploited.

risk analysis A process of analyzing and examining the impact, severity, and the likelihood/frequency of particular risks. Compare with RISK ASSESSMENT. Both RISK ANALYSIS and RISK ASSESSMENT are separate phases of a risk management process.

risk assessment An analysis of threats to and vulnerabilities of an IS and the potential effect of the loss of information or capabilities of a system in order to identify appropriate and cost-effective COUNTERMEASURES.

risk index The difference between the minimum level of CLEARANCE needed for the AUTHORIZATION of IS users and the maximum sensitivity (e.g., CLASSIFICATION and categories) of the system's data.

NOTE: *This is a concept derived from the yellow book of the Rainbow Series, applicable to U.S. defense systems processing CLASSIFIED INFORMATION.*

risk management A process in which an information system's security risks are minimized to a level proportional to the value of the assets protected.

rlogin A UNIX command for logging into a machine across the network. A short form of "remote login."

Role-Based Access Control ACCESS CONTROL model, where accesses to system resources are defined in terms of roles, privileges, sessions, and user-role, role-privileges assignments. Within a session a user activates certain roles and the corresponding privileges.

rootkit Rootkits are software suites that substitute Trojans for commonly used operating system binaries, thereby allowing malicious BACK-DOOR entry to a system. A ROOTKIT typically has four types of tools: (1) Trojans, (2) BACK-DOORS, (3) network interface eavesdropping tools (sniffers), and (4) log cleaners that cover the tracks.

Examples of UNIX rootkit components are altered versions of LOGIN, netstat, ps (Trojan), intetd (BACK DOOR), etc. In Windows NT, a ROOTKIT may patch the NT kernel to usurp system calls to hide a process, registry entry, or Trojan executable file, or redirect calls to Trojan functions. *See also* TROJAN HORSE.

router A system responsible for making decisions about which of the several paths internetwork traffic may follow. A ROUTER may be implemented in hardware, software, or a combination of both. To do this, it uses a routing protocol to gain information about the network, and a set of algorithms to choose the best route based on several criteria known as "routing metrics." See Figure R3. In OSI terminology, a router is a network layer intermediate system. *See also* GATEWAY, BRIDGE, and REPEATER.

Routing Information Protocol An INTERIOR GATEWAY PROTOCOL (IGP) supplied with Berkeley UNIX.

RPC ☞ REMOTE PROCEDURE CALL.

RSA A public key cryptographic algorithm named for its inventors R. Rivest,

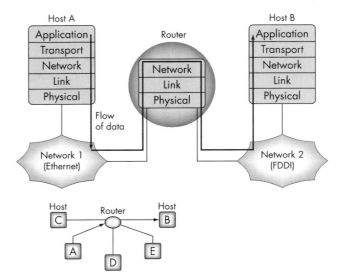

A. Shamir, and L. Adleman. The algorithm can be used for encryption and digital signatures. The security of this algorithm relies on the difficulty of calculating the factors of large numbers. The algorithm was patented in 1983, but the patent has now expired, and so the algorithm is freely available.

RSADSI An abbreviation for RSA Data Security, Inc., the company that held the RSA patent.

> NOTE: (1) RSADSI no longer exists. It is now called RSA Security. (2) The patent for RSA has already expired, and the technology is available publicly. The company released the algorithm publicly a week or so before the patent expired.

rsh The UNIX remote shell command that executes a secured command on a specified machine across a network. Short form of remote shell.

S

S2ML ☞ SECURITY SERVICES MARKUP LANGUAGE.

SA ☞ SECURITY ASSOCIATION; SYSTEM ADMINISTRATOR.

safeguarding statement A statement affixed to a computer output or printout that states the highest CLASSIFICATION being processed at the time the product was produced and requires control of the product, at that level, until the determination of the true CLASSIFICATION by an authorized person. Synonymous with BANNER.

safeguards ☞ SECURITY SAFEGUARDS.

salt A user-specific value cryptographically combined with that user's password. Salt serves several purposes. It makes the hash of two users' passwords different even if their passwords are the same. It also means that an intruder cannot pre-compute hashes of a few thousand guessed passwords and compare that list against a stolen database of hashed passwords. The salt can be a random number that is stored, in the clear, along with the hash of the user's password or it will con-

sist of the user's name or some other user-specific information.

sample key A key used only for off-the-air demonstration.

sandbox An area of a network or a computer system in which programs are allowed to run with limited privileges and have no access and rights to certain system resources or areas. For example, a Java APPLET confined to a sandbox environment may not have access to the hard disk. (See JAVA SANDBOX). An isolated segment of a network used for testing is another example of a sandbox environment.

sanitize The permanent removal of information, including all CLASSIFIED labels, markings, and activity logs, from media.

SATAN ☞ SECURITY ADMINISTRATOR TOOL FOR ANALYZING NETWORKS.

scavenging Acquiring data from object residue.

scratch pad store A short-term storage of keys to guard against tampering, disclosure, and unauthorized use in crypto-equipment.

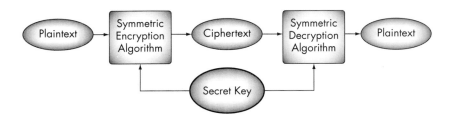

script kiddies   A slang term used for hackers who use tools written by others to attack systems because they themselves lack the technical knowledge and skills to write their own tools.

SDMI   ☞   SECURE DIGITAL MUSIC INITIATIVE.

secrecy   Protects information from people with unauthorized access. *See also* CONFIDENTIALITY.

secret   (1) (noun) A quantity known only to principals that can be used for AUTHENTICATION and encryption of information flow between them. (2) (adjective) A label applied to CLASSIFIED INFORMATION whose unauthorized disclosure may cause serious damage to individual, organizational, or national security.

secret key   The information that is used for both the ENCRYPTION of data and its subsequent DECRYPTION. Typically, a method needs to be used for sharing this secret key between the parties who encrypt and decrypt the data.

secret key cryptography   Also known as SYMMETRIC CRYPTOGRAPHY. A scheme in which the same key is used for ENCRYPTION and DECRYPTION. See Figure S1.

secure communications   Telecommunications secured by TYPE 1 (U.S.) products and/or PROTECTED DISTRIBUTION SYSTEMS.

Secure Digital Music Initiative   A consortium of companies and organizations with an aim to develop an open framework for storing, playing, and distributing digital music and to prevent the distribution of illegal copies of music. At present there are more than 200 members in this consortium representing consumer electronics, Internet service providers, information technology, telecommunications, security technology, and the music industry. It also provides specifications for portable devices. For more details see the information at http://www.sdmi.org.

secure hash algorithm   A specification for a secure hash algorithm in which a condensed message representation, called a MESSAGE DIGEST, can be generated.

Secure Hypertext Transfer Protocol
Developed within the Internet standards process, this protocol defines the security additions to the HTTP protocol. This protocol is an application-level protocol (TCP/IP four-layer model and OSI seven-layer model) and adds encryption and AUTHENTICATION to World Wide Web communications. See RFC 2660.

NOTE: *S-HTTP is now virtually obsolete. HTTPS (HTTP using SSL) is currently the most dominant protocol for protecting Web traffic, and the TLS (TRANSPORT LAYER SECURITY) protocol is being developed (RFC 2817, RFC 2818).*

Secure Socket Layer Protocol   First introduced in 1994 by Netscape (U.S.), us-

SSL Handshake Protocol	SSL, Change Cipher Spec Protocol	SSL Alert Protocol	HTTP
SSL Record Protocol			
TCP			
IP			

FIGURE S2. Secure Socket Layer Protocol stack.

ing a combination of PUBLIC-KEY and SYMMETRIC CRYPTOSYSTEMS to provide CONFIDENTIALITY, DATA INTEGRITY, and AUTHENTICATION of server and client, it provides security services just above the TCP layer. See Figure S2.

secure state A condition of an information system in which objects can be accessed only by authorized subjects in an authorized manner.

secure subsystem A subsystem containing its own implementation of the reference monitor concept for those resources it controls. A secure subsystem may rely on other controls and the base operating system for the control of subjects and the more primitive system objects.

Security Administrator Tool for Analyzing Networks SECURITY ADMINISTRATOR TOOL FOR ANALYZING NETWORKS (SATAN), is a network security analyzer designed by Dan Farmer and Wietse Venema of Sun Microsystems (U.S.). This is a freeware program to help find computer and network system vulnerabilities. SATAN version 1.0 was released in 1995.

security association (1) A relationship between entities represented by a set of information or a contract that describes the rules of utilization of security services for secure communication between these entities. The contract must be shared and agreed by all involved entities. See RFC 2408. (2) Security parameters that control the agreements—such as cryptographic algorithms and key strengths—between the endpoints in an IPsec tunnel.

security controls Hardware, firmware, or software features that allow only authorized subjects to access resources within an IS.

security fault analysis An analysis of the potential (hardware) faults that may occur in a device, and the effects that such faults may have on system security.

Security Features Users Guide A manual that explains the functions of a specific system's security mechanisms.

security filter An IS trusted subsystem in which security policy is enforced on the data passing through it.

security flaw An error in an IS in which the protection mechanism may be weaker than expected, by-passable, or faulty.

security inspection A process to assess whether an IS, including its mechanisms, policies, procedures, and practices, meets its security requirements.

security kernel The part of an operating system responsible for the enforcement of security. Usually used in the context of an operating system constructed with such functions partitioned from the rest of the OS to minimize the chances of security-relevant bugs.

security label   A label containing information describing a subject's or object's sensitivity, such as its hierarchical CLASSIFI-CATION (CONFIDENTIAL, SECRET, TOP SECRET) and any applicable non-hierarchical security categories (e.g., sensitive compartmented information or critical nuclear weapon design information).

> NOTE: *In Australian defense (which is similar to U.S., U.K., and Canada) a label may consist of five parts: (1) the CLASSIFICATION (Unclassified, Restricted, Confidential, Secret, or Top Secret), (2) any compartment/category, (3) any releasability (e.g., Australian Government Access Only-equiv NOFORN) (4) any caveat (e.g., commercial in confidence, medical in confidence), (5) any handling instructions (e.g., handle via XX channels only).*

security model   A precise statement containing a system's security rules. The key defining characteristic of a model in comparison to a security policy is that a model is an abstraction. *See also* SECURITY POLICY.

security net control station   A management system that supervises the execution of network security policy.

security perimeter   A boundary that contains all of an IS's accredited components and devices, excluding separately accredited components.

security policy   As defined in the OR-ANGE BOOK, security policy is the set of laws, rules, and practices that regulate how an organization manages, protects, and distributes sensitive information.

security range   The range of the highest to lowest security levels allowed in or on

an IS, system component, subsystem, or network.

security requirements   Statements describing the security properties that a system must have in order to be acceptable.

security requirements baseline   The minimum security requirements for an IS.

security safeguards   The protective measures and controls required to meet security requirements. Examples include security features, management constraints, personnel security, and security of physical structures, areas, and devices. *See also* ACCRED-ITATION.

Security Services Markup Language   A common language for companies to share information about transactions and end users. An XML-based security services technical committee formed by OASIS is charged with defining S2ML.

security specification   The detailed description of an IS's required safeguards.

security test and evaluation   The examination and analysis of a system's safeguards to determine their adequacy.

seed key   A key for commencing an updating or key generation process.

segment   The unit of end-to-end transmission in the TCP protocol. A segment consists of a TCP header followed by an application data. A segment is transmitted by encapsulation inside an IP DATAGRAM.

self-authentication   The AUTHENTICATION of all of a secure communications system's transmissions.

self/group/public controls   The categorizing of the access control of files. The owner determines what file permissions he or she (self) will have, what permissions a group of users will have, and what permissions the rest of the world (public) will have. Typical permissions include read, write, and execute.

self-synchronizing An ENCRYPTION scheme in which if some CIPHERTEXT is garbled by the addition, deletion, or modification of information, some of the message will be garbled at the receiver, but at some point in the message stream following the CIPHERTEXT modification the message will DECRYPT properly.

sensitive information Information that if misused or modified could unfavorably affect the national interest or corporate interest or the privacy of individuals.

sensitivity label A label that contains information from the security label(s) of a subject and an object and is used by the TRUSTED COMPUTING BASE (TCB) to make MANDATORY ACCESS CONTROL decisions.

separation of duty (1) A condition in which some critical operations require the cooperation of at least two different people. For example, separation of duty exists in a bank vault that has two combination locks if no employee knows the combination for both locks. The principle is that the system will be robust against a single corrupt officer, and the likelihood of two officers being corrupt is acceptably low. (2) Several individuals being assigned security-related tasks and granted the least number of privileges necessary to carry them out.

Serial line IP An Internet protocol used to run IP over serial lines such as telephone circuits of RS-232C cables interconnecting two systems. SERIAL LINE IP (SLIP) is now being replaced by PPP. *See also* POINT-TO-POINT PROTOCOL. *See also* RFC 1055.

server Some resource available on a network to provide some service such as name lookup, file storage, or printing. *See also* CLIENT–SERVER MODEL.

session The set of transactions that is exchanged while a transmission channel is open.

session hijacking An intruder taking over a connection after the original source has been AUTHENTICATED.

session key A key used to encrypt a single message, communications stream, or session.

session layer The OSI layer that provides the pathway for dialogue control between end systems.

SFUG ☞ SECURITY FEATURES USERS GUIDE.

SGML ☞ STANDARD GENERALIZED MARKUP LANGUAGE.

SHA ☞ SECURE HASH ALGORITHM.

shared key A key shared only by the encrypter and decrypter in a shared key (symmetric) CRYPTOSYSTEM. *See also* SECRET KEY.

> NOTE: *In a multicast or a conferencing protocol a key may be shared by a group of more than two people.*

shielded enclosure A room or container which has a boundary that resists the transmission of electromagnetic radiation. The shielding may be employed to prevent the leakage of sensitive emanations from the inside, or to prevent delicate systems from interference, jamming, or other ATTACK originating outside the enclosure.

short title A combination of letters and numbers used to identify certain COMSEC MATERIALS to make handling, accounting, and controlling them easier.

S-HTTP ☞ SECURE HYPERTEXT TRANSFER PROTOCOL.

FIGURE S3. Simple Mail Transfer Protocol.

sign The use of a private key to generate a digital signature.

Signaling System 7 A telephone protocol with three basic functions: (1) supervising, (2) alerting, and (3) addressing. Supervising relates to monitoring the status of a circuit, alerting refers to indications of an incoming call, and addressing relates to routing and destination signals over a network in dial tone or in the form of digital data.

signals security All COMSEC and electronic security.

signature A quantity associated with a message that only someone with knowledge of the signer's PRIVATE KEY could have calculated, but which can be verified to be associated to the signer's PUBLIC KEY (if the message is intact). See DIGITAL SIGNATURE.

signature detection An intrusion detection technique that recognizes an ATTACK based on known characteristics or signatures.

Simple Key Exchange for Internet Protocols Uses PUBLIC KEY CERTIFICATES to exchange symmetric keys between two systems. More details of Simple Key Exchange for Internet Protocols (SKIP) are available at http://www.skip-vpn.org.

Simple Mail Transport Protocol A protocol for sending electronic mail across a network, standardized by the IETF. Details of SIMPLE MAIL TRANSPORT PROTOCOL (SMTP) are given in RFC 821. See Figure S3.

Simple Network Management Protocol A protocol for controlling systems across a network standardized by the IETF. Details of SIMPLE NETWORK MANAGEMENT PROTOCOL (SNMP) are given in RFC 1157.

simple security property A property in the Bell and LaPadula security model that holds if subjects operating at a given security level are prevented from reading objects that have a higher security level. This is sometimes described as "no read up." In the model, subjects are able to read objects that have an equal or lower ("read down") security level.

Simple Watcher A program that goes through the LOG data generated by various security programs, in particular "syslog." It is capable of responding to high-priority events while continuously monitoring the LOG in "real time."

single-level device An IS device that is not trusted to maintain the separation of data with different security levels.

NOTE: *A device may be able to maintain the separation reliably, but if it is not required to, or if it is not trusted to, then it is effectively a single-level device.*

single-point keying A means of distributing keys from a single fill point to multiple, local CRYPTO-EQUIPMENT or devices.

SKIP ☞ SIMPLE KEY EXCHANGE FOR INTERNET PROTOCOLS.

SKIPJACK A SECRET KEY ENCRYPTION algorithm developed by NSA (U.S.) using 64-bit blocks and 80-bit keys. It is embedded in CLIPPER and CAPSTONE CHIPS. It was originally CLASSIFIED SECRET but has since been declassified and published.

SLIP ☞ SERIAL LINE IP.

smart card A credit-card-sized object used for AUTHENTICATION that contains non-volatile storage and computational power. Some smart cards are capable of performing CRYPTOGRAPHIC operations on the card. ISO/IEC 7816 standard contains smart card specifications.

SMI ☞ STRUCTURE OF MANAGEMENT INFORMATION.

SMTP ☞ SIMPLE MAIL TRANSFER PROTOCOL.

smurf A DENIAL-OF-SERVICE ATTACK in which many PINGS (ICMP echo request packets) are broadcast to the network. The "source" field is set to the victim's IP address. Any machines that respond will transmit to the victim, overloading its network interface.

sniffer (1) A program that attaches itself to a computer system and records the first few keystrokes (usually 128) of people logging in. It then typically transmits this data, which may contain password and login information, back to the hacker. (2) Programs that monitor traffic on the Internet.

SNMP ☞ SIMPLE NETWORK MANAGEMENT PROTOCOL.

SOCKS A circuit-level proxy used to protect against application-layer traffic types such as HTTP, FTP, TELNET, etc.

software system test and evaluation process Process that plans, develops, and documents the quantitative demonstration of the fulfillment of all baseline functional performance, operational, and interface requirements.

source (1) The origin. (2) Also, the name of a field in various networking protocols, such as IP, which holds the name or address of the source.

spam (1) To flood a person, newsgroup, or a bulletin board with many unwanted messages. (2) To overflow buffers with a large stream of data.

special mission modification Required or optional modification, relating only to a specific mission, purpose, or operational or environmental need.

specification A technical description of a system's intended behavior, which may help develop the implementation and provide a basis for testing the resulting system.

speech privacy Disguising speech through fixed-sequence permutations or voice/speech inversion so that if it is overheard, it will not be understood.

spiders Software that examines and records the contents of new files by traversing the World Wide Web.

split knowledge Knowledge that is separated among different individuals or teams so that no one individual or team will have access to all of the separated data. *See also* SEPARATION OF DUTY.

spoofing Use by an unauthorized individual of legitimate identification and authentication (I&A) data to impersonate a legitimate user, that is, to appear to have a different identity from one's own. Synonyms are IMPERSONATE and MASQUERADE. *See also* IP SPOOFING.

spread spectrum A transmitted signal's bandwidth that is considerably greater than

123

the frequency content of the original information. Frequency hopping, direct sequence spreading, time scrambling, and combinations of these techniques are forms of spread spectrum.

SPS ☞ SCRATCH PAD STORE.

SRA ☞ SUBREGISTRATION AUTHORITY.

SS 7 ☞ SIGNALING SYSTEM 7.

SSL ☞ SECURE SOCKET LAYER PROTOCOL.

Standard Generalized Markup Language An international standard (metalanguage) for representing text in electronic format in a device-and system-independent format.

star (*) property BELL–LAPADULA SECURITY MODEL rule that prohibits "write downs." That is, a subject operating at one security level is not allowed to write to an object with a lower level. "Write ups" are permitted. Also called CONFINEMENT PROPERTY.

start-up KEK Common KEY ENCRYPTION KEY held by a group of potential communicating entities and used to establish ad hoc tactical networks.

state machine An abstraction or model of a system, comprising inputs, outputs, and internal ("state") memory. At any time, the output is dependent on the current state (or a combination of the current state and the current inputs), and the "next state" is a function of the current state and the inputs. This abstraction is one of the most common ways to describe computer systems, components, and protocols.

state variable Represents either an IS's state or a system resource's state.

steganography Means by which two or more parties may employ subliminal or invisible communication.

storage object An object in which information can be stored (or "written") and subsequently retrieved (or "read").

stream encryption An ENCRYPTION algorithm that ENCRYPTS and DECRYPTS messages of arbitrary size.

strong A CRYPTOGRAPHIC algorithm is said to be strong if it is computationally infeasible to crack, usually assuming that the attacker has knowledge of the algorithm itself, and possibly some known or chosen PLAINTEXT.

strong authentication An AUTHENTICATION where someone eavesdropping on the AUTHENTICATION exchange does not gain sufficient information to impersonate the principal in a subsequent AUTHENTICATION.

structure of management information The rules used to define the objects that can be accessed via a network management protocol.

subject A person, process, or device that transports information among objects or changes information to the system state.

subject security level Sensitivity label(s) of the objects to which the subject has both read and write access. The CLEARANCE level of a subject's user must always be higher than the security level of the subject.

subnet One of the set of hardware networks that compose an IP network. Host addresses on a given subnet share an IP network number with hosts on all other SUBNETS of that IP network, but the local-address part is divided into subnet-number and host-number fields to indicate which SUBNET a host is on. A particular division of the local-address part is not assumed; this could vary from network to network. See Figure S4.

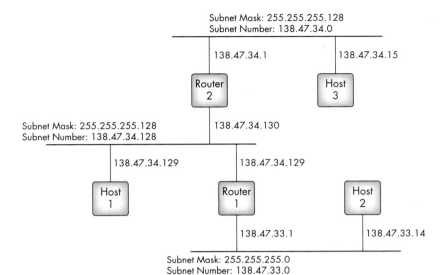

Subnet Mask: 255.255.255.128
Subnet Number: 138.47.34.0

138.47.34.1   138.47.34.15

Router 2   Host 3

Subnet Mask: 255.255.255.128
Subnet Number: 138.47.34.128

138.47.34.130

138.47.34.129   138.47.34.129

Host 1   Router 1   Host 2

138.47.33.1   138.47.33.14

Subnet Mask: 255.255.255.0
Subnet Number: 138.47.33.0

FIGURE S4. Subnet implementation example.

subnet field   The bit field in an Internet address denoting the SUBNET number. The bits making up this field are not necessarily contiguous in the address.

subnet mask   The designation of which bits in the Internet DOTTED DECIMAL NOTATION of address form the SUBNET number. Also known as "netmask." See ADDRESS MASK.

subnet number   A number identifying a SUBNET within a network.

subnetwork   A collection of end systems and intermediate systems under the control of a single administrative DOMAIN and utilizing a single network access protocol. Examples include private X.25 networks and a collection of bridged LANs. See SUBNET.

subregistration authority   The individual in charge of the DISTINGUISHED NAME process.

substitution   An ENCRYPTION algorithm where a ONE-TO-ONE MAPPING is performed on a fixed-size block, for example, where each letter of the alphabet has an enciphered equivalent. Substitution ciphers are not very secure unless the block size is large, and they cannot be combined with permutation ciphers in a series of rounds to build strong ciphers like DES.

subversion   A COMPROMISE that undermines integrity.

superencryption   Process of ENCRYPTING already encrypted information. Occurs when a message that has been encrypted off-line is transmitted over a secured, on-line circuit, or when information encrypted by the originator is multiplexed onto a communications trunk, which is then bulk encrypted.

supersession   The replacement of a COMSEC AID by a different edition.

superuser   An operating system concept in which an individual is allowed to circumvent ordinary security mechanisms. For instance, the system manager must be able to read everyone's files for doing backups.

supervisor state   Synonymous with EXECUTIVE STATE. (Usually the executive state or the supervisor state refers to the state of an operating system.)

suppression measure   A measure to reduce or stop COMPROMISING EMANATIONS in an IS.

surrogate access   ☞ DISCRETIONARY ACCESS CONTROLS.

SWATCH   ☞ SIMPLE WATCHER.

syllabary   List of individual letters, combinations of letters, or syllables, with their equivalent CODE GROUPS, used for spelling out words or proper names that are not in a code's vocabulary. A SYLLABARY may also be a spelling table.

syllabify   To break a word into syllables in order that each might be processed separately in some way.

symmetric cryptography   SECRET KEY CRYPTOGRAPHY. Called symmetric because the same key is used for encryption and DECRYPTION.

SYN   A packet that synchronizes sequence numbers between two session endpoints during the initiation of a TCP session.

SYN/ACK   An acknowledgement package to a TCP SYN request.

system administrator   An individual who installs and maintains an information system, utilizes the IS effectively, provides adequate security parameters, and implements established INFOSEC policies and procedures.

system assets   Any software, hardware, data, or administrative, physical, communications, or personnel resource within an IS.

system development methodologies   Methodologies for managing the complexity of system development. Development methodologies include software engineering aids and high-level design analysis tools.

system high   The highest security level of an IS.

system high mode   An IS security mode of operation in which all users of the IS have all of the following: (1) valid security CLEARANCE for all information within an IS; (2) formal access approval and signed non-disclosure agreements for all the information stored and/or processed (including all compartments, subcompartments, and/or special access programs); and (3) valid NEED-TO-KNOW for some of the information contained within the IS.

system indicator   A distinguishing symbol or group of symbols in an off-line ENCRYPTED message that identify the specific CRYPTOSYSTEM or KEY used in the ENCRYPTION.

system integrity   An attribute of an IS when its function is unaffected by any sort of unauthorized manipulation of the system.

system low   An IS's lowest security level.

system profile   A detailed security description of an IS's general operating environment.

system security   A system's determined degree of security, as a result of an evaluation of all of the system elements and INFOSEC countermeasures.

system security engineering   The effort to provide a system with optimal security and survivability throughout its life cycle.

system security evaluation   A RISK ASSESSMENT of a system to discover its vulnerabilities and possible security threats.

system security management plan
A formal document fully describing the responsibilities for meeting system security requirements for planned security tasks.

system security officer   Synonymous with INFORMATION SYSTEM SECURITY OFFICER.

system security plan   A formal document fully describing the system security requirements for planned security tasks.

T

tampering Altering the proper functioning of equipment through unauthorized modification.

TCB ☞ TRUSTED COMPUTING BASE.

TCP ☞ TRANSMISSION CONTROL PROTOCOL.

TCP segment The unit of data exchanged between TCP modules.

TCSEC ☞ DoD TRUSTED COMPUTER SYSTEM EVALUATION CRITERIA.

telecommunications The preparation, transmission, communication, or related processing of information (writing, images, sounds, or other data) by electrical, electromagnetic, electromechanical, electrooptical, or electronic means.

telecommunications and automated information systems security Types of security that are superseded by INFORMATION SYSTEM SECURITY.

telecommunications security Security related to telecommunications systems. *See also* INFORMATION SYSTEM SECURITY.

telnet The virtual terminal protocol in the Internet suite of protocols. Allows the users of one host to log into a remote host and interact as normal terminal users of that host. In Figure T1, the TELNET client software communicates with the TELNET server on a remote machine through TCP.

TEMPEST The investigating, studying, and controlling of COMPROMISING EMANATIONS from IS equipment.

TEMPEST test A laboratory test to evaluate the nature of compromising emanations associated with an IS.

TEMPEST zone A specific area of a facility for operating equipment with appropriate TEMPEST characteristics (TEMPEST ZONE assignment).

test key Key to test COMSEC EQUIPMENT or systems.

TFTP ☞ TRIVIAL FILE TRANSFER PROTOCOL.

TGT ☞ TICKET-GRANTING TICKET.

threat Any event that is potentially harmful to an IS through unauthorized access, destruction, disclosure, modification of data, and/or denial of service.

threat analysis The analysis of the impact or severity of a threat on the security

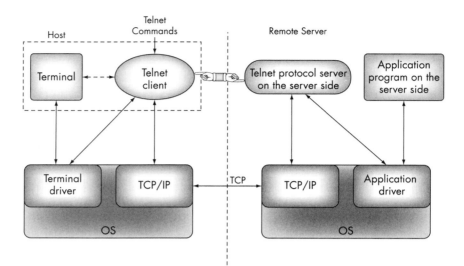

of the system, of its likelihood or frequency, and possibly other factors such as the skills or resources that would be required by an attacker to implement the threat. See RISK ANALYSIS.

threat assessment The determination of whether the level of threat determined by the THREAT ANALYSIS is acceptable. *See also* RISK ASSESSMENT.

threat monitoring The analysis, assessment, and review of information collected to locate system events that possibly violate system security.

ticket A data structure constructed by a trusted intermediary to enable an AUTHENTI-CATION.

ticketed-oriented Each subject maintains a list of TICKETS, which are unforgeable bit patterns. Each subject has one ticket for each object it is authorized to access. *See also* LIST-ORIENTED.

ticket-granting ticket A KERBEROS data structure that is really a ticket to the KEY DISTRIBUTION CENTER. The purpose is to allow a user's workstation to forget a user's long-term SECRET KEY soon after the user logs in.

tiger team A group of people hired by an organization to defeat its own security systems so that the organization can learn the systems' weaknesses. *See also* RED TEAM.

time bomb A resident computer program in which an unauthorized act occurs at a set time.

time-compliance date The deadline for the completion of a mandatory modification to a COMSEC END-ITEM to retain approval for operational use.

time-dependent password A password that is valid only at certain times.

tinkerbell program Programs that issue warnings when traffic enters a network from a particular address or from a particular user.

TLS ☞ TRANSPORT LAYER SECURITY.

TNIEG ☞ Trusted Network Interpretation Environmental Guideline.

token (1) An authentication sequence. (2) A physical item for identification, usually an electronic device that can be inserted in a door or a computer system to gain access.

token authenticator A pocket-sized computer used in a challenge–response authentication scheme. The authentication sequences are called tokens.

top-level specification System behavior described at an abstract level, for example, a functional specification that omits all implementation details.

topology A network configuration that describes the connection of its nodes. Examples include bus, ring, and star topologies.

totient function The number of positive integers less than n that are relatively prime to n.

TPI ☞ Two-person integrity.

Traditional COMSEC Program A program in which NSA (U.S.) controls the development and, sometimes, the production of INFOSEC items. This includes the Authorized Vendor Program. The NSA must approve any changes to the INFOSEC end-items used in products developed and/or produced by these programs.

traffic analysis (1) That part of eavesdropping concerned with the analysis of which parties are communicating and the volumes and timings of those communications, rather than the contents of the messages themselves. Some encryption systems do not protect users against traffic analysis, even though all the content may be encrypted. (2) The study of communications patterns.

traffic encryption key A key that encrypts plaintext, superencrypts previously encrypted text, and/or decrypts ciphertext. Contrast with key encryption key. Similar to session key.

traffic-flow security (1) Security measures and techniques that prevent traffic analysis. (2) Hiding valid messages in an online cryptosystem or secure communications system.

traffic padding The addition of false communications or data units to conceal the amount of real data units being sent.

training key A cryptographic key for training.

tranquility Degree of change of security levels of objects and subjects while an IS is processing an operation. Strong tranquility means that no change is allowed. Weak tranquility allows changes during an operation if the resulting state does not violate security requirements.

transaction (1) The set of exchanges required for one message to be transmitted to one or more recipients. (2) Sequence of tasks needed to be completed for an operation.

transceiver Transmitter–receiver. The physical device that connects a host interface to a local area network such as Ethernet. Ethernet transceivers contain electronics that apply signals to a system's cables and sense collisions. See Figure T2.

TRANSEC ☞ Transmission security.

transmission channel A communication path between a sender and a receiver for the exchange of data and commands.

Transmission Control Protocol The major transport protocol in the Internet suite of protocols providing reliable,

131

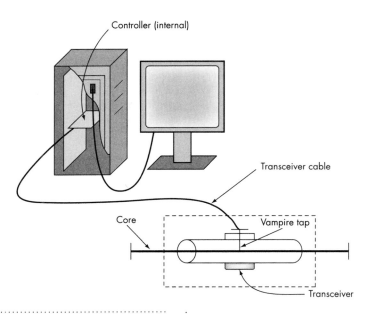

Controller (internal)

Transceiver cable

Core

Vampire tap

Transceiver

CONNECTION-ORIENTED, full-duplex streams. TRANSMISSION CONTROL PROTOCOL (TCP) specifications were given in RFC 793. See Figure T3.

In Figure T3, packets have an IP address (1) that may be fragmented and passed on through the network interface (2). *See also* USER DATAGRAM PROTOCOL, INTERNET FRAGMENT.

transmission security A component of COMSEC resulting from the use of methods other than CRYPTANALYSIS to protect transmissions from interception and exploitation.

transport layer The layer in the OSI reference model that is responsible for reliable end-to-end data transfer between end systems. In the Internet protocol suite, TCP and UDP are TRANSPORT LAYER protocols.

Transport Layer Security A protocol that provides CONFIDENTIALITY and INTEGRITY services between two communicating applications. It was based on the SECURE SOCKET LAYER PROTOCOL (SSL) developed by Netscape. See RFC 2246.

transport service Any reliable stream-oriented data communication service; for example, TCP.

transposition cipher A CIPHER that rearranges the order of encrypted characters but does not change the actual characters.

trap door (1) A hidden software mechanism triggered to circumvent system security measures. May be a legitimate technique that allows users to access source code directly by bypassing lengthy log-on routines. (2) In CRYPTOGRAPHY, a secret that allows to invert a TRAP DOOR FUNCTION. *See also* TRAP DOOR FUNCTION.

trap door function A function that appears irreversible but that has a secret method that, if known, allows someone to reverse the function.

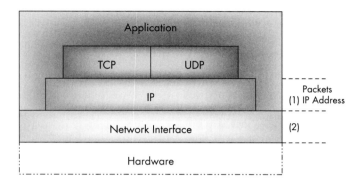

FIGURE T3. A conceptual view of TCP/IP architecture.

trashing (1) Deleting and possibly overwriting an object with pseudo-random data to prevent object reuse. Usage: "Trash the file." (2) Physically searching the garbage for useful information about the target site, such as manuals, internal memos, and other proprietary information.

tripwire A program that counts the bytes in files, hashes of file contents and permissions and issues a warning when there is a change.

Trivial File Transfer Protocol A simple file transfer protocol built on UDP. Details of TRIVIAL FILE TRANSFER PROTOCOL (TFTP) are given in RFC 1350.

Trojan horse A piece of code embedded in a useful program for a malicious purpose, for instance, to steal information. Usually the term Trojan horse is used rather than VIRUS when the offending code does not attempt to replicate itself into other programs.

trust (1) A reliance on a system's ability to meet its specifications or live up to its expectations. (2) Reliance by one principal on another.

trusted (1) Refers to components that are not controlled by the security policy and can violate its rules. (2) Refers to TRUSTWORTHY components that are expected not to violate the security policy. (3) A reliable principle.

trusted applet An APPLET that has full access to system resources on a client computer.

trusted computer system An IS capable of simultaneously processing a range of CLASSIFIED or sensitive information.

trusted computer system evaluation criteria ☞ DoD TRUSTED COMPUTER SYSTEM EVALUATION CRITERIA.

trusted computing base All of a computer system's protection mechanisms responsible for enforcing a security policy.

trusted distribution The distribution of TRUSTED COMPUTING BASE (TCB) hardware, software, and firmware components in which the TCB is protected from modification.

trusted facility management
Administrative procedures, roles, functions, privileges, and databases used for secure system configuration, administration, and operation.

trusted facility manual A document describing a trusted facility's operational requirements, security environment hardware and software configurations and interface and all security procedures, measures, and CONTINGENCY PLANS.

trusted guard A computer system that enforces a certain guard policy, such as preventing the flow of pest programs from an untrusted system to a trusted system. *See also* GUARD.

trusted identification forwarding An identification method used in IS networks in which an authorized user attempting to connect to a receiving host can be verified by the sending host through the transmission of authentication information.

trusted intermediary A third party such as KDC or CA that permits two parties to AUTHENTICATE without the prior configuration of keys between those two parties. A trusted intermediary may also be used for additional functions such as key distribution, contrast, or payment negotiation.

trusted network A network that is within a FIREWALL.

Trusted Network Interpretation Environmental Guideline Evaluation CRITERIA that define the certification criteria for trusted networks. Also referred to as the RED BOOK.

trusted path A secure method for communicating with a TRUSTED COMPUTING BASE. Untrusted (potentially malicious) software cannot masquerade as the TRUSTED COMPUTING BASE (TCB) to the user, or as the user to the TCB. A user would use the trusted path to initiate a login, logout, change of security level, or other security-critical event. The TCB uses the trusted path to indicate the security, current security state or level,

or other security-critical information to the user. The crtl-alt-del secure attention sequence on some Microsoft operating systems initiates a trusted path facility.

trusted process A process that is able to circumvent the system security policy and operates only as intended.

trusted recovery Risk-free recovery after a system failure.

trusted server A server that is TRUSTworthy and helps in network AUTHENTICATION.

trusted software Software that has been produced in a way that makes one confident that there are no TROJAN HORSES in the code.

trusted subject A process that is allowed to bypass security rules. For example, an administrative process, running in behalf of the system administrator, is allowed to bypass BLP rules.

trusted system (1) A system that is assessed (typically through a formal evaluation process) to be able to withstand threats and that is or can be relied on to do so. (2) A system designed, developed, and evaluated in accordance with ORANGE BOOK criteria.

trusted third party ☞ TRUSTED INTERMEDIARY.

trustworthy An attribute describing a system that meets (or has been shown to meet) its specifications, particularly in the areas of reliability, quality, and security.

TSEC ☞ TELECOMMUNICATIONS SECURITY.

TSEC nomenclature A method for identification of the type and purpose of certain items of COMSEC MATERIAL.

tunneling Technology enabling one network's data to be sent through another network's connections by the encapsulation of a network protocol within PACKETS carried by the second network.

Turing test   A test proposed (1950) by Alan Turing (British computer scientist) for testing whether a computer has achieved artificial human intelligence. The test was that a person would communicate by keyboard with either the computer or a human, and if the tester couldn't tell which was the human and which was the computer, then the computer had passed the TURING TEST.

> NOTE: *Turing's philosophy of machine and mind appeared in the paper* COMPUTING MACHINERY AND INTELLIGENCE *published in the philosophical journal* MIND *in 1950.*

two-part code   A code made up of an encoding section, in which the vocabulary items (with their associated CODE GROUPS) are arranged in a systematic order, and a decoding section, in which the CODE GROUPS (with their associated meanings) are arranged in a different systematic order.

two-person control   At least two authorized individuals, each capable of detecting incorrect and unauthorized procedures of a task and each familiar with established security and safety requirements, who constantly survey and control POSITIVE CONTROL MATERIAL.

two-person integrity   At least two authorized persons, each capable of detecting incorrect or unauthorized security procedures related to a task, who must present when certain COMSEC keying material for storage and handling is accessed. *See also* NO-LONE ZONE.

type 1   An NSA (U.S.) approved CLASSIFIED or CONTROLLED CRYPTOGRAPHIC ITEM for securing CLASSIFIED and sensitive U.S. government information. The term refers only to products. TYPE 1 products contain classified NSA algorithms and are available to U.S. government users, their contractors, and federally sponsored non-U.S. government activities subject to export restrictions in accordance with INTERNATIONAL TRAFFIC IN ARMS REGULATIONS.

type 2   NSA (U.S.) approved UNCLASSIFIED cryptographic equipment, assembly, or component for national security systems use as defined in Title 40 U.S.C. Section 1452.

type 3 algorithm   CRYPTOGRAPHIC algorithm that protects unclassified SENSITIVE information or commercial information. It is registered by the (U.S.) NATIONAL INSTITUTE OF STANDARDS AND TECHNOLOGY (NIST) and published as a (U.S.) FEDERAL INFORMATION PROCESSING STANDARD (FIPS).

type 4 algorithm   Unclassified CRYPTOGRAPHIC algorithm, registered by the (U.S.) NATIONAL INSTITUTE OF STANDARDS AND TECHNOLOGY (NIST), but not published as a (U.S.) FEDERAL INFORMATION PROCESSING STANDARD (FIPS).

UA ☞ USER AGENT.

UDP ☞ USER DATAGRAM PROTOCOL.

UDP datagram A UDP DATAGRAM is the unit of end-to-end transmission in the UDP protocol.

UN/CEFACT A United Nations organization headquartered in Geneva that deals with worldwide technical developments and policy in the trade facilitation and electronic business.

unclassified Information that is not CLASSIFIED, meaning it does not require protection from unauthorized disclosure.

Unicode Called Unicode Worldwide Character Standard is a method of setting up binary codes for text or script characters. This system can display, process, and interchange written characters from different world languages. At present UNICODE standard provides distinct code for 34,168 languages derived from 24 language scripts. More details about Unicode are available at http://www.unicode.org.

> NOTE: *UNICODE also supports several characters used in many classical and historical texts written in different languages.*

UNIX A popular multiprogramming operating system, developed at Bell Laboratories in 1969 by Ken Thompson and Dennis Ritchie.

> NOTE: *UNIX is not an acronym. In 1970 "Brian Kernighan suggested the name 'Unix' in a somewhat treacherous pun on 'Multics'" [DMR79].*

untrusted process (1) An untrusted process is one that even if it attempts to do the wrong thing, cannot breach the system security. See the note below. (2) A process that has not been evaluated, and it is unknown whether it adheres to a particular security policy.

> NOTE: *A trusted process is one that can be relied on and that is presumably TRUSTWORTHY. When one develops a system one has to work out which parts can be left untrusted (the more the better). The aim is to have the smallest possible trusted kernel.*

updating An automatic or manual CRYPTOGRAPHIC process that modifies the state of a COMSEC key, equipment, device, or system. This modification is irreversible.

U.S.-controlled facility A controlled-access base or building run by the U.S. government.

U.S.-controlled space   U.S. government-controlled room or floor within a non-U.S.-controlled facility.

usenet   An Internet service that started as a bulletin board and has expanded to include thousands of sites providing service worldwide.

user   A person or process that is authorized to access an IS.

user agent   (1) A user agent is any software that retrieves and processes information from web sites for users. Examples of user agent include web browsers, plug-ins, and media players. (2) A user agent is a commonly used term in e-mail and web architecture and refers to a layer of software that insulates the user from the vagaries of that architecture. User agents described in X.400 and X.500 protocols not only make things simpler for user but also perform specific functions as described in the protocols.

User Datagram Protocol   A transport protocol in the INTERNET suite of protocols. USER DATAGRAM PROTOCOL (UDP), like TCP, uses IP for delivery; however, unlike TCP, UDP provides for the exchange of DATAGRAMS without acknowledgment or guaranteed delivery.

user ID   An IS's method of identifying a specific user by a unique symbol or character string.

user partnership program   A U.S. government program in which the NSA (U.S.) and a U.S. government agency work together to develop secure IS equipment incorporating NSA-approved CRYPTOGRAPHY. The result is that national security information in the user's specific application is safeguarded by the authorized product or system.

user profile   (1) Information about a user. In the context of intrusion detection, a profile generally includes historical patterns of use, against which current patterns of use can be compared to decide whether the current action is an intrusion. (2) Patterns of a user's activity that track abnormal behavior.

user representative   A member of an organization who is authorized to order COMSEC keying material, interface with the keying system, provide information to key users, and ensure that the correct type of key is ordered.

UUCP   UNIX to UNIX Copy Program. A protocol used for communication between consenting UNIX systems.

uudecode   A UNIX utility for reversing the effect of UUENCODE.

uuencode   A UNIX utility for encoding arbitrary binary data as printable characters by encoding six bits of binary data per character.

vaccine A program that searches for and removes virus in a computer system. Sometimes a vaccine can restore previously "infected" files to their original state. In other cases, a file may be irreparable.

validation The process by which one or more departments or agencies and their contractors establish joint usage of an IS through the application of specialized security tests and evaluation procedures, tools, and equipment.

van Eck monitoring Using low levels of electromagnetic emissions from a device to monitor the activity of a computer or other electronic device. Named after Dutch scientist Wim van Eck.

> NOTE: *Details of VAN ECK MONITORING are available in the original paper [WVE85] by Wim van Eck.*

variant A code symbol that has the same PLAINTEXT equivalent as one or more other code symbols.

verified design A design that has been modeled mathematically and formally proved to comply with a security policy.

verify a signature Perform a CRYPTOGRAPHIC calculation using a message, a signature, and a PUBLIC KEY to determine whether the signature was generated by someone knowing the corresponding PRIVATE KEY signing the message.

virtual password An IS password computed from a PASSPHRASE that fills the requirements for password storage (e.g., 64 bits).

virtual private network A protected IS link that uses tunneling, security controls (see INFORMATION ASSURANCE), and endpoint address translation so that to the user it seems as if there is a dedicated line between nodes.

virus A piece of a computer program that replicates by embedding itself in other programs. When those programs are run, the virus is invoked again and spread further.

> NOTE: *Eugene Spafford wrote in a technical report [ES91], that the first published use of the word VIRUS was by David Gerrod in his science fiction short stories which were later expanded and published in the book "When Harlie Was One" [GD72].*

This book described a program named VIRUS that would randomly dial the phone until it found another computer, then break into that system and infect it with a copy of itself. The inventor planned a program VACCINE that could cure VIRUS, but the plan results in disaster, because noise on a phone line causes the VIRUS to mutate so VACCINE is no longer effective.

Fred Cohen first used the term COMPUTER VIRUS in a formal way at University of Southern California [CF84]. According to him: "We define a computer 'virus' as a program that can infect other programs by modifying them to include a possibly evolved copy of itself." In his Ph.D. dissertation [CF85], he credits his adviser, L. Adleman, with originating the terminology.

This dissertation is a mathematical treatment of computer viruses and contains formal definition of a virus and many proofs related to virus defense.

voice system   A biometric system in which a vocal pattern must be matched with a stored pattern to gain access.

VPN   ☞   VIRTUAL PRIVATE NETWORK.

vulnerability   An exploitable weakness in an IS, system security procedures, design, internal controls, or implementation.

vulnerability assessment   The systematic examination of an IS or product to gauge the effectiveness of its security system.

Wassenaar Arrangement The Wassenaar Arrangement is an international agreement among 33 cofounding nations on export controls for conventional arms and
dual-use goods and technologies. By providing greater visibility of arms and dual-
use technology exports, the agreement
aims to ensure regional and international
peace, security, and stability. Member
countries must control their export
policies to conform to the Wassenaar
agreement. The agreement received final
approval in July 1996 and started operations in September 1996. The Wassenaar
Arrangement is headquartered in Vienna,
and plenary meetings are held at least once
a year.

The Dual-Use List, or Basic List
(Tier 1), consists of a Sensitive List
(Tier 2) and a Very Sensitive List (Tier
2 subset), and includes such items as
stealth technology materials and high-
powered computers. Countries are to use
"extreme vigilance" in exports of these
technologies.

The U.S. Department of Commerce
controls the export of dual-use goods and
technologies, and the U.S. Department of

State controls the export of conventional
arms.

The U.S. government controls the
export of CRYPTOGRAPHIC products under
the Wassenaar arrangement. See http://
www.bxa.doc.gov/Wassenaar/ for more
details and a list of items in the Dual-Use
List.

WinNuke A form of ATTACK that affects
only computers running Windows NT
3.51 or Windows NT 4. Rather than re-
turning an error code for bad data in the
TCP header, it sends NT to the Blue Screen
of Death (BSOD).

wiretapping Electronic eavesdropping
on communications. Taps may be ACTIVE
or PASSIVE. They can be implemented with
hardware devices or software. *See also* ACTIVE
THREAT and PASSIVE THREAT.

work factor An estimate of the computational resources required to defeat a given
CRYPTOGRAPHIC system.

worm A self-contained program that
replicates by running copies of itself, usu-

ally on different machines across a computer network.

worm attack An ATTACK in which a worm acts in an unexpected way, possibly making use of security vulnerabilities or causing denials of service.

write To send information from a subject to an object. The basic function in an IS. *See also* ACCESS TYPE.

write access Permission to write to an object in an IS.

X.400 A CCITT (ITU) standard for electronic mail.

X.500 A CCITT (ITU) standard for directory services.

X.509 A CCITT (ITU) standard for security services within the X.500 directory services framework.

X.800 A CCITT (ITU) standard and a supplement to the ISO reference model that provides the OSI security architecture. It provides measures to secure data in communicating open systems by providing security services in each layer of the ISO reference model. It also provides appropriate security mechanisms that can be used to implement services. For more information refer to Security Architecture for Open Systems Interconnection for CCITT Applications (Recommendation X.800), CCITT, Geneva, 1991.

XDR ☞ EXTERNAL DATA REPRESENTATION.

Y

Yellow Pages A directory service part of Sun Microsystems' distributed environment.

NOTE: *This name is now deprecated because of a legal threat from publishers of telephone directories.*

The current name is NIS (Network Information Services).

YP ☞ Yellow Pages.

Z

zero fill   The filling of empty storage locations in an IS with the character representing zero.

zeroize   To remove the key from a CRYPTO-EQUIPMENT or fill device.

zero knowledge proof   A scheme in which one principal can demonstrate knowledge of a secret to another principal, without actually divulging the secret itself.

zombie   (1) UNIX processes that terminate leaving status information in the system [WS93]. For example, a child process that has terminated but its parent PROCESS

is not executing a "wait" system call. In this case the kernel releases the resources such as memory, associated files allocated to the zombie process but keeps its exit status. (2) Multiple processes on multiple hosts that perform DENIAL OF SERVICE ATTACK (DoS) simultaneously. DISTRIBUTED DENIAL OF SERVICE (DDoS) attacks can occur when multiple sites simultaneously perform a DoS attack on the same victim. To construct these attacks, an intruder may plant multiple processes on multiple hosts. These processes, called zombies, all perform the DoS attack simultaneously.

zone of control   An inspectable space.

COMMONLY USED ABBREVIATIONS AND ACRONYMS

APPENDIX

A

ACL Access Control List

ACO Access Control Officer

ADM Advanced Development Model

ADP Automated Data Processing

AE Application Entity

AES Advanced Encryption Standard

AFIWC Air Force Information Warfare Center

AH Authentication Header

AIG Address Indicator Group

AIN Advanced Intelligence Network

AIRK Area Interswitch Rekeying Key

AIS Automated Information System

AISS Automated Information Systems Security

AJ Anti-Jamming

AK Automatic Remote Rekeying

AKDC Automatic Key Distribution Center

AKD/RCU Automatic Key Distribution/ Rekeying Control Unit

AKMC Automated Key Management Center

AKMS Automated Key Management System

ALC Accounting Legend Code

AMS 1. Auto-Manual System
2. Autonomous Message Switch

ANDVT Advanced Narrowband Digital Voice Terminal

ANSI American National Standards Institute

AOSS Automated Office Support Systems

APC Adaptive Predictive Coding

API Application Program Interface

APU Auxiliary Power Unit

ARL Authority Revocation List

ARP Address Resolution Protocol

ARPA Advanced Research Project Agency

ARPANET Advanced Research Projects Agency Network

ASCII   American Standard Code for Information Interchange

ASN1   Abstract Syntax Notation 1

ASPJ   Advanced Self-Protection Jammer

ASSIST Program   Automated Information System Security Incident Support Team

ASU   Approval for Service User

ATM   Asynchronous Transfer Mode

AUTODIN   Automatic Digital Network

AV   Auxiliary Vector

AVP   Authorized Vendor Program

BCA   Brand Certification Authority

BCI   Brand CRL Identifier

BER   Basic Encoding Rule

BIN   Bank Identification Number

BSD   Berkeley Software Distribution

C2   1. Command and Control
2. Controlled Access Protection

C2W   Command and Control Warfare

C3   Command, Control, and Communications

C3I   Command, Control, Communications and Intelligence

C4   Command, Control, Communications, and Computers

CA   1. Controlling Authority
2. Cryptanalysis 3. COMSEC Account
4. Command Authority 5. Certification Authority

CALEA   Communications Assistance for Law Enforcement Act

CAP   Controlled Access Point

CAPI   Cryptographic Application Programming Interface

CAW   Certificate Authority Workstation

CBC   Cipher Blocking Chaining

CC   Common Criteria

CCA   Cardholder Certification Authority

CCEP   Commercial COMSECT Endorsement Program

CCI   Controlled Cryptographic Item

CCITT   Comité Consultatif International Téléphonique et Télégraphique

CCO   Circuit Control Officer

CDC   Certificate Distribution Center

CDR   Certificate Decoder Ring

CDS   Cryptographic Device Services

CDSA   Common Data Security Architecture

CEOI   Communications Electronics Operating Instruction

CEPR   Compromising Emanation Performance Requirement

CER   1. Cryptographic Equipment Room 2. Communications Equipment Room

CERT   Computer Security Emergency Response Team

CESG   Communications Electronics Security Group

CFB   Cipher Feedback

CFD   Common Fill Device

CGI   Common Gateway Interface

CHAP   Challenge Handshake Authentication Protocol

CIAC   Computer Incident Advisory Capability

CIK   Cryptographic Ignition Key

CIP   Crypto-Ignition Plug

CIPSO   Common IP Security Option

CIRK   Common Interswitch Rekeying Key

CIRT   Computer Security Incident Response Team

CIX   Commercial Internet Exchange

CK   Compartment Key

CKG   Cooperative Key Generation

CKL   Compromised Key List

CLMD   COMSEC Local Management Device

CLNP   Connectionless Network Protocol

CMCS   COMSEC Material Control System

CMS   Cryptographic Message Syntax

CNCS   Cryptonet Control Station

CND   Computer Network Defense

CNK   Cryptonet Key

COCOM   Coordinating Committee for Multilateral Export Controls

COI   Community of Interest

COMINT   Communications Intelligence

COMPUSEC   Computer Security

COMSEC   Communications Security

CONOP   Concept of Operations

COPS   Computer Oracle and Password System

COR   1. Central Office of Record (COMSEC) 2. Contracting Officer Representative

COTS   Commercial off-the-shelf

CPS   1. COMSEC Parent Switch 2. Certification Practice Statement

CPU   Central Processing Unit

CRAM   Challenge Response Authentication Mechanism

CRC   Cyclic Redundancy Code

CRC   CRC with 32-bit output

CRL   Certificate Revocation List

CRP   COMSEC Resources Program (Budget)

CRS   Certificate Request Syntax

CSE   Communications Security Element

CSIRT   Computer Security Incident Response Team

CSM   Certificate Services Manager

CSMA   Carrier Sense Multiple Access with Collision Detect

CSS   1. Central Security Service 2. COMSEC Subordinate Switch 3. Constant Surveillance Service (Courier) 4. Continuous Signature Service (Courier) 5. Coded Switch System

CSOR   Computer Security Objects Register

CSP   Cryptographic Security Provider

CSSM   Common Security Services Manager

CSSO   Contractor Special Security Officer

CSTVRP   Computer Security Technical Vulnerability Report Program

CT&E   Certification Test and Evaluation

CTAK   Cipher Text Auto-Key

CTCPEC   Candian Trusted Computer Product Evaluation Criteria

CTTA   Certified TEMPEST Technical Authority

CUP   COMSEC Utility Program

DAA   Designated Approving Authority

DAC   Discretionary Access Control

DAMA   Demand Assigned Multiple Access

DAP   Directory Access Protocol

DARPA   Defense Advanced Research Projects Agency

DASS   Distributed Authentication Security Service

DCID   Director Central Intelligence Directive

DCE   Distributed Computing Environment

DCS   1. Defense Communications System 2. Defense Courier Service

DCSP   Design Controlled Spare Part(s)

DDoS   Distributed Denial of Service Attack

DDI   Deputy Director of Operations, NSA/CSS

DDS   Dual Driver Service (courier)

DDT   Deputy Director of Technology, NSA/CSS

DEA   Data Encryption Algorithm

DEK   Data Encryption Key

DER   Distinguished Encoding Rule

DES   Data Encryption Standard

DIB   Directory Information Base

DII   Defense Information Infrastructure

DISN   Defense Information System Network

DITSCAP   DoD Information Technology Security Certification and Accreditation Process

DN   Distinguished Name

DoD TCSEC   Department of Defense Trusted Computer System Evaluation Criteria

DOI   Domain Of Interpretation

DOS   1. Denial of Service Attack 2. Disk Operating System

DLED   Dedicated Loop Encryption Device

DMA   Direct Memory Access

DMAT   Digital Music Access Technology

DMS   Defense Message System

DN   Distinguished Name

DNS   Domain Name System

DPL   Degausser Products List (a section in the *INFOSEC Products and Services Catalogue*)

DSA   Digital Signature Algorithm

DSN   Defense Switched Network

DSS   Digital Signature Standard

DST   Digital Signature Trust

DSVT   Digital Subscriber Voice Terminal

DTLS   Descriptive Top-Level Specification

DTD   Data Transfer Device

DTS   Diplomatic Telecommunications Service

DUA   Directory User Agent

EAM   Emergency Action Message

EBCDIC   Extended Binary Code Decimal Interchange Code

ebXML   E-business XML standard

ECB   Electronic Code Book

ECC   Elliptic Curve Cryptography

ECCM   Electronic Counter-Countermeasures

ECDSA Elliptic Curve Digital Signature Algorithm

ECM Electronic Countermeasures

ECPL Endorsed Cryptographic Products List (a section in the *INFOSEC, Information System Security Products and Services Catalogue*)

EDAC Error Detection and Correction

EDE Encrypt/Decrypt/Encrypt

EDESPL Endorsed Data Encryption Standard Products List

EDI Electronic Data Interchange

EDM Engineering Development Model

EES Escrowed Encryption Standard

EFD Electronic Fill Device

EFTO Encrypt For Transmission Only

EGADS Electronic Generation, Accounting and Distribution System

EGP Exterior Gateways Protocol

EKMS Electronic Key Management System

ELINT Electronic Intelligence

ELSEC Electronic Security

E Model Engineering Development Model

EMSEC Emission Security

EPL Evaluated Products List (a section in the *INFOSEC Products and Services Catalogue*)

ERTZ Equipment Radiation TEMPEST Zone

ESP Encapsulating Security Payload

ETL Endorsed Tools List

ETPL Endorsed TEMPEST Products List

EUCI Endorsed for Unclassified Cryptographic Information

EV Enforcement Vector

EW Electronic Warfare

FDDI Fiber Distributed Data Interface

FDIU Fill Device Interface Unit

FIPS Federal Information Processing Standard

FIRST Forum Of Incident Response and Security Teams

FIX Federal Internet Exchange Points

FOCI Foreign Owned, Controlled, or Influenced

FOIA Freedom of Information Act

FOUO For Official Use Only

FPKI Federal Public Key Infrastructure

FSRS Functional Security Requirements Specification

FSTS Federal Secure Telephone Service

FTP File Transfer Protocol

FTS Federal Telecommunications System

FTAM File Transfer Access Management

FTLS Formal Top-Level Specification

GASSP Generally Accepted Systems Security Principles

GCA Geopolitical Certificate Authority

GCCS Global Command and Control System

GCD Greatest Common Divisor

GETS Government Emergency Telecommunications Service

GPS Global Positioning System

GSM Global System for Mobile Communications

GSS-API Generic Security Service Application Program Interface

GTS Global Telecommunications Service

GWEN Ground Wave Emergency Network

HDM Hierarchical Development Methodology

HMAC Hashed Message Authentication Code

HTML Hypertext Markup Language

HTTP Hypertext Transfer Protocol

HUS Hardened Unique Storage

HUSK Hardened Unique Storage Key

IA Information Assurance

I & A Identification and Authentication

IAB Internet Activity Board

IANA Internet Assigned Number Authority

IBAC Identity Based Access Control

ICANN Internet Corporationn for Assigned Names and Numbers

ICMP Internet Control Message Protocol

ICRL Indirect Certificate Revocation List

ICU Interface Control Unit

IDEA International Data Encryption Algorithm

IDES Intrusion Detection Expert System

IDIOT Intrusion Detection In Our Time

IDM Intrusion Detection Model

IDS Intrusion Detection System

IEEE Institute of Electrical and Electronics Engineers

IEMATS Improved Emergency Message Automatic Transmission System

IESG Internet Engineering Steering Group

IETF Internet Engineering Task Force

IFCC Internet Fraud Complaint Center (U.S.)

IFF Identification, Friend or Foe

IFFN Identification, Friend, Foe, or Neutral

IGP Interior Gateway Protocol

IIRK Interarea Interswitch Rekeying Key

IK Interswitch Rekeying Key

IKE Internet Key Exchange

ILS Integrated Logistics Support

IMAP Internet Message Access Protocol

INFOSEC Information System Security

InterNIC Internet Network Information Center

IO Information Operations

IOB Intelligence Oversight Board (The U.S. President's)

IOTP Internet Open Trading Protocol

IP Internet Protocol

IPM Interpersonal Messaging

IPNG Internet Protocol Next Generation

IPRA Internet Policy Registration Authority

IPsec Internet Protocol Security

IPSO Internet Protocol Security Option

IR Information Ratio

IRC Internet Relay Chat

IRTF Internet Research Task Force

IS Information System

ISAKMP Internet Security Association and Key Management Protocol

ISDN   Integrated Services Digital Network

ISO   International Organization for Standardization

ISOC   Internet Society

ISS   1. Information System Security 2. Internet Security Systems 3. Internet Security Scanner

ISSA   Information System Security Association

ISSM   Information System Security Manager

ISSO   Information System Security Officer

IT   Information Technology

ITAR   International Traffic in Arms Regulation

ITSEC   Information Technology Security Evaluation Criteria

ITU   International Telecommunications Union

IV   Initialization Vector

JVM   Java Virtual Machine

JIVA   Joint Intelligence Virtual Architecture

JSIWC   Joint Service Information Warfare Command

KAK   Key-Auto-Key

KDC   Key Distribution Center

KEA   Key Exchange Algorithm

KEK   Key Encryption Key

KG   Key Generator

KMASE   Key Management Application Service Element

KMC   Key Management Center

KMID   Key Management Identification Number

KMODC   Key Management Ordering and Distribution Center

KMP   Key Management Protocol

KMPDU   Key Management Protocol Data Unit

KMS   Key Management System

KMSA   Key Management System Agent

KMUA   Key Management User Agent

KP   Key Processor

KPK   Key Production Key

KSOS   Kernelized Secure Operating System

KVG   Key Variable Generator

LCMS   Local COMSEC Management Software

LDAP   Lightweight Directory Access Protocol

LEAD   Low-Cost Encryption/ Authentication Device

LEAF   Law Enforcement Access Field

LKG   Loop Key Generator

LMD   Local Management Device

LMD/KP   Local Management Device/Key Processor

LME   Layer Management Entry

LMI   Layer Management Interface

LOCK   Logical CoProcessing Kernel

LOD   Legion Of Doom

LPC   Linear Predictive Coding

LPD   Low Probability of Detection

LPI   Low Probability of Intercept

LRA   Local Registraion Authority

LRIP Limited Rate Initial Preproduction

LSI Large Scale Integration

MAC 1. Mandatory Access Control 2. Media Access Control

MAN Metropolitan Area Network

MATSYM Material Symbol

MCA Merchant Certification Authority

MCCB Modification/Configuration Control Board

MCG Meta-Certificate Group

MCTL Military Critical Technology List

MDC Manipulation Detection Code

MEECN Minimum Essential Emergency Communications Network

MEP Management Engineering Plan

MER Minimum Essential Requirements

MHS Message Handling System

MI Message Indicator

MIB Management, Information Base

MIC Message Integrity Code

MIJI Meaconing, Intrusion, Jamming, and Interface

MIME Multipurpose Internet Mail Extensions

MINTERM Miniature Terminal

MISSI Multilevel Information Systems Security Initiative

MLI Multilevel Integrity

MLS Multilevel Security

MNCKS Mobile Network Computer Reference Specifications

MOSS MIME Object Security Service

MQV Menezes–Qu–Vanstone key agreement scheme

MRT Miniature Receiver Terminal

MSE Mobile Subscriber Equipment

MSP Message Security Protocol

MTU Maximum Transmission Unit

Multics Multiplexed Information and Computing Service

MVTO Multiversion Timestamp Ordering

NACAM National COMSEC Advisory Memorandum

NACSI National COMSEC Instruction

NACSIM National COMSEC Information Memorandum

NAK Negative Acknowledge

NAT Network Address Translator

NC Network Computer

NCCD Nuclear Command and Control Document

NCRP Network Computer Reference Specification

NCS 1. National Communications System 2. National Cryptologic School 3. Net Control Station

NCSA National Computer Security Association

NCSC National Computer Security Center

NFS Network File System

NIAP National Information Assurance Partnership

NIC Network Information Center

NISAC National Industrial Security Advisory Committee

NIST National Institute of Standards and Technology

NKSR Nonkernel Security Related

NLZ   No-Lone Zone

NOIC   National Organization of Internet Commerce

NSA   National Security Agency

NSAD   Network Security Architecture and Design

NSCID   The National Security Council Intelligence Directive

NSD   National Security Directive

NSDD   National Security Decision Directive

NSEP   National Security Emergency Preparedness

NSI   National Security Information

NSM   Network Security Monitor

NSO   Network Security Officer

NSTAC   National Security Telecommunications Advisory Committee

NSTISSAM   National Security Telecommunications and Information Systems Security Advisory/Information Memorandum

NSTISSC   National Security Telecommunications and Information Systems Security Committee

NSTISSD   National Security Telecommunications and Information Systems Security Directive

NSTISSI   National Security Telecommunications and Information Systems Security Policy

NTCB   Network Trusted Computing Base

NTIA   National Telecommunications and Information Administration

NTISSAM   National Telecommunications and Information Systems Security Advisory/Information Memorandum

NTISSD   National Telecommunications and Information Systems Security Directive

NTISSI   National Telecommunications and Information Systems Security Instruction

NTISSP   National Telecommunications and Information Systems Security Policy

NW3C   National White Collar Crime Center (U.S.)

OASIS   Organization for the Advancement of Structured Information Standards

OADR   Originating Agency's Determination Required

OCSP   Online Certificate Status Protocol

OFB   Output Feedback Mode

OID   Object Identifier

OPCODE   Operations Code

OPSEC   Operations Security

OPUS   Obvious Password Utility System

ORA   Organizational Registration Authority

OSF   Open Software Foundation

OSI   Open System Interconnect

OSPF   Open Short Path First

OTAD   Over-the-Air Key Distribution

OTAR   Over-the-Air Key Rekeying

OTAT   Over-the-Air Key Transfer

OTP   1. One-Time Pad
2. One-Time Password

OTT   One-Time Tape

P2P   Peer-to-peer

P3P   Platform for Privacy Preferences Projects

PAA   Policy Approving Authority

PAAP   Peer Access Approval

PAE   Peer Access Enforcement

PAL   Permissive Action Link

PAN   Primary Account Number

PAP   Password Authentication Protocol

PC   Personal Computer

PCA   Policy Creation Authority

PCI   Private Communication Technology

PCMCIA   Personal Computer Memory Card International Association

PCZ   Protected Communications Zone

PDR   Preliminary Design Review

PDS   1. Protected Distribution Systems 2. Practices Dangerous to Security

PDU   Protocol Data Unit

PEM   Privacy Enhanced Mail

PES   Positive Enable System

PFS   Public Key Forward Secrecy

PGP   Pretty Good Privacy

PICA   Platform Independent Cryptography

PICS   Platform for Internet Control Selection

PIN   Personal Identification Number

PKA   Public Key Algorithm

PKC   Public Key Cryptography

PKCS   Public Key Cryptography Standard

PKI   Public Key Infrastructure

PKIX-CMP   Internet X.509 Public Key Infrastructure Certificate Management Protocols

PKSD   Programmable Key Storage Device

P Model   Preproduction Model

PNEK   Post-Nuclear Event Key

POP3   Post Office Protocol, version 3

PPP   Point to Point Protocol

PPL   Preferred Products List (a section in the *INFOSEC Products and Services Catalogue*)

PPTP   Point to Point Tunneling Protocol

PRBAC   Partition Rule-Based Access Control

PROM   Programmable Read-Only Memory

PROPIN   Proprietary Information

PSL   Protected Services List

PWDS   Protected Wireline Distribution System

QoS   Quality of Service

RA   Registration Authority

RACE   Rapid Automatic Cryptographic Equipment

RADIUS   Remote Authentication Dial-In User Service

RAMP   Rating Maintenance Program

RARP   Reverse Address Resolution Protocol

RAT   Remote Access Trojan

RBAC   Role Based Access Control

RC2   Rivest Cipher 2

RC4   Rivest Cipher 4

RCP   UNIX command

RFC   Requests For Comments

RFS   Remote Procedure Call

RIP   Routing Information Protocol

RPC   Remote Procedure Call

RSA Rivest–Shamir–Aldeman Algorithm

RQT Reliability Qualifications Tests

S2ML Security Services Markup Language

SA Systems Administrator

SABI Secret and Below Interoperability

SAID Security Association Identifier

SAO Special Access Office

SAP 1. System Acquisition Plan
2. Special Access Program

SARK SAVILLE Advanced Remote Keying

SASL Simple Authentication and Security Layer

SATAN Security Administrator Tool for Analyzing Networks

SBU Sensitive But Unclassified

SCA Subordinate Certification Authority

SCI Sensitive Compartmented Information

SCIF Sensitive Compartmented Information Facility

SDE Secure Data Exchange

SDMI Secure Digital Music Initiative

SDNRIU Secure Digital Net Radio Interface Unit

SDNS Secure Data Network System

SDR System Design Review

SET Secure Electronic Transaction

SFA Security Fault Analysis

SFUG Security Features Users Guide

SGML Standard Generalized Markup Language

SHA Secure Hash Algorithm

SHS Secure Hash Standard

SHTTP Secure HyperText Transfer Protocol

SI Special Intelligence

SIGSEC Signals Security

SIGINT Signals Intelligence

SISS Subcommittee on Information Systems Security

SKIP Simple Key Exchange for Internet Protocols

SLIP Serial Line Interface Protocol (now PPP)

SMI Structure of Management Information

SMIME Secure MIME

SMTP Simple Mail Transport Protocol

SMU Secure Mobile Unit

SNMP Simple Network Management Protocol

SPK Single Point Key(ing)

SPI Security Parameters Index

SPS Scratch Pad Store

SRA Sub-Registration Authority

SRR Security Requirements Review

SS 7 Signaling System 7

SSI Server Side Include

SSL Secure Socket Layer Protocol

SSO 1. System Security Officer
2. Special Security Officer

ST&E Security Test and Evaluation

STE Secure Terminal Equipment

STS Subcommittee on Telecommunications Security

STT Secure Transaction Technology

STU Secure Telephone Unit

SWATCH Simple Watcher

TA Traffic Analysis

TAC Terminal Access Controller

TACTED Tactical Trunk Encryption Device

TAG TEMPEST Advisory Group

TAISS Telecommunications and Automated Information Systems Security

TCB Trusted Computing Base

TCD Time Compliance Data

TCP Transmission Control Protocol

TCMM Trusted Capability Maturity Model

TCSEC DoD Trusted Computer System Evaluation Criteria

TD Transfer Device

TDEA Triple Data Encryption Algorithm

TED Trunk Encryption Device

TEK Traffic Encryption Key

TEP TEMPEST Endorsement Program

TEMPEST Telecommunications Electronics Material Protected from Emanating Spurious Transmissions

TESS The Exponential Encryption System

TFM Trusted Facility Manual

TFS Traffic Flow Security

TFTP Trivial File Transfer Protocol

TGS Ticket-Granting Server

TGT Ticket-Granting Ticket

TIS Trusted Information Systems

TLS 1. Top-Level Specification
2. Transport Layer Security

TLSP Transport Layer Security Protocol

TNI Trusted Network Interpretation

TNIEG Trusted Network Interpretation Environment Guideline

TPC Two-Person Control

TPEP Trusted Products Evaluation Program

TPI Two-Person Integrity

TPM Trust Policy Manager

TRANSEC Transmission Security

TRB Technical Review Board

TRI-TAC Tri-Service Tactical Communications System

TSCM Technical Surveillance Countermeasures

TSEC Telecommunications Security

TSIG Trusted Systems Interoperability Group

TSK Transmission Security Key

TSR Terminate and Stay Resident

TTP Trusted Third Party

UA User Agent

UDP User Data Protocol

UIRK Unique Interswitch Rekeying Key

UIS User Interface System

UN/CEFACT United Nations Center for Trade Facilitation and Electronic Business

UPP User Partnership Program

URI Uniform Resource Identifier

URL Uniform Resource Locator

URN Uniform Resource Name

USDE Undesigned Signal Data Emanations

UUCP UNIX to UNIX Copy

VAN Value Added Network

VPN Virtual Private Network

V Model Advanced Development Model

VMS Virtual Memory System

VPN Virtual Private Network

VST VINSON Subscriber Terminal

VTT VINSON Trunk Terminal

W3 World Wide Web (WWW)

W3C World Wide Web Consortium

WIPO World Intellectual Property Organization

WWW World Wide Web

XDM/X Model Experimental Development Model/Exploratory Development Model

XDR External Data Representation

YP Yellow Pages

A SELECT ANNOTATED LIST
OF SECURITY-RELATED RFCS
SORTED BY RFC NUMBER

APPENDIX

B

This list contains select security-related Internet Request for Comments (RFCs) arranged in increasing order of RFC number. The RFC citations given below contain the information necessary for a reader to identify, at a quick glance, specific details of an RFC. The reader may use this information to further examine an RFC. The RFCs may be obtained in a number of ways: using HTTP, FTP, or e-mail from the IETF Web site at

http://www.ietf.org

In addition, there are many mirror sites from which RFCs can be obtained. RFC citations appear in the following format:

- Author(s), RFC #: Title of RFC. Date of Issue, Number of Pages, [Status: sss] [Obsoletes RFC #].

    Annotation.

Key to citations: # is the RFC number. Obsoletes RFC # refers to other RFCs that this one replaces; the Status field *sss* gives the document's current status.

Many RFCs are obsoleted by new RFCs, this list provides only the new RFC and identifies the most recent RFC it obsoletes.

- D.L. Mills, RFC 1004: A Distributed-Protocol Authentication Scheme, April 1987, 8 p. [Status: Experimental].

  This RFC discusses authentication problems in the Internet and proposes mediated access-control and authentication procedures as solution to these problems.

- S. Kent, RFC 1108: Security Options for the Internet Protocol, 1991 November, 17 p. [Status: Historic], [Obsoletes RFC 1038].

  This RFC documents the Internet options of the U.S. Department of Defense Basic Security Option and the top-level description of the Extended Security Option for use on the Department of Defense common user data networks.

- J. Reynolds, RFC 1135: The Helminthiasis of the Internet, December 1989, 33 p. [Status: Informational].

  This RFC provides information about the infection, infestation, decay, and compromise of the Internet by worms, viruses, and other forms of malicious attacks; it also contains methods to rid the Internet of such infestations.

- R. Fougner, RFC 1170: Public Key Standards and Licenses, January 1991, 2 p. [Status: Informational].

  This RFC contains a statement about issuing of exclusive sublicensing rights to some patents to Public Key Partners.

- C. Mills, D. Hirsh, and G. Ruth, RFC 1272: Internet accounting: background, November 1991, 19 p. [Status: Informational].

  This RFC provides information about the Internet Accounting Architecture including methods to provide semantics to measure network utilization, syntax, and data reporting.

- R.D. Pethia, S. Crocker, and B.Y. Fraser, RFC 1281: Guidelines for the Secure Operation of the Internet, November 1991, 10 p. [Status: Informational].

  This RFC provides a set of guidelines to aid in the secure operation of the Internet.

- B. Kaliski, RFC 1319: The MD2 Message-Digest Algorithm, April 1992, 17 p. [Status: Informational].

  This RFC describes the MD2 Message-Digest Algorithm.

- R. Rivest, RFC 1320: The MD4 Message-Digest Algorithm, April 1992, 20 p. [Status: Informational].

  This RFC describes the MD4 Message Digest Algorithm.

- R. Rivest, RFC 1321: The MD5 Message-Digest Algorithm, April 1992, 21 p. [Status: Informational].

  This RFC describes the MD5 Message Digest Algorithm.

- B. Lloyd, W. Simpson, RFC 1334: PPP Authentication Protocols, October 1992, 16 p. [Status: Standards Track].

  This RFC defines the Password Authentication Protocol and the Challenge-Handshake Authentication Protocol for authentication.

- J. Galvin, K. McCloghrie, and J. Davin, RFC 1352: SNMP Security Protocols, July 1992, 41 p. [Status: Historic].

  This RFC defines the protocols to support security services like data integrity, data origin authentication, and data confidentiality in context with the SNMP specification and SNMP administrative model.

- J. Curran and A. Marine, RFC 1355: Privacy and Accuracy Issues in Network Information Center Databases, August 1992, 4 p. [FYI 15], [Status: Informational].

  This RFC sets operational and administrative framework and guidelines for public Network Information Center (NIC) databases.

- D. Borman, RFC 1411: Telnet Authentication: Kerberos Version 4, January 1993, 4 p. [Status: Experimental].

  This RFC describes telnet authentication using Kerberos version 4.

- K. Alagappan, RFC 1412: Telnet Authentication: SPX, January 1993, 4 p. [Status: Experimental].

  This RFC describes telnet authentication using SPX protocol.

- M. St. Johns, RFC 1413: Identification Protocol, February 1993, 8 p. [Status: Standards Track], [Obsoletes RFC 912, RFC 931].

  This RFC describes means to determine the identity of a user of a particular TCP connection.

- M. St. Johns and M. Rose, RFC 1414: Identification MIB, February 1993, 7 p. [Status: Standards Track].

  This RFC defines an MIB for use in identifying the users associated with the TCP connections.

- J. Linn, RFC 1421: Privacy enhancement for Internet electronic mail: Part I: Message encryption and authentication procedures, February 1993,

42 p. [Status: Standards Track], [Obsoletes RFC 989, RFC 1040 and RFC 1113].

This RFC describes message encryption and authentication to provide PEM services for e-mail.

■ S.T. Kent and J. Linn, RFC 1422: Privacy enhancement for Internet electronic mail: Part II: Certificate-based key management, February 1993, 32 p., 9 Ref. [Status: Standards Track], [Obsoletes RFC 1114].

This RFC describes certificate-based key management for e-mail transfer through the Internet.

■ D. Balenson, RFC 1423: Privacy enhancement for Internet electronic mail: Part III: Algorithms, modes, and identifiers, February 1993, 14 p., 14 Ref. [Status: Standards Track], [Obsoletes RFC 1115].

This RFC deals with cryptographic algorithms, modes, and identifiers for Privacy Enhanced Mail (PEM) within the context of the Internet.

■ B. Kaliski, RFC 1424: Privacy Enhancement for Internet Electronic Mail: Part IV: Key Certification and Related Services, February 1993, 9 p., 3 Ref. [Status: Standards Track].

This RFC discusses key certification, certificate revocation list storage, and CRL retrieval for PEM.

■ J. Galvin and K. McCloghrie, RFC 1446: Security Protocols for version 2 of the Simple Network Management Protocol (SNMPv2), April 1993, 51 p. [Status: Historic].

This RFC discuses Security Protocols for version 2 of the Simple Network Management Protocol.

■ D. Eastlake, RFC 1455: Physical Link Security Type of Service, May 1993, 6 p. [Status: Experimental].

This RFC documents defines a Physical Link Security Type of Service experimental protocol. It adds to the types of services described in RFC 1349.

■ R. Housley, RFC 1457: Security Label Framework for the Internet, May 1993, 14 p. [Status: Informational].

This RFC presents a security-labeling framework for the Internet.

■ F. Kastenholz, RFC 1472: The Definitions of Managed Objects for the Security Protocols of the Point-to-Point Protocol, June 1993, 12 p. [Status: Standards Track].

This RFC describes, for point-to-point protocols, the details of managed objects for security protocols management on subnetwork interfaces.

■ C. Finseth, RFC 1492: An Access Control Protocol, Sometimes Called TACACS, July 1993, 21 p. [Status: Informational].

This RFC describes an access control protocol, TACACS.

■ C. Kaufman, RFC 1507: DASS: Distributed Authentication Security Service, September 1993, 119 p. [Status: Experimental].

This RFC describes DASS that provides authentication services in a distributed environment to offer greater security and flexibility.

■ J. Kohl and C. Neumann, RFC 1510: The Kerberos Network Authentication Service (V5), September 1993, 112 p. [Status: Standards Track].

This RFC describes the underlying concept and model of the Kerberos Network Authentication System and specifies version 5 of Kerberos protocol.

■ J. Linn, RFC 1511: Common Authentication Technology Overview, September 1993, 2 p. [Status: Informational].

This RFC gives an overview of current authentication technology and discusses related service interfaces as well as protocols.

■ E. Gavron, RFC 1535: A Security Problem and Proposed Correction with Widely Deployed DNS Software, October 1993, 5 p. [Status: Informational].

This RFC discusses errors and flaw in some current distributed name resolver clients and suggests corrections using DNS.

■ R. Braden, D. Clark, S. Crocker, and C. Huitema, RFC 1636: Report of IAB Workshop on Security in the Internet Architecture (February 8–10, 1994), June 1994, 52 p., 0 Ref. [Status: Informational].

This RFC documents Internet architecture workshop report on security issues in the Internet architecture. The workshop was held on February 8–10, 1994 at USC Information Sciences Institute.

■ N. Haller and R. Atkinson, RFC 1704: On Internet Authentication, October 1994, 17 p., 35 Ref. [Status: Informational].

This RFC discusses various authentication technologies and suggests the type of authentication suitable for use in protocols and applications on the Internet.

■ R. Hidden, RFC 1710: Simple Internet Protocol Plus White Paper, October 1994, 23 p., 17 Ref. [Status: Informational].

This RFC describes the Simple Internet Protocol plus (SIPP), which is considered to be the next version of Internet Protocol by IETF.

■ J. Myers, RFC 1731: IMAP4 Authentication Mechanisms, December 1994, 6 p. [Status: Standards Track].

This RFC describes identification and authentication mechanisms for IMAP4 protocol. It includes authentication of a user to IMAP4 server and mechanisms to provide secure interactions.

■ J. Myers, RFC 1734: POP3 AUTHentication command, December 1994, 5 p. [Status: Standards Track].

This RFC describes the optional POP3 AUTH command for authentication to the server and optional negotiation of protection mechanism for interaction between client and server.

■ D. Eastlake, 3rd, S. Crocker, and J. Schiller, RFC 1750: Randomness Recommendations for Security, December 1994, 25 p. [Status: Informational].

Many passwords, cryptographic security keys, and similar security objects use items that require random numbers. This RFC describes the problems associated with using traditional pseudo random number generating techniques to generate random numbers that are used in these items.

■ D. McDonald, RFC 1751: A Convention for Human-Readable 128-bit Keys, December 1994, 15 p. [Status: Informational].

This RFC provides a convention for 128-bit cryptographic keys that makes it easier for humans to read and remember these keys.

■ N. Haller, RFC 1760: The S/KEY One-Time Password System, February 1995, 12 p. [Status: Informational].

This RFC describes Bellcore's S/KEY* One-Time Password system that provides protection against passive attacks on authentication subsystem.

■ Rubin, RFC 1805: Location-Independent Data/Software Integrity Protocol, June 1995, 6 p. [Status: Informational].

This RFC describes a protocol to add integrity assurance to software or data that may be distributed across the Internet with the help of a trusted third party.

■ H. Danisch RFC 1824: The Exponential Security System TESS: An Identity-Based Cryptographic Protocol for Authenticated Key-Exchange, August 1995, 21 p., 14 Ref. [Status: Informational].

This RFC describes the details of identity-based systems for the secure authenticated exchange and distribution of cryptographic keys and generation of signatures.

- P. Metzger, W. Simpson, RFC 1828: IP Authentication using Keyed MD5, August 1995, 5 p. [Status: Standards Track].

  This RFC describes the use of MD5 algorithm in IP Authentication Header to provide integrity and authentication for IP datagrams.

- P. Karn, P. Metzger, W. Simpson, RFC 1829: The ESP DES-CBC Transform, August 1995, 10 p, [Status: Standards Track].

  This RFC describes the use of DES-CBC security transform to provide confidentiality for IP datagrams using IP Encapsulating Security Payload (ESP).

- J. Galvin, S. Murphy, S. Crocker, N. Freed, RFC 1847: Security Multiparts for MIME: Multipart/Signed and Multipart/Encrypted, October 1995, 11 p.- [Status: Standards Track].

  This RFC describes how security services provided by other protocols may be applied to the MIME body parts by defining signed and encrypted subtypes of the MIME multipart content type. This results in security for both single and multipart messages.

- S. Crocker, N. Freed, J. Galvin, S. Murphy, RFC 1848: MIME Object Security Services, October 1995, 48 p. [Status: Standards Track].

  This RFC describes MIME Object Security Services (MOSS) between the sender and receiver at the application layer. This protocol applies digital signature (using public key cryptography) and encryption services (using symmetric key) to MIME objects. This protocol provides mechanisms to support many public key management schemes.

- P. Karn, P. Metzger, W. Simpson, RFC 1851: The ESP Triple DES Transform, September 1995, 11 p. [Status: Experimental].

  This RFC describes the use of triple DES-CBC algorithm to provide IP datagram payload protection under ESP.

- P. Metzger, W. Simpson, RFC 1852: IP Authentication using Keyed SHA, September 1995, 6 p. [Status: Experimental].

  This RFC describes Authentication Header use of keyed Secure Hash Algorithms (SHA).

- W. Simpson, RFC 1853: IP in IP Tunneling, October 1995, 8 p., 9 Ref. [Status: Informational].

  This document discusses techniques, such as those used in Amateur Packet Radio network to build a large mobile network, for connecting IP Protocol/Payload number 4 Encapsulation to IP Security and other protocols. The techniques are valid when the source and the destination application may have different capabilities and policies.

■ G. Ziemba, D. Reed, P.Traina, RFC 1858: Security Considerations for IP Fragment Filtering, October 1995, 10 p. [Status: Informational].

This RFC describes two methods of attacks that use IP fragmentation to disguise TCP packets from IP filters and presents methods to prevent these attacks.

■ J. Myers, M. Rose, RFC 1864: The Content-MD5 Header Field, October 1995, 4 p, 3 Ref. [Status: Standards Track], [Obsoletes RFC 1544].

This RFC specifies how the MD5 algorithm may be used as an integrity check for MIME mail by using an optional header field, Content-MD5, which can be used as a message integrity check (MIC). This MIC can be used to verify that the data sent and the received decoded data are the same.

■ N. Berge, RFC 1875: UNINETT PCA Policy Statements, December 1995, 10 p. [Status: Informational].

This RFC describes the policy statements submitted by the UNINETTPCA.

■ G. Waters, Editor, RFC 1910: User-based Security Model for SNMPv2, February 1996, 44 p. [Status: Experimental].

This RFC describes a User-based Security Model for SNMPv2. This model provides mechanisms to achieve SNMP administrative-framework-defined level of security for protocol interactions.

■ M. Leech et al., RFC 1928: SOCKS Protocol Version 5, March 1996, 9 p. [Status: Standards Track].

This RFC describes a SOCKS Protocol Version 5 that extends the SOCKS Protocol version 4 to include UDP, IPv6 addresses, and provision of strong authentication schemes.

■ M. Leech, RFC 1929: Username/Password Authentication for SOCKS V5, March 1996, 2 p. [Status: Standards Track].

This RFC describes a protocol for username/password authentication in the initial socks connection setup for SOCKS Version 5.

■ S. Bellovin, RFC 1948: Defending Against Sequence Number Attacks, May 1996, 6 p. [Status: Informational].

This RFC describes a modification to the existing TCP implementations that should be useful against IP spoofing attacks.

■ A. Ballardie, RFC 1949: Scalable Multicast Key Distribution, May 1996, 18 p. [Status: Experimental].

This RFC describes how the Core Based Tree (CBT) multicast protocol, which provides explicit mechanisms for security, for example its mechanisms for secure joining of CBT group tree can be used to provide a scalable solution to the multicast key distribution problem.

- P. McMahon, RFC 1961: GSS-API Authentication Method for SOCKS Version 5, June 1996, 9 p. [Status: Standards Track].

This RFC specifies the SOCKS V5 GSS-API authentication protocol for initial SOCKS connection. It also discusses how a GSS-API may be used to provide integrity, authentication, and optional confidentiality under SOCKS.

- J. Linn, RFC 1964: The Kerberos Version 5 GSS-API Mechanism, June 1996, 20 p. [Status: Standards Track].

This RFC describes issues such as elements of protocols and procedures for interoperability for implementing GSS-API peers on top of Kerberos Version 5.

- G. Meyer, RFC 1968: The PPP Encryption Control Protocol (ECP), June 1996, 11 p. [Status: Standards Track].

This RFC discusses Encryption Control Protocol (ECP) and negotiation of encryption algorithm(s) over PPP link after a connection has been established. Note that different method of encryption may be negotiated in each direction of the link for considerations, such as speed, cost, memory, etc.

- K. Sklower, RFC 1969: The PPP DES Encryption Protocol (DESE), G. Meyer, June 1996, 10 p. [Status: Informational].

This RFC describes the methods for encryption of PPP encapsulated packets using DES.

- IAB and IESG, RFC 1984: IAB and IESG Statement on Cryptographic Technology and the Internet, August 1996, 5 p. [Status: Informational].

This RFC contains a statement by IAB and IESG to encourage policies by governments to provide access to uniform strong cryptographic technology for all Internet users in all countries.

- D. Atkins, W. Stallings, and P. Zimmermann, RFC 1991: PGP Message Exchange Formats, August 1996, 21 p. [Status: Informational].

This RFC describes the PGP v 2.x message exchange formats. It describes the format of messages that have been encrypted and/or signed with PGP.

- M. Elkins, RFC 2015: MIME Security with Pretty Good Privacy (PGP), October 1996, 8 p. [Status: Standards Track].

This RFC describes the ways to use PGP to provide privacy and authentication using MIME.

■ C. Adams, RFC 2025: The Simple Public-Key GSS-API Mechanism (SPKM), October 1996, 45 p. [Status: Standards Track].

This RFC describes mechanisms to be used by peer protocols, who implement a GSS-API using a Simple Public-key mechanism instead of using a symmetric key infrastructure.

■ R. Baldwin, R. Rivest, RFC 2040: The RC5, RC5-CBC, RC5-CBC-Pad, and RC5-CTS Algorithms, October 1996, 29 p. [Status: Informational].

This RFC describes four ciphers, the RC5, RC5-CBC, RC5-CBC-Pad, and RC5-CTS with clarity and enough details to ensure interoperability between different implementations.

■ C. Rigney, A. Rubens, W. Simpson, S. Willens, RFC 2058: Remote Authentication Dial In User Service (RADIUS), January 1997, 64 p. [Status: Standards Track].

This RFC describes Remote Authentication Dial In User Service (RADIUS) Protocol. The details of authentication, authorization, and configuration information of connection between a Network Access Server as a client and a RADIUS Server are given.

■ C. Rigney, RFC 2059: RADIUS Accounting, January 1997, 25 p. [Status: Informational].

This RFC describes delivery of accounting information in a RADIUS Protocol.

■ F. Baker, R. Atkinson, RFC 2082: RIP-2 MD5 Authentication, January 1997, 12 p. [Status: Standards Track].

This RFC proposes that RIP-2 use keyed MD5 as a standard authentication algorithm but the authentication mechanism of RIP-2 be kept as algorithm independent.

■ G. Bossert, S. Cooper, W. Drummond, RFC 2084: Considerations for Web Transaction Security, January 1997, 6 p. [Status: Informational].

This RFC discusses Web transaction security. It contains details of security services such as confidentiality, integrity, user authentication, and authentication of servers/services as extensions to HTTP or as separate protocol on top of HTTP.

■ M. Oehler, R. Glenn, RFC 2085: HMAC-MD5 IP Authentication with Replay, Prevention, February 1997, 6 p. [Status: Standards Track].

This RFC describes mechanisms to prevent replay attacks using keyed-MD5 transform based on HMAC-MD5 along with IP Authentication Header.

■ J. Myers, RFC 2086: IMAP4 ACL extension, January 1997, 8 p. [Status: Standards Track].

This RFC describes the ACL extension of the IMAP4 that allows manipulation of an access control list.

■ H. Harney, C. Muckenhirn, RFC 2093: Group Key Management Protocol (GKMP) Specification, July 1997, 23 p. [Status: Experimental].

This RFC proposes Group Key Management Protocol (GKMP) that cooperatively creates keys between more than two protocol entities within a group and distributes grouped symmetric keys among communicating peers on the Internet.

■ H. Harney, C. Muckenhirn, RFC 2094: Group Key Management Protocol (GKMP) Architecture, July 1997, 22 p. [Status: Experimental].

This RFC describes architecture for managing grouped cryptographic keys among peer protocols for multicast communication.

■ H. Krawczyk, M. Bellare, R. Canetti, RFC 2104: HMAC: Keyed-Hashing for Message Authentication, February 1997, 11 p. [Status: Informational].

This RFC describes a protocol HMAC: Keyed-Hashing for Message Authentication for message authentication which is a MAC mechanism based on cryptographic hashing functions.

■ C. Adams, RFC 2144: The CAST-128 Encryption Algorithm, May 1997, 15 p. [Status: Informational].

This RFC describes a DES like Substitution-Permutation Network (SPN) cryptosystem, CAST-128 encryption algorithm.

■ S. Murphy, M. Badger, B. Wellington, RFC 2154: OSPF with Digital Signatures, June 1997, 29 p. [Status: Experimental].

This RFC describes extensions to OSPF protocol. These extensions add features such as digital signatures to Link State Data and certification for router data. The RFC also lists LSA processing, key management in addition to details of transition from OSPF v2.

■ Gwinn, RFC 2179: Network Security For Trade Shows, July 1997, 10 p. [Status: Informational].

This RFC is a set of guidelines to assist vendors and participants in trade shows for protection against network and system attacks.

■ B. Fraser, RFC 2196: Site Security Handbook Editor, September 1997, 75 p. [Status: Informational], [Obsoletes: 1244].

This RFC contains guidelines and recommendations to develop policies and procedures for security of sites and systems that are connected to the Internet.

- P. Cheng, R. Glenn, RFC 2202: Test Cases for HMAC-MD5 and HMAC-SHA-1, September 1997, 9 p. [Status: Informational].

  This RFC provides two sets of test cases and the corresponding results to be used as conformance tests for HMAC-MD5 and HMAC-SHA-1 implementations.

- M. Eisler, A. Chiu, L. Ling, RFC 2203: RPCSEC_GSS Protocol Specification, September 1997, 23 p. [Status: Standards Track].

  This RFC describes RPCSEC_GSS security protocol that allows RPC protocols to access the GSS-API.

- J. Myers, RFC 2222: Simple Authentication and Security Layer (SASL), October 1997, 27 p. [Status: Standards Track].

  This RFC describes a procedure to add authentication to connection-based protocols. If negotiated it adds a new security layer between the protocol and the connection.

- M. Horowitz, S. Lunt, RFC 2228: FTP Security Extensions, October 1997, 27 p. [Status: Standards Track].

  This RFC provides authentication, integrity, and confidentiality as security extensions to the FTP protocol and introduces new optional commands as well as new class of reply types for protected replies.

- R. Atkinson, RFC 2230: Key Exchange Delegation Record for the DNS, November 1997, 11 p. [Status: Informational].

  This RFC describes the syntax of key exchange record and methods to delegate key exchange services to different nodes through secure DNS.

- C. Newman, RFC 2245: Anonymous SASL Mechanism, November 1997, 5 p. [Status: Standards Track].

  This RFC describes anonymous access by a client of a server within SASL framework. The RFC includes a grammar and an example access scenario.

- P. Ferguson, D. Senie, RFC 2267: Network Ingress Filtering: Defeating Denial of Service Attacks which employ IP Source Address Spoofing, January 1998, 10 p. [Status: Informational].

  This RFC discusses a method for using traffic filtering to allow valid source IP addresses from input links to routers to prevent DoS attacks.

- R. Rivest, RFC 2268: A Description of the RC2(r) Encryption Algorithm, March 1998, 11 p. [Status: Informational].

This RFC describes a secret key block encryption algorithm RC2 as a proposed replacement for DES. The algorithm has 64-bit input and 64-bit output blocks and a key size of up to 128 bytes.

■ U. Blumenthal, B. Wijnen, RFC 2274: User-based Security Model (USM) for version 3 of the Simple Network Management Protocol (SNMPv3), January 1998, 76 p. [Status: Standards Track], [Obsoletes: 2264].

This RFC describes the user-based security model for SNMP which includes procedure for providing SNMP message-level security and an MIB for remote management.

■ B. Wijnen, R. Presuhn, K. McCloghrie, RFC 2275: View-based Access Control Model (VACM) for the Simple Network Management Protocol (SNMP) January 1998, 36 p. [Status: Proposed Standard], [Obsoletes: 2265].

This RFC describes the View-based Access Control Model for the SNMP architecture, which include procedures for controlling access to management information and an MIB for remote management.

■ L. Blunk, J. Vollbrecht, RFC 2284: PPP Extensible Authentication Protocol (EAP), March 1998, 15 p. [Status: Proposed Standard].

This RFC describes the PPP Extensible Authentication Protocol (EAP) to authenticate multiprotocol datagrams over point-to-point links.

■ J. Kapp, RFC 2286: Test Cases for HMAC-RIPEMD160 and HMAC-RIPEMD128, February 1998, 7 p. [Status: Informational].

This RFC provides two sets of test cases and the corresponding results to be used as conformance tests for HMAC-RIPEMD160 and HMAC-RIPEMD128 implementations.

■ N. Haller, C. Metz, P. Nesser, M. Straw, RFC 2289: A One-Time Password System, February 1998, 25 p. [Status: Draft Standard], [Obsoletes: 1938].

This RFC describes an authentication method that uses a secret pass-phrase from a user to generate a sequence of one-time passwords. This method is not vulnerable to replay attacks because the secret pass-phrase does not cross the network for authentication.

■ S. Dusse, P. Hoffman, B. Ramsdell, L. Lundblade, L. Repka, RFC 2311: S/MIME Version 2 Message Specification, March 1998, 37 p. [Status: Informational].

This RFC describes specifications and protocols for adding cryptographic signature and encryption services to MIME messages.

- S. Dusse, P. Hoffman, B. Ramsdell, J. Weinstein, RFC 2312: S/MIME Version 2 Certificate Handling, March 1998, 20 p. [Status: Informational].

  This RFC describes the procedures used by S/MIME to manage certificates.

- B. Kaliski, RFC 2315: PKCS #7: Cryptographic Message Syntax Version 1.5, March 1998, 32 p. [Status: Informational].

  This RFC describes syntax for data that may need to be encrypted such as in digital signatures and digital envelops.

- S. Bellovin, RFC 2316: Report of the IAB Security Architecture Workshop, April 1998, 9 p. [Status: Informational].

  This RFC contains a report of the IAB security architecture workshop that was held with goals to define security architecture for the Internet and identify current areas of strength, weakness and to provide guidance.

- N. Brownlee, E. Guttman, RFC 2350: Expectations for Computer Security Incident Response, June 1998, 38 p. [Status: Best Current Practice].

  This RFC outlines expectations and framework for presenting the important subjects related to incident response from Computer Security Incident Response Teams (CSIRTs). It also provides formal templates and completed examples of information for presenting reports to users.

- G. Montenegro, V. Gupta, RFC 2356: Sun's SKIP Firewall Traversal for Mobile IP, June 1998, 24 p. [Status: Informational].

  This RFC describes traversal of mobile IP through a SKIP firewall. The document lists support required at firewall mobile IP home agent and mobile IP node and also methods for a mobile IP node to access past a SKIP firewall to construct a secure channel into its home network.

- D. McDonald, C. Metz, B. Phan, RFC 2367: PF_KEY Key Management API, Version 2, July 1998, 68 p. [Status: Informational].

  This RFC describes the PF_KEY Key Management API, Version 2 which can be used for IP Security and other network security services.

- S. Kent, R. Atkinson, RFC 2401: Security Architecture for the Internet Protocol, November 1998, 66 p. [Status: Standards Track], [Obsoletes: 1825].

  This RFC describes the architecture of IPsec compliant systems including the high level description of IPsec and methods to provide security services such as access control, connectionless integrity, data origin authentication, rejection of replayed packets, and confidentiality for traffic at the IP layer.

■ S. Kent, R. Atkinson, RFC 2402: IP Authentication Header, November 1998, 22 p. [Status: Standards Track], [Obsoletes: 1826].

This RFC describes the structure, fields, format, and other details of the IP Authentication Header (AH). The AH provides integrity and data origin authentication for IP datagrams.

■ C. Madson, R. Glenn, RFC 2403: The Use of HMAC-MD5–96 within ESP and AH, November 1998, 7 p. [Status: Standards Track].

This RFC describes the use of the HMAC algorithm and the MD5 algorithm, to provide the data origin authentication and integrity protection for IPsec ESP and IPsec AH.

■ C. Madson, R. Glenn, RFC 2404: The Use of HMAC-SHA-1–96 within ESP and AH, November 1998, 7 p. [Status: Standards Track].

This RFC describes the use of the HMAC algorithm and the SHA-1 algorithm, to provide the data origin authentication and integrity protection for IPsec ESP and IPsec AH.

■ C. Madson, N. Doraswamy, RFC 2405: The ESP DES-CBC Cipher Algorithm With Explicit IV, November 1998, 10 p. [Status: Standards Track].

This RFC describes the DES Cipher algorithm in Cipher Block Chaining Mode, with an explicit IV, to provide confidentiality under IPsec Encapsulating Security Payload.

■ S. Kent, R. Atkinson, RFC 2406: IP Encapsulating Security Payload (ESP), November 1998, 22 p. [Status: Standards Track], [Obsoletes: 1827].

This RFC describes the IP Encapsulating Security Payload (ESP) protocol that provides many security services such as confidentiality, data origin authentication, connectionless integrity, an anti-replay service for IPv4 and IPv6.

■ D. Piper, RFC 2407: The Internet IP Security Domain of Interpretation for ISAKMP, November 1998, 32 p. [Status: Standards Track].

This RFC describes the Internet IP Security DOI (IPSEC DOI) for ISAKMP. Related protocols using ISAKMP in a DOI negotiate security associations, choose security protocols and share many other important functions and attributes.

■ D. Maughan, M. Schertler, M. Schneider, J. Turner, RFC 2408: Internet Security Association and Key Management Protocol (ISAKMP), November 1998, 86 p. [Status: Standards Track].

This RFC describes the Internet Security Association and Key Management Protocol (ISAKMP) protocol for key management, authentication, and security association for secure communication in an internet environment.

■ D. Harkins, D. Carrel, RFC 2409: The Internet Key Exchange (IKE), November 1998, 41 p. [Status: Standards Track].

This RFC describes a hybrid protocol that uses parts of Oakley and SKEME to get authenticated keying material for use with ISAKMP, IPsec ESP and AH.

■ R. Glenn, S. Kent, RFC 2410: The NULL Encryption Algorithm and Its Use With IPsec, November 1998, 6 p. [Status: Standards Track].

This RFC describes the NULL encryption algorithm, to help IPsec ESP provide authentication and integrity for IP datagrams.

■ B. Kaliski, J. Staddon, RFC 2437: PKCS #1: RSA Cryptography Specifications Version 2.0, October 1998, 39 p. [Status: Informational], [Obsoletes: 2313].

This RFC describes specifications for implementing the RSA algorithm in computer and communication systems. The description includes cryptographic primitives, encryption schemes, signature schemes, and ASN.1 syntax.

■ C. Newman, RFC 2444: The One-Time-Password SASL Mechanism, October 1988, 7 p. [Status: Standards Track], [Updates: 2222].

This RFC describes the One-Time-Password (OTP) SASL mechanism to formally integrate OTP into SASL enabled protocols. The OTP, by giving only one-time password is useful for authentication when a client or a server is untrusted, such as a client application in a publicly available computer or an Internet kiosk.

■ R. Pereira, R. Adams, RFC 2451: The ESP CBC-Mode Cipher Algorithms, November 1998, 14 p. [Status: Standards Track].

This RFC describes application of CBC-mode cipher algorithms to encrypt the IP datagram payload for the IPsec ESP Protocol.

■ E. Baize, D. Pinkas, RFC 2478: The Simple and Protected GSS-API Negotiation Mechanism, December 1988, 18 p. [Status: Standards Track].

This RFC describes a simple and protected security negotiation mechanism between GSS-API peers.

■ C. Adams, RFC 2479: Independent Data Unit Protection Generic Security Service Application Program Interface (IDUP-GSS-API), December 1988, 70 p. [Status: Informational].

This RFC describes the Independent Data Unit Protection Generic Security Service Application Program Interface (IDUP-GSS-API), which provides data origin authentication with data integrity, data confidentiality with data integrity, and support for non-repudiation services.

■ N. Freed, RFC 2480: Gateways and MIME Security Multiparts, January 1999, 6 p. [Status: Standards Track].

This RFC discusses the problems of using MIME security multiparts and gateways to connect to non-MIME environments and provides specifications for gateway behavior that should solve these problems.

■ P. Hoffman, RFC 2487: SMTP Service Extension for Secure SMTP over TLS, January 1999, 8 p. [Status: Standards Track].

This RFC describes an extension to the SMTP service to provide secure SMTP communication using TLS between SMTP client and server.

■ E. Guttman, L. Leong, G. Malkin, RFC 2504: Users' Security Handbook, February 1999, 33 p. [Status: Informational].

This RFC contains guidelines for users to keep their data, computers, and networks secure.

■ C. Adams, S. Farrell, RFC 2510: Internet X.509 Public Key Infrastructure Certificate Management Protocols, March 1999, 72 p. [Status: Standards Track].

This RFC describes the Internet X.509 Public Key Infrastructure (PKI) Certificate Management Protocols. It contains details of data structures used for PKI management messages, functions done in PKI management, and a simple protocol for transporting PKI messages.

■ M. Myers, C. Adams, D. Solo, D. Kemp, RFC 2511: Internet X.509 Certificate Request Message Format, March 1999, 25 p. [Status: Standards Track].

This RFC describes the details and the syntax of the Internet X.509 Certificate Request Message Format.

■ P. Karn, W. Simpson, RFC 2521: ICMP Security Failures Messages, March 1999, 7 p. [Status: Experimental].

This RFC specifies message format and error procedures for ICMP security failures messages when using IP security protocols.

■ P. Karn, W. Simpson, RFC 2523: Photuris: Extended Schemes and Attributes, March 1999, 19 p. [Status: Experimental].

This RFC provides Extensible Exchange Schemes and authentication attributes for implementation of Photuris.

■ S. Chokhani, W. Ford, RFC 2527: Internet X.509 Public Key Infrastructure Certificate Policy and Certification Practices Framework, March 1999, 45 p. [Status: Informational].

This RFC establishes an outline of Certificate Policy and Certification Practices in Internet X.509 Public Key Infrastructure. This outline contains guidelines to include topics in preparing certificate policy definition or a certification practice statement.

■ R. Housley, W. Polk, RFC 2528: Internet X.509 Public Key Infrastructure Representation of Key Exchange Algorithm (KEA) Keys in Internet X.509 Public Key Infrastructure Certificates, March 1999, 9 p. [Status: Informational].

This RFC outlines the format and semantics of fields of Key Exchange Algorithm keys in the Internet X.509 public key infrastructure certificates.

■ D. Eastlake, RFC 2537: RSA/MD5 KEYs and SIGs in the Domain Name System (DNS), March 1999, 6 p. [Status: Standards Track].

This RFC describes a standard method for storage of RSA keys and RSA/MD5 based signatures in the DNS.

■ D. Eastlake, RFC 2539: Storage of Diffie–Hellman Keys in the Domain Name System (DNS), March 1999, 7 p. [Status: Standards Track].

This RFC describes a standard method for storage of Diffie–Hellman keys in the DNS.

■ D. Eastlake, RFC 2540: Detached Domain Name System (DNS) Information, March 1999, 6 p. [Status: Experimental].

This RFC defines a standard format for representing information retrieved such as public cryptographic keys from DNS for archival purposes.

■ D. Eastlake, RFC 2541: DNS Security Operational Considerations, March 1999, 7 p. [Status: Informational].

This RFC discusses various operational aspects of DNS security such as security of high-level zones; and lifetime, size, and storage for keys and signatures used for the KEY and SIG DNS resource records.

■ J. Myers, RFC 2554: SMTP Service Extension for Authentication, March 1999, 11 p. [Status: Standards Track].

This document describes an SMTP service extension [ESMTP] for authentication and an optional negotiation for a security layer for protocol interactions.

■ M. Myers, R. Ankney, A. Malpani, S. Galperin, C. Adams, RFC 2560: X.509 Internet Public Key Infrastructure Online Certificate Status Protocol—OCSP, June 1999, 23 p. [Status: Standards Track].

This RFC describes a protocol that helps applications determine the status of a certificate from a server without requiring CRLs.

■ U. Blumenthal, B. Wijnen, RFC 2574: User-based Security Model (USM) for version 3 of the Simple Network Management Protocol (SNMPv3), April 1999, 86 p. [Status: Draft Standard], [Obsoletes 2274].

This RFC describes the User-based Security Model (USM) for SNMP version 3, provision of SNMP message level security, and a MIB for remotely managing the parameters of this USM.

■ M. Allman, S. Ostermann, RFC 2577: FTP Security Considerations, May 1999, 8 p. [Status: Informational].

This RFC contains suggestions for improving security of FTP servers.

■ R. Finlayson, RFC 2588: IP Multicast and Firewalls, May 1999, 12 p. [Status: Informational].

This document discusses how firewall handles IP Multicast traffic that includes issues like surrounding the traversal of IP Multicast traffic across a firewall.

■ C. Newman, RFC 2595: Using TLS with IMAP, POP3 and ACAP, June 1999, 15 p. [Status: Standards Track].

This RFC describes use of TLS with IMAP, POP 3, and ACAP for secure communication.

■ J. Franks, P. Hallam-Baker, J. Hostetler, S. Lawrence, P. Leach, A. Luotonen, and L. Stewart, RFC 2617: HTTP Authentication: Basic and Digest Access Authentication, June 1999, 34 p. [Status: Draft Standard], [Obsoletes: 2069].

This RFC describes basic and digest access authentication methods within the HTTP authentication framework.

■ B. Aboba, G. Zorn, RFC 2618: RADIUS Authentication Client MIB, June 1999, 14 p. [Status: Standards Track].

This RFC describes extensions to the Management Information Base (MIB) for use with network management protocols. These extensions help IP based management stations manage RADIUS authentication client.

■ G. Zorn, B. Aboba, RFC 2619: RADIUS Authentication Server MIB, June 1999, 16 p. [Status: Standards Track].

This RFC describes extensions to the Management Information Base (MIB) for use with network management protocols. These extensions help IP based management stations manage RADIUS authentication server.

■ B. Aboba, G. Zorn, RFC 2620: RADIUS Accounting Client MIB, June 1999, 13 p. [Status: Informational].

This RFC describes extensions to the Management Information Base (MIB) for use with network management protocols. These extensions help IP based management stations manage RADIUS account client.

■ G. Zorn, B. Aboba, RFC 2621: RADIUS Accounting Server MIB, June 1999, 15 p. [Status: Informational].

This RFC describes extensions to the Management Information Base (MIB) for use with network management protocols. These extensions help IP based management stations manage RADIUS account servers.

■ M. Eisler, RFC 2623: NFS Version 2 and Version 3 Security Issues and the NFS Protocol's Use of RPCSEC_GSS and Kerberos V5, June 1999, 19 p. [Status: Standards Track].

This RFC describes NFS security issues, functioning of NFS over Kerberos v5 using RPCSEC_GSS, and how the Version 2 and Version 3 of the NFS use RPCSEC_GSS.

■ V. Smyslov, RFC 2628: Simple Cryptographic Program Interface (Crypto API), June 1999, 30 p. [Status: Informational].

This RFC describes a simple application program interface to cryptographic functions so as to separate cryptographic libraries from applications.

■ E. Rescorla, A. Schiffman, RFC 2659: Security Extensions For HTML, August 1999, 4 p. [Status: Experimental].

This RFC describes security extensions to HTML for embedding S-HTTP negotiation parameters related to cryptographic enhancements.

■ M. Blaze, J. Feigenbaum, J. Ioannidis, A. Keromytis, RFC 2704: The KeyNote Trust-Management System Version 2, September 1999, 37 p. [Status: Informational].

This RFC describes version 2 of the KeyNote trust-management system.

■ P. Srisuresh, RFC 2709: Security Model with Tunnel-mode IPsec for NAT Domains, October 1999, 11 p. [Status: Informational].

This RFC describes a security model by which IP Network Address Translator devices recognize tunnel-mode IPsec security.

■ Medvinsky, M. Hur, RFC 2712: Addition of Kerberos Cipher Suites to Transport Layer Security (TLS), October 1999, 7 p. [Status: Standards Track].

This document proposes addition of Kerberos Cipher Suites to the TLS protocol.

■ B. Aboba, D. Simon, RFC 2716: PPP EAP TLS Authentication Protocol, October 1999, 24 p. [Status: Experimental].

This RFC document describes the way EAP-TLS provides TLS mechanisms within EAP.

■ C. Villamizar, C. Alaettinoglu, D. Meyer, S. Murphy, RFC 2725: Routing Policy System Security, December 1999, 41 p. [Status: Standards Track].

This RFC document suggests an authentication and authorization model to assure integrity of data in a routing policy system.

■ J. Zsako, RFC 2726: PGP Authentication for RIPE Database Updates, December 1999, 11 p. [Status: Standards Track].

This RFC suggests PGP authentication of the updates to the RIPE database.

■ J. Linn, RFC 2743: Generic Security Service Application Program Interface Version 2, Update 1, January 2000, 101 p. [Status: Standards Track], [Obsoletes 2078].

This RFC describes update 1 of GSS-API version 2.

■ J. Wray, RFC 2744: Generic Security Service API Version 2: C-bindings, January 2000, 101 p. [Status: Standards Track], [Obsoletes: 1509].

This RFC describes GSS-API C language bindings.

■ C. Alaettinoglu, C. Villamizar, R. Govindan, RFC 2754: RPS IANA Issues, January 2000, 7 p. [Status: Informational].

This RFC describes RPSL objects in the IRR and lists operations required from IANA.

■ A. Chiu, M. Eisler, B. Callaghan, RFC 2755: Security Negotiation for WebNFS, January 2000, 12 p. [Status: Informational].

This RFC document describes protocol for security negotiation between WebNFS client and WebNFS server.

■ R. Zuccherato, RFC 2785: Methods for Avoiding the Small-Subgroup Attacks on the Diffie–Hellman Key Agreement Method for S/MIME, March 2000, 11 p. [Status: Informational].

This RFC describes methods to avoid "Small-Subgroup" attacks on the Diffie–Hellman Key Agreement Method for S/MIME.

■ M. St. Johns, RFC 2786: Diffie–Hellman USM Key Management Information Base and Textual Convention, March 2000, 20 p. [Status: Experimental].

This RFC describes an experimental part of the Diffie–Hellman USM Key Management Information Base and textual conventions to do Diffie–Hellman key exchange for use with network management protocols.

■ K. Davidson, Y. Kawatsura, RFC 2802: Digital Signatures for the v1.0 Internet Open Trading Protocol (IOTP), April 2000, 29 p. [Status: Informational].

This RFC describes the details of the computation and verification of digital signatures in version 1.0 of the Internet Open Trading Protocol (IOTP).

■ M. Nystrom, RFC 2808: The SecurID(r) SASL Mechanism, April 2000, 11 p. [Status: Informational].

This RFC defines an SASL authentication mechanism using hardware token card or its software implementation. This RFC uses SecurID, a hardware token card produced by RSA Securities Inc.

■ R. Khare, S. Lawrence, RFC 2817: Upgrading to TLS Within HTTP/1.1, May 2000,1 p. [Status: Standards Track], [Updates: 2616].

This RFC describes the use of Upgrade mechanism in HTTP/1.1 to start Transport Layer Security (TLS) connection over an existing TCP connection by using the same port 80 instead of port 443 used for HTTPS.

■ E. Rescorla, RFC 2818: HTTP Over TLS, May 2000, 7 p. [Status: Informational].

This RFC describes the functioning of HTPP/TLS. It describes how HTTP protocol may be used on top of TLS protocol to provide secure connection(s).

■ R. Shirey, RFC 2828: Internet Security Glossary, May 2000, 212 p. [Status: Informational].

This RFC contains definition and description of Internet security terms with a purpose to provide standardization and comprehensibility for writing in Internet security and Internet Standards documents.

■ M. Wahl, H. Alvestrand, J. Hodges, R. Morgan, RFC 2829: Authentication Methods for LDAP, May 2000, 16 p. [Status: Standards Track].

This RFC describes suggested and recommended seurity combinations for authentication in LDAP implementations.

■ J. Hodges, R. Morgan, M. Wahl, RFC 2830: Lightweight Directory Access Protocol (v3): Extension for Transport Layer Security, May 2000, 12 p. [Status: Standards Track].

This RFC describes the Start Transport Layer Security in initiation of connection in an LDAP association.

- P. Leach, C. Newman, RFC 2831: Using Digest Authentication as a SASL Mechanism, May 2000, 27 p. [Status: Standards Track].

  This RFC describes methods to use HTTP Digest Authentication as SASL mechanism to authentication, for example on Web, mail, LDAP, etc.

- J. Kabat, M. Upadhyay, RFC 2853: Generic Security Service API Version 2: Java Bindings, June 2000, 96 p. [Status: Standards Track].

  This RFC describes the Java bindings of GSS-API.

- Keromytis, N. Provos, RFC 2857: The Use of HMAC-RIPEMD-160–96 within ESP and AH, June 2000, 7 p. [Status: Standards Track].

  This RFC describes how the HMAC algorithm and the RIPEMD-160 algorithm together may be used to authenticate under IPSEC protocol.

- R. Bush, D. Karrenberg, M. Kosters, R. Plzak, RFC 2870: Root Name Server Operational Requirements, June 2000, 10 p. [Status: Best Current Practice], [Obsoletes: 2010].

  This RFC provides recommendations for operation of the root name servers.

- H. Prafullchandra, J. Schaad, RFC 2875: Diffie–Hellman Proof-of-Possession Algorithms, July 2000, 23 p. [Status: Standards Track].

  This RFC describes two proof-of-possession algorithms to generate an integrity check value using Diffie–Hellman algorithm.

- B. Kaliski, RFC 2898: PKCS #5: Password-Based Cryptography Specification Version 2.0, September 2000, 34 p. [Status: Informational].

  This RFC document contains a republication of "PKCS #5: Password-Based Cryptography Specification Version 2.0". This RFC adds security consideration section to the above document. Note that PKCS series of documents are produced by the RSA Laboratories.

- Eastlake, RFC 2931: DNS Request and Transaction Signatures (SIG (0) s), September 2000, 10 p. [Status: Standards Track], [Updates: 2535].

  This RFC describes minor changes to the Domain Name System SIG Resource Records that are used to digitally sign DNS requests and transactions/responses.

- T. Ts'o, editor, J. Altman, RFC 2941: Telnet Authentication Option, September 2000, 15 p. [Status: Standards Track], [Obsoletes: 1416].

This RFC describes a telent authentication option that can be used to decide whether to use encryption and forwarding of credentials for authentication, and to negotiate an authentication type and mode among the connecting points.

■ N. Freed, RFC 2979: Behavior of and Requirements for Internet Firewalls, October 2000, 7 p. [Status: Informational].

This RFC contains guidelines to make Internet firewalls consistent and interoperable among various implementations.

■ C. Adams, RFC 2984: Use of the CAST-128 Encryption Algorithm in CMS, October 2000, 6 p. [Status: Standards Track].

This RFC document describes methods to incorporate CAST-128 encryption algorithm into the S/MIME Cryptographic Message Syntax (CMS). The CAST-128 encryption algorithm is an additional algorithm within CMS for symmetric content and key encryption.

■ M. Nystrom, B. Kaliski, RFC 2985: PKCS#9: Selected Object Classes and Attribute Types Version 2.0, November 2000, 42 p. [Status: Informational].

This RFC document contains a republication of "PKCS #9: Certification Request Syntax Specification v2.0". This RFC adds security consideration section to the above document. Note that PKCS series of documents are produced by the RSA Laboratories.

■ M. Nystrom, B. Kaliski, RFC 2986: PKCS#10: Certification Request Syntax Specification Version 1.7, November 2000, 14 p. [Status: Informational], [Obsoletes: 2314].

This RFC document contains a republication of "PKCS #10: Certification Request Syntax Specification v1.7". This RFC adds security consideration section to the above document. Note that PKCS series of documents are produced by the RSA Laboratories.

■ H. Ohta, M. Matsui, RFC 2994: A Description of the MISTY1 Encryption Algorithm, November 2000, 10 p. [Status: Informational].

This RFC describes an encryption algorithm including key scheduling and data randomizing for a 128-bit key, 64-bit block, secret-key cryptosystem MISTY1. The algorithm uses variable number of rounds for encryption.

■ B. Wellington, RFC 3007: Secure Domain Name System (DNS) Dynamic Update, November 2000, 9 p. [Status: Standards Track], [Obsoletes: 2137], [Updates: 2535, 2136].

This RFC describes methods that use secure communication and authentication to do DNS dynamic updates securely.

- B. Wellington, RFC 3008: Domain Name System Security (DNSSEC) Signing Authority, November 2000, 7 p. [Status: Standards Track], [Updates: 2535].

  This RFC document revises Domain Name System Security (DNSSEC) Signing Authority model to simplify the secure resolution process. A major change is that in a secure zone, zone data must sign the zone key.

- T. Killalea, RFC 3013: Recommended Internet Service Provider Security Services and Procedures, November 2000, 13 p. [Status: Best Current Practice].

  This RFC is a set of guidelines and recommendations from IETF and describe best current practices related to security. These guidelines and recommendations are for Internet Service Providers (ISPs) and the Internet users.

- G. Pall, G. Zorn, and RFC 3078: Microsoft Point-To-Point Encryption (MPPE) Protocol, March 2001,12 p. [Status: Informational].

  This RFC document describes the Microsoft Point-to-Point Encryption (MPPE) including, the use of RSA C4 algorithm to provide data confidentiality, MPPE Key Change Algorithm, and change of session keys.

- G. Zorn, RFC 3079: Deriving Keys for use with Microsoft Point-to-Point Encryption (MPPE), March 2001, 21 p. [Status: Informational].

  This RFC document describes the derivation of initial MPPE session keys to encrypt PPP packets over point-to-point links. The session keys are changed frequently and the frequency of change is negotiated between the communicating parties.

- K. Chan, J. Seligson, D. Durham, S. Durham, S. Gai, K. McCloghrie, S. Herzog, F. Reichmeyer, R. Yavatkar, and A. Smith, RFC 3084: COPS Usage for Policy Provisioning (COPS-PR), March 2001, 34 p. [Status: Standards Track].

  This document describes the Common Open Policy Service (COPS) protocol that includes message formats and objects that carry the modeled policy data to support policy provisioning. It makes no assumption about the underlying policy data model being communicated.

- E. Lewis, RFC 3090: DNS Security Extension Clarification on Zone Status, March 2001, 11 p. [Status: Standards Track].

  This RFC updates sections of RFC 2535 by defining the criteria to designate a zone as a secure zone. This definition is independent of the underlying key algorithm used.

- R. Braden, L. Zhang, RFC 3097: RSVP Cryptographic Authentication— Updated Message Type Value, April 2001, 4 p. [Status: Standards Track].

This RFC memo suggests an updated message type value in RSVP Cryptographic Authentication by changing the message type of the challenge and integrity response messages in RFC 2747.

■ D. Eastlake 3rd, RFC 3110: RSA/SHA-1 SIGs and RSA KEYs in the Domain Name System (DNS), May 2001, 7 p. [Status: Standards Track].

This RFC defines a new DNS signature algorithm to produce RSA/SHA1 SIG resource records and RSA KEY resource records.

LIST OF
SECURITY
STANDARDS

APPENDIX

C

ANSI STANDARDS

ANSI X3. 92

"American National Standard for *Data Encryption Algorithm* (DEA)," American National Standards Institute, 1981.

ANSI X3.105

"American National Standard for Information Systems—*Data Link Encryption*," American National Standards Institute, 1983.

ANSI X3.106

"American National Standard for Information Systems—*Data Encryption Algorithm-Modes of Operation*," American National Standards Institute, 1983.

ANSI X9.17

"American National Standard for *Financial Institution Key Management* (Wholesale)," American Bankers Association, 1985 (Revised).

ANSI X9.19

"American National Standard for *Retail Message Authentication*," American Bankers Association, 1985.

ANSI X9.23

"American National Standard for *Financial Institution Message Encryption*," American Bankers Association, 1988.

ANSI X9.24

"Draft Proposed American National Standard for *Retail Key Management*," American Bankers Association, 1988.

ANSI X9.26

"American National Standard for Financial Institution *Sign-On Authentication for Wholesale Financial Transaction*," American Bankers Association, 1990 (Revised).

ANSI X9.30

"Working Draft: *Public Key Cryptography Using Irreversible Algorithms for the Financial Services Industry*," American Bankers Association, August 1994.

ANSI X9.31

"Working Draft: *Public Key Cryptography Using Reversible Algorithms for the Financial Services Industry*," American Bankers Association, March 1993.

ANSI X9.8

"American National Standard for *Personal Information Number (PIN) Management and Security*," American Bankers Association, 1982.

ANSI X9.9

"American National Standard for *Financial Institution Message Authentication* (Wholesale)," American Bankers Association, 1986. (Revised)

ECMA STANDARDS (BLUE COVER)

ECMA-106

Private Telecommunication Networks (PTN), Signalling Protocol at the S Reference Point, Circuit Mode Basic Services (SSIG-BC), 3rd edition (December 1993).

ECMA-151

Data Compression for Information Interchange, Adaptive Coding with Embedded Dictionary, DCLZ Algorithm (June 1991).

ECMA-205

Commercially Oriented Functionality Class for Security Evaluation (COFC) (December 1993).

ECMA-206

Association Context Management including Security Context Management (December 1993)

ECMA-219

Authentication and Priviledge Attribute Security Application with Related Key Distribution Functions, Parts 1, 2, and 3, 2nd edition (March 1996).

ECMA-307

Corporate Telecommunication Networks, Signalling Interworking between QSIG and H.323, Generic Functional Protocol for the Support of Supplementary Services (June 2000).

ECMA-308

Corporate Telecommunication Networks, Signalling Interworking between QSIG and H.323, Call Transfer Supplementary Services (June 2000).

ECMA-309

Corporate Telecommunication Networks, Signalling Interworking between QSIG and H.323, Call Diversion Supplementary Services (June 2000).

FIPS STANDARDS

FIPS PUB ZZZ

Advanced Encryption Standard (AES).

FIPS PUB 112

Password Usage, 1985 May 30.

FIPS PUB 196

Entity Authentication Using Public Key Cryptography, 1997 February 18.

FIPS PUB 46

Data Encryption Standard (DES), January 1997.

FIPS PUB 46-3

Data Encryption Standard (DES), 1999 October 25.

FIPS PUB 81

DES Modes of Operation.

FIPS PUB 113

Computer Data Authentication.

FIPS PUB 140-1

Security Requirements For Cryptographic Modules.

FIPS PUB 171
Key Management Using ANSI X9.17.

FIPS PUB 180–1
Secure Hash Standard (SHS).

FIPS PUB 181
Automated Password Generator (APG).

FIPS PUB 185
Automated Password Generator (APG).

FIPS PUB 186
Digital Signature Standard (DSS).

FIPS PUB 186–2
Automated Password Generator (APG).

ISO STANDARDS

ISO 7498–2:1989
Information processing systems, Open Systems Interconnection, Basic Reference Model, Part 2: Security Architecture.

ISO/IEC 10164–7:1992
Information technology, Open Systems Interconnection, Systems Management: Security alarm reporting function.

ISO/IEC 10164–8:1993
Information technology, Open Systems Interconnection, Systems Management: Security audit trail function.

ISO/IEC DIS 10181–1
Information technology, Open Systems Interconnection, Security Frameworks for Open Systems: Overview.

ISO/IEC DIS 10181–2
Information technology, Open Systems Interconnection, Security Frameworks for Open Systems, Part 2: Authentication Framework.

ISO/IEC DIS 10181–3
Information technology, Open Systems Interconnection, Security frameworks in open systems, Part 3: Access control.

ISO/IEC DIS 10181–4
Information technology, Open Systems Interconnection, Security frameworks in Open Systems, Part 4: Nonrepudiation.

ISO/IEC DIS 10181–5
Information technology, Security frameworks in open systems, Part 5: Confidentiality.

ISO/IEC DIS 10181–6
Information technology, Security frameworks in open systems, Part 6: Integrity.

ISO/IEC DIS 10181–7
Information technology, Open Systems Interconnection, Security Frameworks for Open Systems: Security Audit Framework.

ISO/IEC 10745:1995
Information technology, Open Systems Interconnection, Upper layers security model.

ISO/IEC DIS 11586–1
Information technology, Open Systems Interconnection, Generic Upper Layers Security, Part 1: Overview, Models and Notation.

ISO/IEC DIS 11586–2
Information technology, Open Systems Interconnection, Generic Upper Layers Security, Part 2: Security Exchange Service Element (SESE) Service Specification.

ISO/IEC DIS 11586–3
Information technology, Open Systems Interconnection, Generic Upper Layers Security, Part 3: Security Exchange Service Element (SESE) Protocol Specification.

ISO/IEC DIS 11586–4

Information technology, Open Systems Interconnection, Generic Upper Layers Security, Part 4: Protecting Transfer Syntax Specification.

ISO/IEC DIS 11586–5

Information technology, Open Systems Interconnection, Generic Upper Layers Security: Security Exchange Service Element Protocol Implementation Conformance Statement (PICS) Proforma.

ISO/IEC DIS 11586–6

Information technology, Open Systems Interconnection, Generic Upper Layers Security: Protecting Transfer Syntax Implementation Conformance Statement (PICS) Proforma.

ISO/IEC 9796:1991

Information technology, Security techniques, Digital signature scheme giving message recovery.

ISO/IEC 9797:1994

Information technology, Security techniques, Data integrity mechanism using a cryptographic check function employing a block cipher algorithm.

ISO/IEC 9798–1:1991

Information technology, Security techniques, Entity authentication mechanisms, Part 1: General model.

ISO/IEC 9798–2:1994

Information technology, Security techniques, Entity authentication, Part 2: Mechanisms using symmetric encipherment algorithms.

ISO/IEC 9798–3:1993

Information technology, Security techniques, Entity authentication mechanisms, Part 3: Entity authentication using a public key algorithm.

ISO/IEC 9798–4:1995

Information, Security techniques, Entity authentication, Part 4: Mechanisms using a cryptographic check function.

ISO/IEC 9979:1991

Data cryptographic techniques, Procedures for the registration of cryptographic algorithms.

ISO/IEC 10116:1991

Information technology, Modes of operation for an n-bit block cipher algorithm.

ISO/IEC 10118–1:1994

Information technology, Security techniques, Hash-functions, Part 1: General.

ISO/IEC 10118–2:1994

Information technology, Security techniques, Hash-functions, Part 2: Hash-functions using an n-bit block cipher algorithm.

ISO/IEC DIS 11770–2

Information technology, Security techniques, Key management, Part 2: Mechanisms using symmetric techniques.

ISO/IEC DTR 13335–1

Information technology, Guidelines for the management of IT security, Part 1: Concepts and models for IT security.

ISO/IEC DTR 13335–2

Information technology, Guidelines for the management of IT security, Part 2: Planning and managing IT security.

ISO/IEC DTR 13335–3

Information technology, Guidelines for the management of IT security, Part 3: Techniques for the management of IT security.

ISO/IEC DIS 14980

Information technology, Code of practice for information security management.

ISO DIS 10118a

"Information Technology, *Security Techniques: Hash Functions,*" International Organization for Standardization, 1989 (Draft).

ISO DIS 10118b

"Information Technology, *Security Techniques: Hash Functions,*" International Organization for Standardization, April 1991 (Draft).

ISO DIS 8730

"*Banking: Requirements for Message Authentication* (Wholesale)," Association for Payment Clearing Services, London, July 1987.

ISO DIS 8731–1

"*Banking:-Approved Algorithms for Message Authentication, Part 1:* DEA," Association for Payment Clearing Services, London, 1987.

ISO DIS 8731–2

"*Banking:-Approved Algorithms for Message Authentication, Part 2:* Message Authenticator Algorithm," Association for Payment Clearing Services, London, 1987.

ISO DIS 8732

"*Banking:-Key Management* (Wholesale)," Association for Payment Clearing Services, London, Dec 1987.

ISO N179

"*AR Fingerprint Function,*" working document, ISO-IEC/JTC1/SC27/WG2, International Organization for Standardization, 1992.

ISO N98

"*Hash Functions Using a Pseudo Random Algorithm,*" working document, ISO-IEC/JTC1/SC27/WG2, International Organization for Standardization, 1992.

ISO/IEC 10118

"*Information Technology, Security Techniques: Hash Functions,* Part 1: General and Part 2: Hash Functions Using an *n*-Bit Block Cipher Algorithm," International Organization for Standardization, 1993.

ISO/IEC 9796

"Information Technology, Security Techniques: *Digital Signature Scheme Giving Message Recovery,*" International Organization for Standardization, Jul 1991.

ISO/IEC 9797

"Data Cryptographic Techniques, *Data Integrity Mechanism Using a Cryptographic Check Function Employing a Block Cipher Algorithm,*" International Organization for Standardization, 1989.

ISO/IEC JTC1/SC 21

ISO/IEC JTC1/SC 21, Amendment 1 to ISO/IEC 9594–8:1995, *Information Technology, Open Systems Interconnection, The Directory: Authentication Framework, AMENDMENT 1: Certificate Extensions.*

ISO/IEC 8825

ISO/IEC 8825: *Information Technology-Open Systems Interconnection-Specification of ASN.1 Encoding Rules,* 1987 (also ITU-T X.690 series Recommendations).

ISO/IEC 9594–8

ISO/IEC 9594–8: *Information Technology, Open Systems Interconnection, The Directory, Authentication Framework,* 1988 (revised 1993) (also ITU-T Recommendation X.509).

ITU STANDARDS

[X.273]

Recommendation X.273, Information technology, Open Systems Interconnection, Network layer security protocol (9).

[X.274]

Recommendation X.274, Information technology, Telecommunication and information exchange between systems, transport layer security protocol (6).

[X.736]

Recommendation X.736, Information technology, Open Systems Interconnection, Systems management: Security alarm reporting function (6).

[X.736 SUMMARY]

Summary of Recommendation X.736, Information technology, open systems interconnection, systems management: security alarm reporting function (1).

[X.740]

Recommendation X.740, Information technology, Open Systems Interconnection, systems management: security audit trail function (6).

[X.800]

Recommendation X.800, Security architecture for Open Systems Interconnection for CCITT applications (6).

[X.802]

Recommendation X.802, Information technology, Lower layers security model (2).

[X.803]

Recommendation X.803, Information Technology, Open Systems Interconnection, Upper layers security model (2).

ATM NETWORKING STANDARDS

B–ICI

Broadband Intercarrier Interface.

P–NNI

Public Network-to-Network Interface.

IEEE 1363 STANDARD

IEEE P1363:

Standard Specifications for Public Key Cryptography.

RAINBOW SERIES

CSC-STD-002–85

DoD Password Management Guideline, 12 April 1985.

CSC-STD-004–85

Technical Rational Behind CSC-STD-003–85: Computer Security Requirements, Guidance for Applying the DoD TCSEC in Specific Environments, 25 June 1985.

NTISSAM COMPUSEC/1–87

Advisory Memorandum on Office Automation Security Guidelines.

NCSC-TG-004

Glossary of Computer Security Terms, 21 October 1988.

NCSC-TG-005

Trusted Network Interpretation (TNI) of the Trusted Computer System Evaluation Criteria (TCSEC), [Red Book] 1987.

NCSC-TG-009

Computer Security Subsystem Interpretation of the TCSEC 16 September 1988.

NCSC-TG-010

A Guide to Understanding Security Modeling in Trusted Systems, October 1992.

NCSCTG-011

Trusted Network Interpretation Environments Guideline, August 1990.

NCSC-TG-017

A Guide to Understanding Identification and Authentication in Trusted Systems, September 1991.

NCSC-TG-020-A

Trusted UNIX Working Group (TRU-SIX) Rationale for Selecting Access Control List Features for the UNIX® System, 7 July 1989.

NCSC-TG-021

Trusted Database Management System Interpretation of the TCSEC (TDI), April 1991.

NCSC-TG-022

A Guide to Understanding Trusted Recovery in Trusted Systems, 30 December 1991.

NCSC-TG-023

A Guide to Understanding Security Testing and Test Documentation in Trusted Systems.

NCSC-TG-024 Vol 1/4

A Guide to Procurement of Trusted Systems: An Introduction to Procurement Initiators on Computer Security Requirements, December 1992.

NCSC-TG-024 Vol 3/4

A Guide to Procurement of Trusted Systems: Computer Security Contract Data Requirements List and Data Item Description Tutorial, 28 February 1994.

NCSC-TG-026

A Guide to Writing the Security Features User's Guide for Trusted Systems, September 1991.

NCSC-TG-027

A Guide to Understanding Information System Security Officer Responsibilities for Automated Information Systems, May 1992.

NCSC-TG-028

Assessing Controlled Access Protection, 25 May 1992.

OTHER NCSC PUBLICATIONS

C1 Technical Report 001

Technical Report, Computer Viruses: Prevention, Detection, and Treatment, 12 March 1990.

C Technical Report 79–91

Technical Report, Integrity in Automated Information Systems, September 1991.

C Technical Report 32–92

The Design and Evaluation of INFOSEC systems: The Computer Security Contribution to the Composition Discussion, June 1992.

C Technical Report 111–91

Integrity-Oriented Control Objectives: Proposed Revisions to the TCSEC, October 1991.

NCSC Technical Report 002

Use of the TCSEC for Complex, Evolving, Mulitpolicy Systems.

NCSC Technical Report 003

Turning Multiple Evaluated Products Into Trusted Systems.

NCSC Technical Report 004

A Guide to Procurement of Single Connected Systems, Language for RFP Specifications and Statements of Work, An Aid to Procurement Initiators, Includes Complex, Evolving, and Multipolicy Systems.

NCSC Technical Report 005 Volume 1/5

Inference and Aggregation Issues In Secure Database Management Systems.

NCSC Technical Report 005 Volume 2/5

Entity and Referential Integrity Issues In Multilevel Secure Database Management.

NCSC Technical Report 005 Volume 3/5
Polyinstantiation Issues In Multilevel
Secure Database Management Systems.

NCSC Technical Report 005 Volume 4/5
Auditing Issues In Secure Database Management Systems.

NCSC Technical Report 005 Volume 5/5
Discretionary Access Control Issues In
High Assurance Secure Database Management Systems.

PUBLIC KEY CRYPTOGRAPHIC STANDARD (PKCS)

PKCS #1:
RSA Encryption and Signature.

PKCS #3:
Diffie–Hellman Key Agreement.

PKCS #5:
Password-based Encryption.

PKCS #6:
Extended Certificate Syntax.

PKCS #7:
Cryptographic Message Syntax.

PKCS #8:
Private Key Information Syntax.

PKCS #9:
Selected Attribute Syntaxes.

PKCS #10:
Certificate Request Syntax.

PKCS #11:
Abstract Token Interface API.

OTHER DOCUMENTS

CCEB
Common Criteria for Information Technology Security Evaluation, Version 2.0. May 1998.

CEC91
Commission of the European Communities. *Information Technology Security Evaluation Criteria (ITSEC)*, Version 1.2, 1991.

CEC93
Commission of the European Communities. *Information Technology Security Evaluation Manual (ITSEM)*, 1993.

CSSC
Canadian System Security Centre. *The Canadian Trusted Computer Product Evaluation Criteria*, Version 3.0e, 1993.

DoD 5200.28-STD
Department of Defense (DoD) Trusted Computer System Evaluation Criteria (TCSEC), [Orange Book], DoD 5200.28-STD, December 1985.

DoD 5200.28-STD
U.S. Department of Defense. *DoD Trusted Computer System Evaluation Criteria, (Orange Book)* DoD 5200.28-STD, 1985.

DoD 5220.22-M
U.S. Department of Defense. *Industrial Security Manual for Safeguarding Classified Information*, DoD 5220.22-M, June 1987.

CFR 120–130
Department of State, "*International Traffic in Arms Regulations* (ITAR)," 22 CFR 120–130, Office of Munitions Control, Nov 1989.

DoT85
Department of the Treasury, "*Criteria and Procedures for Testing, Evaluating, and Certifying Message Authentication Decisions for Federal E.F.T Use*," Department of Treasury, 1 May 1985.

DoT86

Department of the Treasury, *"Electronic Funds and Securities Transfer Policy, Message Authentication and Enhanced Security,"* Order No. 106–09, Department of Treasury, 2 Oct 1986.

NIST92

National Institute of Standards and Technology & National Security Agency. *Federal Criteria for Information Technology Security,* Version 1.0, 1992.

SET Book 3

SET, *Secure Electronic Transaction Specification*

Book3: Formal Protocol Definition, Version 1.0, May 31, 1997.

SHS92

"Proposed Federal Information Processing Standard for Secure Hash Standard," *Federal Register,* v.57, n. 21,31 Jan 1992, pp. 3747–3749.

TRU87 X800

Secure Architecture for Open Systems Interconnection for CCITT Applications (Recommendation X.800), CCITT, Geneva, 1991.

LIST OF ANNOTATED WEB RESOURCES

APPENDIX

D

The following collection of World Wide Web resources may interest the reader. I have consulted many of these sites while searching for the most appropriate and up-to-date description of terms, and if a site seemed to me to have potential value for the reader, I have included it in this list. The sites are of diverse origin, from government, nonprofit organizations, and commercial organizations, and they include both U.S. and international sites.

This list is by no means complete; the Web is a vast and dynamic place, and any list will be obsolete in a short time. However, I believe this list has staying power because many sites in the list are stable and generic, such as www.cert.org, www.ietf.org, www.ieee.org. These URLs will not change frequently, and this list of resources is quite comprehensive.

This listing is organized as follows: it is sorted alphabetically, and the name of the resource is given in bold letters, followed by a brief description of the contents of the site. Following these is the URL of the site. These URLs were active at the date of this writing.

■ **A brief history of codes and ciphers used in the Second World War**

This Web site was created by Tony Sales, and it describes the history, science, and engineering of cryptanalysis in World War II. It contains links to Enigma, original World War II documents such as the German manual for the naval use of Enigma, technical lectures by Tony Sales, links related to Bletchley Park, including the Bletchley Park Cryptographic Dictionary, and many other sources of historical interest.

http://www.codesandciphers.org.uk/

■ **ACM special interest group on security audit and control**

This is the home page of the special interest group on security audit and control of the Association of Computing Machinery (ACM). ACM is the oldest and perhaps most widely known computer science professional organization. The Web page of the special interest group is home to many security resources.

http://www.acm.org/sigsac/#top

■ **Advanced Computing Systems Association (USENIX)**

This Web site of USENIX (Advanced Computing Systems Association) has links to various sources of information and conferences.

http://www.usenix.org/

■ **American National Standards Institute**

This is the official Web site of the American National Standards Institute and contains access to information on the ANSI Federation and the latest national and international standards and related activities.

http://www.ansi.org/

■ **An Introduction to Secure Socket Layer (SSL)**

This Web site, maintained by Netscape Corporation, contains introduction, resources, and documentation related to the Secure Sockets Layer (SSL) protocol. SSL is used on the World Wide Web for authenticated and encrypted communication between clients and servers.

http://developer.netscape.com/docs/manuals/security/sslin/index.htm

■ **Canadian Communications Security Establishment**

This Web site is maintained by the Communications Security Establishment (CSE) of the Canadian government with a purpose to provide information technology security (ITS) solutions to the government of Canada. It has links to Canadian Common Criteria Scheme, information technology educational resources, and various other information.

http://www.cse.dnd.ca/

■ **Cipher, An IEEE electronic newsletter of the Technical Committee on Security and Privacy (IEEE/CS)**

This Web site contains **Cipher**, IEEE's electronic newsletter of the Technical Committee on Security and Privacy (IEEE/CS) and provides a past-issue archive, cipher book reviews, cipher news briefs, a cipher reader's guide to literature, and other information.

http://www.ieee-security.org/cipher.html

■ **Common Criteria for IT Security Evaluation (CC)**

This is NIST's Web site on the Common Criteria Project for IT security evaluation (CC) and contains various CC-related documents. It also contains links to "official" CC Project Web site at http://www.commoncriteria.org and the NIAP Web site at http://niap.nist.gov.

http://csrc.ncsl.nist.gov/cc

■ **Common Data Security Architecture**

This Web site is maintained by Intel and has information about Intel Common Data Security Architecture (CDSA) including downloads, documentation, FAQs, technical information, adopters, and specifications.

http://www.intel.com/ial/security/index.htm

■ **Computer Emergency Response Team (CERT), Australia**

This is the official site of Australian CERT. Although regional in nature, it contains a list of downloadable security-related software and links to many technical reports, security contacts, and other valuable information.

http://www.auscert.org.au/

■ **Computer Emergency Response Team (CERT), Coordination Center**

This is the official Web site of CERT. In addition to containing security advisories, alerts, and incident notes, this site is a good source of technical papers and information about Internet security. It also contains CERT statistics, current intruder trends, and many reports issued by CERT staff related to security. A very good site, I highly recommend it for regular browsing.

http://www.cert.org/

■ **Computer Society Institute**

This Web site is maintained by the Computer Security Institute. It has links to security archives, technical reports, news, and a host of other resources.

http://www.gocsi.com/

■ **Cyptography organization**

This Web site is maintained by Michael Paul Johnson and contains North American Cryptography archives. In addition, it contains links to various cryptographic resources and sites.

http://cryptography.org/

■ **Cryptographic policies of countries**

Crypto law survey by Bert-Jaap Koops. This page contains reports that analyze cryptographic policies of different countries. An excellent and information-filled report with good analysis.

http://cwis.kub.nl/~frw/people/koops/lawsurvy.htm

■ **Draft of UNCITRAL Model Law for electronic commerce: issues and solutions**

An article that explains proposal Draft UNCITRAL Model Law for electronic commerce and deals with the legal issues related to the law. Written by Richard Hill and Ian Walden, this article was published in the March 1996 issue of *The Computer Lawyer*.

http://www.batnet.com/oikoumene/arbunc.html

■ **Electronic Frontier Foundation**

This Web site is maintained by the Electronic Frontier Foundation (EFF), a nonprofit, non-partisan organization with a purpose to protect fundamental civil liberties, including privacy and freedom of expression in the arena of computers and the Internet. This site contains links to some excellent resources and discussions.

http://www.eff.org/

■ **European Committee for Standardization**

The Web site of the European Committee for Standardization, responsible for voluntary technical harmonization in Europe in conjunction with worldwide bodies and European partners. This body also develops procedures for mutual recognition and conformity assessment to standards. Contains information on where to obtain European standards.

http://www.cenorm.be/

■ **Federation of American Scientists (FAS)**

This Web site of the Federation of American Scientists contains papers, discussions, and important links to a variety of topics including military analysis, special weapons, and intelligence.

http://www.fas.org/

■ **Forum of Incident Response and Security Teams**

This is the official Web site of FIRST and contains information about FIRST, recent events, conferences, contacts, and other information.

http://www.first.org/

■ **IEEE Computer Society, Security and Privacy Section**

Maintained by IEEE computer Society, this Web site provides publications center, communities, standards, career services center, and information about education and certifications.

http://www.computer.org/cspress/catalog9.htm#sec-priv

■ **IEEE Computer Society Technical Committee on Security and Privacy**

This Web site, maintained by IEEE Computer Society Technical Committee on Security and Privacy (TCSP), provides links to Cipher, the TCSP electronic newsletter, upcoming conferences, TCSP contacts, and various reports of the society.

http://www.ieee-security.org/index.html

■ **IEEE Standard Specifications for Public-Key Cryptography**

This is the official Web site for IEEE P1363 (IEEE has now adopted it as a standard) home page maintained by IEEE and contains Standard Specifications for Public-Key Cryptography. The complete IEEE 1363 and other draft documents are available through this Web site.

http://grouper.ieee.org/groups/1363/

■ **IETF Working group on Authenticated Firewall Traversal**

This Web site contains a general introduction to the IETF working group on authenticated firewall traversal.

http://www.ietf.cnri.reston.va.us/html.charters/aft-charter.html

■ **IETF Working group on Common Authentication Technology**

This Web site contains a general introduction to the IETF working group on authentication technology.

http://www.ietf.cnri.reston.va.us/html.charters/cat-charter.html

■ **IETF Working group on Intrusion Detection Exchange Format**

This Web site contains a general introduction to the IETF working group on intrusion-detection exchange format.

http://www.ietf.cnri.reston.va.us/html.charters/idwg-charter.html

■ **IETF Working group on IP Security Protocol**

This Web site contains a general introduction to the IETF working group on IP security protocol.

http://www.ietf.cnri.reston.va.us/html.charters/ipsec-charter.html

■ **IETF Working group on IP Security Policy**

This Web site contains a general introduction to the IETF working group on IP security policy.

http://www.ietf.cnri.reston.va.us/html.charters/ipsp-charter.html

■ **IETF Working group on IP Security Remote Access**

This Web site contains a general introduction to the IETF working group on IP security remote access.

http://www.ietf.cnri.reston.va.us/html.charters/ipsra-charter.html

■ **IETF Working group on Kerberized Internet Negotiation of Keys**

This Web site contains a general introduction to the IETF working group on kerberized Internet negotiation of keys.

http://www.ietf.cnri.reston.va.us/html.charters/kink-charter.html

■ **IETF Working group on Kerberos WG**

This Web site contains a general introduction to the IETF working group on Kerberos WG.

http://www.ietf.cnri.reston.va.us/html.charters/krb-wg-charter.html

■ **IETF Working group on Multicast Security**

This Web site contains a general introduction to the IETF working group on multicast security.

http://www.ietf.cnri.reston.va.us/html.charters/msec-charter.html

■ **IETF Working group on an Open Specification for Pretty Good Privacy**

This Web site contains a general introduction to the IETF working group on an open specification for pretty good privacy.

http://www.ietf.cnri.reston.va.us/html.charters/openpgp-charter.html

■ **IETF Working group on One Time Password Authentication**

This Web site contains a general introduction to the IETF working group on one time password authentication.

http://www.ietf.cnri.reston.va.us/html.charters/otp-charter.html

■ **IETF Working group on Public-Key Infrastructure (X.509)**

This Web site contains a general introduction to the IETF working group on Public-Key Infrastructure (X.509)

http://www.ietf.cnri.reston.va.us/html.charters/pkix-charter.html

■ **IETF Working group on Securely Available Credentials**

This Web site contains a general introduction to the IETF working group on securely available credentials.

http://www.ietf.cnri.reston.va.us/html.charters/sacred-charter.html

■ **IETF Working group on Secure Shell**

This Web site contains a general introduction to the IETF working group on secure shell.

http://www.ietf.cnri.reston.va.us/html.charters/secsh-charter.html

■ **IETF Working group on S/MIME Mail Security**

This Web site contains a general introduction to the IETF working group on S/MIME mail security.

http://www.ietf.cnri.reston.va.us/html.charters/smime-charter.html

■ **IETF Working group on Secure Network Time Protocol**

This Web site contains a general introduction to the IETF working group on secure network protocol.

http://www.ietf.cnri.reston.va.us/html.charters/stime-charter.html

■ **IETF Working group on Security Issues in Network Event Logging**

This Web site contains a general introduction to the IETF working group on security issues in network event logging.

http://www.ietf.cnri.reston.va.us/html.charters/syslog-charter.html

■ **IETF Working group on Transport Layer Security**

This Web site contains a general introduction to the IETF working group on transport layer security.

http://www.ietf.cnri.reston.va.us/html.charters/tls-charter.html

■ **IETF Working group on Web Transaction Security**

This Web site contains a general introduction to the IETF working group on Web transaction security.

http://www.ietf.cnri.reston.va.us/html.charters/wts-charter.html

■ **IETF Working group on XML Digital Signatures**

This Web site provides a general introduction of XML digital signatures.

http://www.ietf.cnri.reston.va.us/html.charters/xmldsig-charter.html

■ **Information about cryptology and encryption challenges**

This is the official Web site of RSA Security (the organization that developed the RSA algorithm) and is an excellent source of information related to information security in general and cryptography in particular. In addition to security-related news, it contains information about RSA conferences and contains pointers to RSA products and services.

http://www.rsa.com

■ **Information about prime numbers**

This page contains detailed links to information about prime numbers.

http://www.utm.edu/research/primes/

■ **Information about Secure Socket Layer (SSL)**

This site is maintained by Netscape Corporation and contains draft SSL 3.0 specifications. The Web page also contains links to additional information to aid implementation of SSL 3.0.

http://www.netscape.com/eng/ssl3

■ **Information on Certification and Public Key infrastructure**

This Web site of commercial vendors Entrust and Verisign contains good information related to Internet security, certification, and public key infrastructure.

http://www.entrust.com
http://verisign.com

■ **Information on IBM's Remote Access Control Facility**

This site contains information about IBM's Remote Control Access Control Facility (RACF) Software. This software is available for both the OS/390 and Z/OS operating systems. This site contains links to a PDF file *OS/390 Security Server Introduction,* a good source of information related to access control in operating systems.

http://www-1.ibm.com/servers/eserver/zseries/zos/racf/

■ **Information on Microsoft's Security**

This is the Microsoft Web site related to security. It contains links to important resources for security developers, security bulletins, and security-related columns.

http://microsoft.com/security

■ **Information on Multics**

This Web site is a good source of information about the Multics operating system. In addition to containing a list of documents related to Multics, it contains a history of Multics, and the name and links to Web pages of people who contributed to Multics. There are 1411 names, 510 mail addresses, 109 home pages. It also contains links to a collection of 15 select technical papers about Multics.

http://www.multicians.org/multics.html

■ **Information on Internet Protocol Version 6 (IPv6)**

These Web site provides general information on IPv6, including IPv6 specifications and the latest news and links.

http://www.ipv6.org/

Another good source for information on IPv6 is the Sun Microsystems site at

http://playground.sun.com/pub/ipng/html/ipng-main.html

■ **Information related to Public Key Infrastructure**

This page contains links to various sites and documents, related to Public Key Infrastructure (PKI) and extensive links to Certification Authorities (CAs) licensed by various agencies. An excellent source of information related to CAs.

http://www.pki-page.org/

■ **Information Security Forum**

This Web site is maintained by Information Security Forum (previously known as European Security Forum). The Information Security Forum meets the demand for business-based solutions to information security problems.

http://www.securityforum.org

■ **Information Systems Security Association**

The Web site of the Information Systems Security Association (ISSA), a nonprofit international organization of information security professionals and practitioners, provides education forums, publications, and peer-interaction opportunities.

http://www.issa-intl.org/

■ **Information Security Solutions Europe**

This Web site is maintained by the European Forum for Electronic Business. The link below is of the Information Security Solutions Europe (ISSE) conference, which presents the latest developments and concerns for IT Security, including Encryption, Data Protection, Biometrics, Business Models for Trusted Services, Risk Management, PKI, Smart Cards, Digital Signatures, Legal Issues.

http://www.eema.org/isse/

■ **INFOSEC publication, European Commission**

This site is published by INFOSEC, DG Information Society of the European Commission, and contains detailed information and links related to European Trust Services (ETS) and various other reports. The site also contains common criteria (now an international standard IS 15408), which supersedes Information Technology Security Evaluation Criteria (ITSEC). In addition, a report of a recent evaluation of ETS is also available at

http://www.cordis.lu/infosec/src/ets.htm.
http://www.cordis.lu/infosec/home.html

■ **Infosyssec, The security portal for Information System Security Professionals**

An excellent resource on information security. This Web site contains links to security-related standards, reports, general interest articles, and many other resources.

www.infosyssec.net/infosyssec/secstan1.htm

■ **Institute of Information Security**

This Web site is maintained by the Institute of Information Security and provides a forum to discuss security-related issues and links to extensive resources, newsletters, education, and archives.

http://www.instis.com/

■ **International Association for Cryptologic Research**

The official Web site of the International Association for Cryptologic Research (IACR), this site contains information about IACR publications, conferences, membership, etc.

http://www.iacr.org/~iacr/

■ **(The) International PGP Home Page**

This Web site is maintained for the promotion of PGP use and has many mirror sites around the world. A very good source for documentation, download, FAQ, Internet links, language, products, and services related to PGP.

http://www.pgpi.org/

■ **International Organization for Standardization**

The official site of the International Organization for Standardization (ISO), this site contains detailed history and news about ISO9000, and other important information.

http://www.iso.ch/

■ **International Telecommunication Union**

This is the home page of the International Telecommunication Union (ITU) and contains links and information related to telecommunication technology, regulations and standards information. Publications can be purchased through the ITU Publications Online subscription service.

http://www.itu.int/home/index.html

■ **Internet Research Task Force**

The home page of the Internet Research Task Force (IRTF) provides an overview of IRTF and links to the Internet Engineering Task Force (IETF) and Internet Society (ISOC). The IRTF is managed by the IRTF Chair in consultation with the Internet Research Steering Group (IRSG).

http://www.irtf.org/

■ **Introduction to Cryptographic Standards**

This site is a pointer to an article by Richard Ankney that introduces cryptographic standards.

http://chacs.nrl.navy.mil/ieee/cipher/standards/cipher-crypto-stds.html

■ Introduction to Elliptic Curve Cryptography

This Web site is maintained by Integrated Sciences Incorporated, and the page (see the address below) contains an excellent (though general) introduction to elliptic curve cryptography. The concepts are explained with graphs, and the site also contains links to research papers and other sources related to password verification.

http://world.std.com/~dpj/elliptic.html

■ Java Cryptography Architecture

This server is maintained by Sun Microsystems and contains detailed technical information on Java cryptography architecture, API specifications, and reference.

http://java.sun.com/products/jdk/1.1/docs/guide/security/CryptoSpec.html

■ Keyed hash functions for message authentication

The site for IBM research contains pointers to some excellent papers. A list of papers related to keyed hash functions for message authentication are available at

http://www.research.ibm.com/security/keyed-md5.html.

■ List of all RFCs

This site is the IETF repository for Internet Requests for Comments (RFCs). The RFCs can be obtained by RFC number. The site also contains a complete index of RFCs. The site itself does not have an index or search feature, but these features are available at the RFC Editor Web page.

http://ietf.org/rfc.html

■ National Institute of Standards and Technology (NIST)

This site contains information about a variety of computer security issues, products, and research of concern to federal agencies, industry, and users. This site is run and maintained by NISTs Computer Security Division as a service to the computer security and IT community.

http://csrc.ncsl.nist.gov/

■ National Cryptologic Museum

This is the official Web site of the National Cryptologic Museum and is maintained by the National Security Agency.

http://www.nsa.gov/museum/

■ National Security Agency

This is the official Web site of the U.S. National Security Agency (NSA).

http://www.nsa.gov

■ **National Security Institute's Security Resource Net**

The National Security Institute's Web site is an excellent resource for Internet security. This site contains industry and product news, computer alerts, travel advisories, a calendar of events, a directory of products and services, and access to an extensive virtual security library.

http://nsi.org/

■ **Navy's Center for High Assurance Computing Systems**

This is the home page of the Center for High Assurance Computer Systems, within the Information Technology Division of the Naval Research Laboratory. The Center for High Assurance Computing Systems conducts interdisciplinary research and development in security-related systems. This site contains links to government and security-related Web servers; of particular interest are downloadable copies of High Assurance Workshop Reports.

http://chacs.nrl.navy.mil/main_fra.html.

■ **NIST's Advanced Encryption Standard (AES) Development Effort**

This Web site contains a Draft Federal Information Processing Standard (FIPS) for the AES for public review and comment. The site also contains important links including links to pages for public comments to the Rijndael (AES) algorithm, an AES discussion forum, and archived AES home pages.

http://csrc.nist.gov/encryption/aes/

■ **NIST's Computer Security Publications**

This is an excellent site that contains links to the NIST computer security resources clearing-house Web server, Rainbow series publications, FIPS, special publications, interagency reports, ITL bulletins, POSIX, and other miscellaneous resources.

http://csrc.ncsl.nist.gov/publications.html

■ **PKCS set of documents**

The Web site of RSA Security contains documents PKCS#1 through PKCS#11 for download. Here is a list of document names and the corresponding URL.

ftp://ftp.rsa.com/pub/pkcs/ps/

■ **PKCS #1: RSA Encryption and Signature**

This Web site contains an introduction to the RSA encryption standard.

ftp://ftp.rsa.com/pub/pkcs/ps/pkcs-1.ps

■ **PKCS #3: Diffie–Hellman Key Agreement**

Introduction to the Diffie–Hellman key agreement standard.

ftp://ftp.rsa.com/pub/pkcs/ps/pkcs-3.ps

■ **PKCS #5: Password-based Encryption**

Introduction to password-based encryption standards.

ftp://ftp.rsa.com/pub/pkcs/ps/pkcs-5.ps

■ **PKCS #6: Extended Certificate Syntax**

Introduction to extended certificate syntax standards.

ftp://ftp.rsa.com/pub/pkcs/ps/pkcs-6.ps

■ **PKCS #7: Cryptographic Message Syntax**

ftp://ftp.rsa.com/pub/pkcs/ps/pkcs-7.ps

■ **PKCS #8: Private Key Information Syntax**

Introduction to private key information syntax.

ftp://ftp.rsa.com/pub/pkcs/ps/pkcs-8.ps

■ **PKCS #9: Selected Attribute Syntaxes**

Introduction to selected attribute syntaxes.

ftp://ftp.rsa.com/pub/pkcs/ps/pkcs-9.ps

■ **PKCS #10: Certificate Request Syntax**

Introduction to certificate request syntax.

ftp://ftp.rsa.com/pub/pkcs/ps/pkcs-10.ps

■ **PKCS #11: Abstract Token Interface API**

Introduction to abstract token interface API.

ftp://ftp.rsa.com/pub/pkcs/ps/pkcs-11.ps

■ **Quantum Cryptography**

This paper by Gilles Brassard, of McGill University, provides an extensive annotated bibliography of papers on quantum cryptography and related topics.

http://www.cs.mcgill.ca/~crepeau/CRYPTO/Biblio-QC.html

■ **Rainbow Series Library**

This Web site contains a listing and links to the documents in the Rainbow series. Documents are available in text, postscript, and PDF format. It also contains a postscript gzip archive.

www.radium.ncsc.mil/tpep/library/rainbow/

■ **Resource for Computer Threat and Vulnerability**

This site is maintained by Internet Security Systems and contains excellent information and literature about computer threats and vulnerabilities, news about latest vulnerabilities, patches, and other information. The security alerts and virtual library are extensive and useful. The search options on the main page provide capabilities to search by product, platform, and months.

http://xforce.iss.net/

■ Resource on Mac-Crypto (Macintosh Cryptography)

This Web site provides Macintosh Crypto Web resources and contains links to past crypto conferences of 2001, 1998, 1997, 1996.

http://www.vmeng.com/mc/

■ SANS Institute

This is the Web site of the SANS (System Administration, Networking, and Security) Institute, a cooperative research and training organization. It contains excellent resources related to Internet security.

http://www.sans.org/

■ Secure Electronic Marketplace for Europe

This Web site is maintained by Secure Electronic Marketplace for Europe (SEMPER) and the Web site http://www.semper.org/sirene/ maintained by SIRENE (SIcherheit in REchner-NEtzen / Security in Computer Networks) and an excellent source of information and standards in computer network security. SIRENE is a loosely collaborating group of researchers from different organizations with a common interest in security and privacy. Information on electronic commerce, payment systems, and security is available at

http://www.semper.org/sirene/outsideworld/ecommerce.html#syst
http://www.semper.org/

■ Security-related news and information

This site is an on-line news service organized by SC Magazine and a global security portal. Key links associated with a reported news item direct the reader to further relevant sources of information.

http://www.infosecnews.com/

■ Simple Key management for Internet Protocols (SKIP)

This Web site contains information about SKIP: Simple Key management for Internet Protocols, including technical specifications, the latest news and items about SKIP, interoperability testing, and technical papers.

http://skip.incog.com/

■ **Software Industry Issues: Digital Signatures**

This Web site is maintained by Software Industry organization. The URL of the page given below contains comprehensive information about digital signature laws, reference material, commercial sites, vendor CPSs, and other encryption and privacy information.

http://www.softwareindustry.org/issues/1digsig.html#sl

■ **SRI technical report on UNIX security**

This site contains the Stanford Research Institute (SRI) report "Improving the Security of Your UNIX System" by David A. Curry. The report has some very useful information related to security of UNIX systems.

www.sri.ucl.ac.be/SRI/documents/unix-secure

■ **The IETF Security Area**

This Web page represents the security area of the IETF. This page contains links to Security Area Working Group Web pages and other status information related to security.

http://web.mit.edu/network/ietf/sa/

■ **The UK ITSEC scheme**

This is the official Web site of the UK Information Technology Security Evaluation & Certification Scheme and contains a good description of assurance levels for software products and guidelines in achieving them. The site also has a list of certified products, a collection documents, and latest news releases.

http://www.itsec.gov.uk/

■ **Theory and practice related to random number generation**

This server is maintained by a team of mathematicians and computer scientists led by Peter Hellekalek at the University of Salzburg's mathematics department and contains links to tests, literature, news, and software related to random number generation.

http://random.mat.sbg.ac.at/

■ **Useful Resources on ASN.1**

This Web site maintained by OSS Nokalava, a New Jersey, USA-based company, contains excellent information about ASN.1 including questions and answers, glossary, and reference books.

http://www.oss.com/asn1/index.html

■ **U.S. federal guidelines for searching and seizing computers**

This site is maintained by EPIC and contains U.S. federal guidelines for searching and seizing computers. EPIC has made an analysis of this document, available from http://cpsr.org

/cpsr/privacy/epic/guidelines_analysis.txt. A printed version appears in the Bureau of National Affairs publication *Criminal Law Reporter*, Vol. 56, No. 12 (December 21, 1994).

http://www.epic.org/security/computer_search_guidelines.txt

■ **Virus Bulletin**

This is the home page of the Virus Bulletin and contains information on developments in the field of computer viruses and antivirus products.

http://www.virusbtn.com/

■ **Web site of Internet Engineering Task Force**

This is the official Web site of the Internet Engineering Task Force (IETF). It contains a host of information related to IETF purpose and mission, activities, working groups, etc. In addition it contains links to Internet drafts and Internet Request for Comments.

http://www.ietf.org

■ **Workshop on Selected Areas in Cryptography (SAC)**

This Web site contains information on workshops on Selected Areas in Cryptography (SAC) and has links and papers of SAC '99 through SAC '94.

http://adonis.ee.queensu.ca:8000/sac/

■ **World Wide Web Consortium**

The official site of World Wide Web Consortium (W3C) contains W3C news and links to information about W3C technologies. W3C develops specifications, guidelines, software, and tools to use the full potential of the Web for information, commerce, communication, and collective understanding. An excellent site to keep up to date related to Web standards and technologies.

BIBLIOGRAPHY

Why add a bibliography to a dictionary? Internet security is passing from its adolescence to adulthood. Its literature is rich and is growing every day. The goal of preparing this bibliography is to stress the importance of some excellent references available as books, technical reports, research papers, and government documents. A separate list provides published standards and RFCs.

This bibliography does not document the evolutionary or historical record of Internet security; it is also not an attempt to cite the works of established researchers or specific organizations. Several of these documents were referenced while I formulated the most appropriate description of a term. For anything that was unclear I consulted with the experts on the Technical Advisory Committee to come up with the final description. Some valuable references may not be explicitly cited in the description of terms, but these are listed in the bibliography due to their relevance and inherent importance to the field of Internet security. An interested reader should scan through these titles for references of interest.

BOOKS

AJM93   A.J. Menezes. *Elliptic Curve Public Key Cryptosystem,* Kluwer Academic Publishers, Boston, 1993.

AJM97   A.J. Menezes, P.C. Van Oorschot, and S.A. Vanstone. *Handbook of Applied Cryptography.* CRC Press, Boca Raton, FL, 1997.

AK81   A. Konheim. *Cryptography: A Primer,* John Wiley & Sons, 1981.

AR97   A. Rubin, D. Geer, and M. Ranum. *Web Security Sourcebook.* Wiley, New York, 1997.

AT87   A. Tanenbaum. *Operating Systems: Design and Implementation,* Prentice Hall, Englewood Cliffs, NJ, 1987.

Bibliography

AT88   A. Tanenbaum. *Computer Networks,* Prentice Hall, Englewood Cliffs, NJ, 1988.

BP91   B. Plattner, C. Lanz, H. Lubich, M. Muller, T. Walker. *X.400 Message Handling: Standards, Interworking, Applications,* Addison-Wesley, Reading, MA, 1991.

BS00   B. Schneier, *Secrets and Lies,* Wiley, New York, 2000.

BS96   B. Schneier. *Applied Cryptography: Protocols, Algorithms, and Source Code in C,* Wiley, New York, 1996.

CK95   C. Kaufman, R. Perlman, and M. Speciner. *Network Security: Private Communications in a Public World,* Prentice Hall, Englewood Cliffs, NJ, 1995.

CM82   C. Meyer and S. Matyas. *Cryptography: A New Dimension in Computer Data Security,* Wiley, New York, 1982.

CO91   T. Cormen, C. Leiserson, and R. Rivest, *Introduction to Algorithms,* MIT Press, Cambridge, MA, 1991.

CP89   C. Pfleeger. *Security in Computing,* Prentice Hall, Englewood Cliffs, NJ, 1989.

CP97   C. Pfleeger. *Security in Computing.* Prentice Hall, Englewood Cliffs, NJ, 1997.

CS89   C. Stoll. *The Cuckoo's Egg: Tracing a Spy Through the Maze of Computer Espionage,* Doubleday, New York, 1989.

CS91   C. Sandler, T. Badgett, and L. Lefkowitz. *VAX Security,* Wiley, New York, 1991.

DA97   D. Atkins, P. Buis, C. Hare, R. Kelley, C. Nachenberg, A.B. Nelson, P. Philips, T. Ritchey, T. Sheldon, and J. Snyder. *Internet Security.* New Riders, Indianapolis, IN, 2nd edition, 1997.

DAC92   D.A. Curry. *Unix System Security.* Addison-Wesley, Reading, MA, 1992.

DC95   D. Chapman and E. Zwicky. *Building Internet Firewalls,* O'Reilly & Associates, Inc., Sebastopol, CA, 1995.

DC00   D. Comer. *Internetworking with TCP/IP, Volume I: Principles, Protocols and Architecture.* Prentice Hall, Englewood Cliffs, NJ, 2000.

DD89   D. Davies and W. Price. *Security for Computer Networks.* Wiley, New York, 1989.

DED82   D.E. Denning and E.R. Dorothy. *Cryptography and Data Security,* Addison-Wesley, Reading, MA, 1982.

DEK69   D.E. Knuth., *The Art of Computer Programming: Seminumerical Algorithms,* Volume 2, Addison-Wesley, Reading, MA, 1969.

DF92   D. Ferbrache. *A Pathology of Computer Viruses.* Springer-Verlag, London, 1992.

DG99   D. Gollmann. *Computer Security.* Wiley, New York, 1999.

DK67   D. Kahn. *The Codebreakers: The Story of Secret Writing,* Macmillan, New York, 1967.

DP93   D. Piscitello and A.L. Chapin. *Open Systems Networking: TCP/IP and OSI*, Addison-Wesley, Reading, MA, 1993.

DR91   D. Russel, and G.T. Gangemi. *Computer Security Basics*, O'Reilly & Associates, Inc., Sebastopol, CA, July 1991.

DWD84   D.W. Davies and W.L. Price. *Security for Computer Networks*, Wiley, New York, 1984.

FC94   F. Cohen. *A Short Course on Computer Viruses*. Wiley, New York, 1994.

GM97   G. McGraw and E.W. Felten. *Java Security*. Wiley, New York, 1997.

GD72   Gerrold, David, *When Harlie Was One*, Ballantine Books, New York, 1972. The first edition.

HFG56   H.F. Gaines. *Crypatnalysis*, Dover, New York, 1956.

JAC89   J.A. Cooper. *Computer and Communications Security: Strategies for the 1990s*, McGraw-Hill, New York, 1989.

JF99   J. Feghhi, J. Feghhi and P. Williams. *Digital Certificates: Applied Internet Security*. Addison-Wesley, Reading, MA, 1999.

JM94   J. McLean. Security models. In J. Marciniak, editor, *Encyclopedia of Software Engineering*. Wiley, New York, 1994.

JS89   J. Seberry and J. Pieprzyk. *Cryptography: An Introduction to Computer Security*, Prentice Hall, Englewood Cliffs, NJ, 1989.

MG88   M. Gasser. *Building a Secure Computer System*, Van Nostrand Reinhold, New York, 1988.

NL96   N. Lynch, *Distributed Algorithms*, Morgan Kauffman, San Francisco, 1996.

PRZ95   P.R. Zimmerman. *The Official PGP User's Guide*, MIT Press, Cambridge, MA, 1995.

RF91   R. Farrow. *UNIX System Security: How to Protect Your Data and Prevent Intruders*, Addison-Wesley, Reading, MA, 1991

RP92   R. Perlman. *Interconnections: Bridges and Routers*, Addison-Wesley, Reading, MA, 1992.

RS97a   R. Summers. *Secure Computing: Threats and Safeguards*, McGraw-Hill, New York, 1997.

RS97b   R. Smith. *Internet Cryptography*. Addison-Wesley, Reading, MA, 1997.

RSA97   RSA Data Security, Inc. "Government Encryption Standard DES Takes a Fall." *RSA Data Press Release*, June 17, 1997.

SB96   S. Bradner and A. Mankin. *IPng: Internet Protocol Next Generation*. Addison-Wesley, Reading, MA, 1996.

SG96 S. Garfinkel and G. Spafford. *Practical Unix & Internet Security.* O'Reilly & Associates, Sebastopol, CA, 2nd edition, 1996.

SG97 S. Garfinkel and G. Spafford. *Web Security & Commerce.* O'Reilly and Associates, Cambridge, MA, 1997.

SL84 S. Levy. *Hackers: Heroes of the Computer Revolution,* Doubleday, New York, 1984.

ST92 Bruce Sterling, *The Hacker Crackdown: Law and Disorder on the Electronic Frontier,* Bantam Books, New York, 1992.

TB91 T. Beth, M. Frisch, and G. Simmons, eds. *Public Key Cryptography: State of the Art and Future Directions.* Springer-Verlag, New York, 1991.

TM92 T. Madron. *Network Security in the 90s: Issues and Solutions for Managers,* Wiley, New York, 1992.

WC94 W. Cheswick and S. Bellovin. *Firewalls and Internet Security: Repelling the Wily Hacker.* Addison-Wesley, Reading, MA, 1994.

WF94 W. Ford. *Computer Communications Security: Principles, Standard Protocols, and Techniques,* Prentice Hall, Englewood-Cliffs, NJ, 1994.

WF97 W. Ford and M. Baum. *Secure Electronic Commerce: Building the Infrastructure for Digital Signatures and Encryption,* Prentice Hall, Englewood Cliffs, NJ, 1997.

WJ00 W. Jansen and T. Karygiannis, *NIST Special Publication 800–19–Mobile Agent Security.*

WRC94 W.R. Cheswick and S.M. Bellovin. *Firewall and Internet Security.* Addison-Wesley, Reading, MA, 1994.

WS93 W. Stevens, *Advanced Programming in the Unix Environment,* Addison-Wesley, Reading, MA, 1993.

WS94 W. Stevens. *TCP/IP Illustrated, Volume 1: The Protocols.* Addison-Wesley, Reading, MA, 1994.

CONFERENCE PROCEEDINGS AND JOURNALS

AB82 A. Birrell, R. Needham, and M. Schroeder. Grapevine: An exercise in distributed computing, *Communications of the ACM,* Vol 25 #4, April 1992.

ADB86 A.D. Birrell, B.W. Lampson, R.M. Needham, and M.D. Schroeder. A global authentication service without global trust, *Proceedings of the 1986 IEEE Symposium on Security and Privacy,* IEEE Computer Society Press, Oakland, CA, April 1986, pp. 223–230.

AJ97 A. Jurisic and A. Menezes. Elliptic curves and cryptography. *Dr. Dobb's Journal,* April 1997.

AR97 A. Rubin. An experience teaching a graduate course in cryptography. *Cryptologia,* April 1997.

AS88   A. Shimizu and S. Miyaguchi. Fast data encipherment algorithm FEAL, *Advances in Cryptography-Eurocrypt 87*, Lecture Notes in Computer Science, Vol 304, Springer-Verlag, Berlin, 1988.

BAL91   B.A. LaMacchia and A.M. Odlyzko. Computation of discrete logarithms in prime fields, *Designs, Codes, and Cryptography*, 1, 1991, pp. 46–62.

BBE92   Bennett, C.H., G. Brassard, and A. K. Ekert. Quantum cryptography, *Scientific American*, October 1992, pp. 50–57.

BD89   B. Den Boer. Cryptanalysis of FEAL, *Advances in Cryptology-Eurocraft 88*, Lecture Notes in Computer Science, Vol 330, Springer-Verlag, Berlin, 1989.

BD92   B. Den Boer and A. Bosselaers. An Attack on the last two rounds of MD4, *Advances in Cryptology—CRYPTO '91 Proceedings*, Springer-Verlag, Berlin, 1992, pp. 194–203.

BL73   B. Lampson. A note on the confinement problem, *Communications of the ACM*, Vol 16 #10, October 1973, pp. 613–615.

BL74   B. Lampson. Protection, *ACM Operating Systems Review*, Vol 8 #1, January 1974, pp. 18–24.

BL91   B. Lampson, M. Abadi, M. Burrows, and E. Wobber. Authentication in distributed systems: theory and practice, *Proceedings of the 13th ACM Symposium on Operating System Principles*, October 1991.

BSK88   B.S. Kaliski, R. Rivest, and A. Sherman. Is the data encryption standard a group? (results of cycling experiments on DES), *Journal of Cryptology*, Vol 1, 1988, pp. 3–36.

CB93   C. Boyd. Multisignatures revisited, *Cryptography and Coding III*, M.J. Ganley, ed., Clarendon Press, Oxford, 1993, pp. 21–30.

CC98   Christian Collberg, Clark Thomborson, and Douglas Low. Manufacturing cheap, resilient, and stealthy opaque constructs. In *SIGPLAN-SIGACT POPL'98.* ACM Press, San Diego, CA, January 1998.

CCITT   *Recommendations X. 509: The Directory: Authentication Framework*, 1989. CCITT Blue Book, Volume VIII, Fascicle VIII.8.

CEL94   C.E. Landwehr, A.R. Bull, J.P. McDermott, and W.S. Choi. A taxonomy of computer program security flaws, with examples. *ACM Computing Surveys*, 26 (3), 1994.

CF84   Cohen, Fred, Computer viruses: theory and experiments, *Proceedings of the 7th National Computer Security Conference*, pp. 240–263, 1984.

CI90   C. I'Anson and C. Mitchell. Security defects in CCITT recommendation X.509: the directory authentication framework. *Computer Communications Review*, April 1990.

CN97   C. Nachenberg. Computer virus–antivirus corevolution. *Communications of the ACM,* January 1997.

CS48   C. Shannon. A mathematical theory of communication, *Bell System Journal,* Vol 27, 1948, pp. 379–423 and 623–656.

DB85   D. Baleson. Automated distribution of cryptographic keys using the financial institution key management standard, *IEEE Communications,* Vol 23 #9, September 1985, pp. 41–46.

DC87   D.R. Clark and D.R. Wilson. A comparison of commercial and military computer security policies. *Proceedings of the 1987 IEEE Symposium on Security and Privacy,* pp. 184–194, 1987.

DC94   D. Coppersmith. The data encryption standard (DES) and its strength against attacks. *IBM Journal of Research and Development,* May 1994.

DCF89   D.C. Feldmeier and P.R. Karn. UNIX password security—ten years later, *Advances in Cryptology–CRYPTO '89 Proceedings,* Springer-Verlag, Berlin.

DD84   D. Davis, R. Ihaka, and P. Fenstermacher. Cryptographic randomness from air turbulence in disk drives, *Advances in Cryptology–CRYPTO '94,* Lecture Notes in Computer Science #839, Springer-Verlag, New York, 1984.

DEB96   D.E. Bell and L.J. LaPadula. Mitre technical report 2547 (secure computer system): Volume II. *Journal of Computer Security,* 4 (2/3) pp. 239–263, 1996.

DED76   D.E. Denning. A lattice model of secure information flow, *Communications of the ACM,* Vol 19 #5, May 1976, pp. 236–243.

DED81   D.E. Denning and G.M. Sacco. Timestamps in key distribution protocols, *Communications of the ACM,* Vol 24 #8, August 1981, pp. 533–536.

DED88   D.E. Denning, T.F. Lunt, R.R. Schell, W.R. Shockley, and M. Heckman. The SeaView security model. In *Proceedings of the 1988 IEEE Symposium on Security and Privacy,* pp. 218–233, 1988.

DF90   D. Framer and E.H. Spafford. The COPS security checker system. In *The Summer Usenix Conference,* Anaheim, CA, 1990.

DF92   D. Ferraiolo and R. Kuhn. Role-based access controls, *Proceedings Volume II, 15th National Computer Security Conference,* 1992.

DFCB   D.F.C. Brewer and M.J. Nash. The Chinese wall security policy. In *Proceedings of the 1989 IEEE Symposium on Security and Privacy,* pp. 206–214, 1989.

DMR79   Dennis M. Ritchie. The evolution of the Unix time-sharing system. *Language Design and Programming Methodology Conference,* Sydney, Australia, September 1979. The conference proceedings were published as *Language Design and Programming Methodology,* Lecture Notes in Computer Science #79, Springer-Verlag, New York, 1980. Reprinted in *AT&T Bell Laboratories Technical Journal* 63 No. 6 Part 2, October 1984, pp. 1577–1593.

DO87   D. Otway and O. Rees. Efficient and timely authentication, *Operating Systems Review*, Vol 21 #1, January 1987, pp. 8–10.

DSS91   Proposed federal information processing standard for digital signature standard (DSS), *Federal Register*, v. 56, n. 169, 30 Aug 1991, pp. 42980–42982.

DSS94   Approval of federal information processing standards publication 186, digital signature standard (DSS), *Federal Register*, v. 58, n. 96, 19 May 1994, pp. 26208–26211.

EB91   E. Biham and A. Shamir. Differential cryptanalysis of DES-like cryptosystems, *Journal of Cryptology*, Vol 4 #1, 1991, pp. 3–72.

EB92   E. Biham and A. Shamir. Differential cryptanalysis of Snefru, Khafre, REDOC-II, LOCI, and Lucifer, *Advances in Cryptology–CRYPTO '91 Proceedings*, Springer-Verlag, Berlin, 1992.

EB93   E. Biham and A. Shamir. Differential cryptanalysis of the full 16-round DES, *Advances in Cryptology–CRYPTO '92 Proceedings*, Springer-Verlag, Berlin, 1993.

FH73   F. Hapgood. The computer hackers, *Harvard Magazine*, October 1973, pp. 26–29 and 46.

FIPS92   Proposed reaffirmation of federal information processing standard (FIPS) 46–1, data encryption standard (DES), *Federal Register*, v. 57, n. 177, 11 Sep 1992, p. 41727.

FIPS94   Proposed revision of federal information processing standard (FIPS) 180, secure hash standard, *Federal Register*, v. 59, n. 131, 11 July 1994, pp. 35317–35318.

GB90   G. Brassard and C. Crepeau. Sorting out zero-knowledge, *Advances in Cryptology–EUROCRYPT '89 Proceedings*, Springer-Verlag, New York, 1990, pp. 181–191.

GP79   G. Popek and C. Kline. Encryption and secure computer networks. *ACM Computing Surveys*, December 1979.

HSJ91   H.S. Javitz and A. Valdes. The SRI IDES statistical anomaly detector. In *Proceedings of the 1991 IEEE Symposium on Research in Security and Privacy*, pp. 316–326, 1991.

HV89   H. Vaccaro and G. Liepins. Detection of anomalous computer session activity. *Proceedings of the IEEE Symposium on Research in Security and Privacy*, May 1989.

JA92   J. Adam. Virus threats and countermeasures. *IEEE Spectrum*, August 1992.

JAG82   J.A. Goguen and J. Meseguer. Security policies and security models. In *Proceedings of the 1982 IEEE Symposium on Security and Privacy*, pp. 11–20, 1982.

JB93   J. Boyar, C. Lund, and R. Peralta. On the communication complexity of zero-knowledge proofs, *Journal of Cryptology*, v. 6, n. 2, 1993, pp. 65–85.

Bibliography

JD00   J. Daemen and V. Rijmen, The block cipher Rijndael, *Smart Card Research and Applications*, LNCS 1820, J.-J. Quisquater and B. Schneier, eds., Springer-Verlag, New York, 2000, pp. 288–296.

JD01   J. Daemen and V. Rijmen. Rijndael, the advanced encryption standard. *Dr. Dobb's Journal*, Vol 26, No. 3, March 2001, pp. 137–139.

JGS88   J.G. Steiner, C. Neuman, and J.I. Schiller. Kerberos: an authentication service for open network systems, *Proceedings of the USENIX Winter Conference*, February 1988, pp. 191–202.

JJT91   J.J. Tardo and K. Algappan. SPX: global authentication using public key certificates, *Proceedings of the 1991 IEEE Symposium on Security and Privacy*, May 1991, pp. 232–244.

JK97   J. Kephart, G. Sorkin, D. Chess, and S. White. Fighting computer viruses. *Scientific American*, November 1997.

JL90   J. Linn. Practical authentication for distributed computing, *IEEE Symposium on Security and Privacy*, Oakland, CA, May 1990.

JM87   J. McLean. Reasoning about security models. In *Proceedings of the 1987 IEEE Symposium on Security and Privacy*, pp. 123–131, 1987.

JM90   J. McLean. The specification and modeling of computer security. *IEEE Computer*, 23 (1) pp. 9–16, January 1990.

JM93   John C. Munson and Taghi M. Kohshgoftaar. Measurement of data structure complexity. *Journal of Systems Software*, 20:217–225, 1993.

KI93   K. Ilgun. USTAT: a real-time intrusion detection system for UNIX. *Proceedings, 1 993 IEEE Computer Society Symposium on Research in Security and Privacy*, May 1993.

LB86   L. Blum, M. Blum, and M. Shub. A simple unpredictable pseudo-random number generator, *SIAM Journal on Computing*, Vol 15 #2, 1986.

LG88   L. Guillou and J. Quisquater. A practcal zero-knowledge protocol fitted to security microprocessor minimizing both transmission and memory, *Advances in Cryptology–EUROCRYPT '88*, Springer-Verlag, Berlin, 1988.

LG97   L. Gong, M. Mueller, H. Prafullchandra, and L. Schemers. Going beyond the sandbox: an overview of new security architecture in the Java Development Kit 1.2. In *USENIX Symposium on Internet Technologies and Systems*, Monterey, CA, December 1997.

LL81   L. Lamport. Password authentication with insecure communication, *Communications of the ACM*, Vol 24 #11, November 1981, pp. 770–772.

MA87   M. Abrams, S. Jajodia, and H. Podell,. eds. *Information Security: An Integrated Collection of Essays.* IEEE Computer Society Press, Los Alamitos, CA, 1995.

MB90   M. Burrows, M. Abadi, and R.M. Needham. A logic of authentication, *ACM Transactions on Computer Systems,* Vol 8 #1, February 1990, pp. 18–36.

MB94   M. Blaze. Protocol failure in the escrowed encryption standard, *Proceedings of the Second ACM Conference on Computer and Communications Security,* November 1994.

MB96   M. Blaze, J. Feigenbaum, and J. Lacy. Decentralized trust management. *Proceedings of IEEE Symposium on Security and Privacy,* May 1996, pp. 164–173.

MEH78   M.E. Hellman. An overview of public-key cryptography, *IEEE Transactions on Communications,* Vol 16 #6, November 1978, pp. 24–32.

MEH79   M.E. Hellman. DES will be totally insecure within ten years, *IEEE Spectrum,* Vol 16, 1979, pp. 32–39.

MEH81   M.E. Hellman and R.C. Merkle. On the security of multiple encryption, *Communications of the ACM,* Vol 24, 1981, pp. 465–467.

MG89   M. Gasser, A. Goldstein, C. Kaufman, and B. Lampson. The digital distributed system security architecture, *Proceedings of the 12th National Computer Security Conference,* NIST/NCSC, October 1989, pp. 305–319.

MG90   M. Gasser and E. McDermott. An architecture for practical delegation in a distributed system, *1990 Symposium on Security and Privacy.*

MOR80   M.O. Rabin. Probabilistic algorithm for primality testing, *Journal of Number Theory,* Vol 12, 1980, pp. 128–138.

MS83   M. Schroeder, A. Birrell, and R. Needham. Experience with Grapevine: the growth of a distributed system, *ACM Transactions on Computer Systems,* Vol 2 #1, February 1984.

NAT91   National Research Council, System Security Study Committee, *Computers at Risk: Safe Computing in the Information Age,* National Academy Press, Washington, D.C., 1991.

NIST91   National Institute of Standards and Technology, *Glossary of Computer Security Terminology.* NISTIR4659, 1991.

NK87   N. Koblitz. Elliptic curve cryptosystems, *Mathematics of Computation,* 48(177), 1987, pp. 203–209.

PD90   P. Denning, ed. *Computers Under Attack: Intruders, Worms, and Viruses,* ACM Press, Addison-Wesley, Reading, MA, 1990.

PJ95   P. Janson and G. Tsudik. Secure and minimal protocols for authenticated key distribution, *Computer Communications Journal,* 1995.

PW89   P. Wallich, Quantum cryptography, *Scientific American,* May 1989, pp. 28–30.

RB93   R. Bird, I. Gopal, A. Herzberg, P. Janson, S. Kutten, R. Molva, and M. Yung. Systematic design of a family of attack-resistant authentication protocols, *IEEE Journal on Selected Areas in Communications,* Vol 11 #5, June 1993, pp. 679–693.

RH94   R. Hauser, P. Janson, R. Molva, G. Tsudik, and E. Van Herreweghen. Robust and secure password/ key change method, *Proc. of the Third European Symposium on Research in Computer Security (ESORICS)*, Lecture Notes in Computer Science, Springer-Verlag, Berlin, November 1994, pp. 107–122.

RJA98   R.J Anderson and F.A.P. Petticolas. On the limits of stenography. *IEEE Journal on Selected Areas in Communications*, 16 (4) pp. 474–481, February 1998.

RJR84   R.R. Jueneman, S.M. Matyas, and C.H. Meyer. Message authentication with manipulation detection codes, *Proceedings of the 1983 Symposium on Security and Privacy*, IEEE Computer Society Press, 1984, pp. 33–54.

RKT93   R.K. Thomas and R.S. Sandhu. A kernelized architecture for multilevel secure object-oriented databases supporting write-up. *Journal of Computer Security*, 2 (2, 3) pp. 231–275, February 1993.

RL94   R. Lee and J. Israel. Understanding the role of identification and authentication in NetWare 4, *Novell Application Notes*, Vol 5 #10, October 1994, pp. 27–51.

RLR78   R.L. Rivest, A. Shamir, and L. Adleman. A method for obtaining digital signatures and public-key cryptosystems, *Communications of the ACM*, Vol 21 #2, February 1978, pp. 120–126.

RLR90   R.L. Rivest. The MD4 message digest algorithm. *Proceedings, CRYPTO '90*, August 1990, Springer-Verlag, New York, 1990.

RLR91   R.L. Rivest. The MD4 message digest algorithm, *Advances in Cryptology-CRYPTO '90 Proceedings*, Lecture Notes in Computer Science 537, Springer-Verlag, New York, 1991, pp. 303–311.

RLR94   R.L. Rivest. The RC5 encryption algorithm. *Proceedings, Second International Workshop on Fast Software Encryption*, December 1994, Springer-Verlag, New York, 1995.

RLR95   R.L. Rivest. The RC5 encryption algorithm. *Dr. Dobb's Journal*, January 1985.

RM78   R. Merkle. Secure communication over insecure channels, *Communications of the ACM*, Vol 21, April 1978, pp. 294–299.

RM79   R. Morris and K. Thompson. Password security: a case history, *Communications of the ACM*, Vol 22, November 1979, pp. 594–597.

RM90   R. Merkle. A fast software one-way hash function, *Journal of Cryptology*, Vol 3 #1, 1990, pp. 43–58.

RM92   R. Molva, G. Tsudik, E. Van Herreweghen, and S. Zatti. KryptoKnight authentication and key distribution system, *European Symposium on Research in Computer Security*, 1992, pp. 155–174.

RM97   R. MacGregor, C. Ezvan, L. Liguori, and J. Han. *Secure Electronic Transactions: Credit Card Payment on the Web in Theory and Practice*. IBM RedBook SG24–4978–00, 1997. Available at www.redbooks.ibm.com/SG244978.

RMD178   R.M. Davis. The data encryption standard in perspective, *IEEE Communications Society Magazine*, Vol 1 #6, 1978, pp. 5–9.

RMN78   R.M. Needham and M.D. Schroeder. Using encryption for authentication in large networks of computers. *Communications of the ACM*, 21 (12) pp. 993–999, 1978.

RMN87   R.M. Needham and M.D. Schroeder. Authentication revisited, *Operating Systems Review*, Vol 21 #1, January 1987, p. 7.

RO97   R. Oppliger. Internet security: firewalls and beyond. *Communications of the ACM*, May 1997.

RRJ85   R.R. Jueneman, S.M. Matyas, and C.H. Meyer. Message authentication, *IEEE Communications*, Vol 23 #9, September 1985, pp. 29–40.

RS77   R. Solovay and V. Strassen. A fast Monte-Carlo test for primality, *SIAM Journal on Computing*, Vol 6., March 1977, pp. 84–85.

RSS 96   R.S. Sandhu, E.J. Coyne, H.L. Feinstein, and C.E. Youman. Role-based access control models. *IEEE Computer*, 29 (2) pp. 38–47, February 1996.

RSS93   R.S. Sandhu. Lattice-based access control models. *IEEE Computer*, 26 (11) pp. 9–19, November 1993.

SA83   S. Akl. Digital Signatures: a tutorial survey. *Computer*, February 1983.

SAB94   S.A Brands. Untraceable off-line cash in wallet with observers, *Advances in Cryptology–CRYPTO '93*, Springer-Verlag, New York, 1994, pp. 302, 318.

SC92   S. Chokhani. Trusted product evaluations. *Communications of the ACM*, 35 (7) pp. 64–76, July 1992.

SF93   S. Fumy and P. Landrock. Principles of key management. *IEEE Journal on Selected Areas in Communications*, June 1993.

SF97   S. Forrest, S. Hofmeyr, and A. Somayaji. Computer immunology. *Communications of the ACM*, October 1997.

SGS92   S.G. Stubblebine and V.D. Gligor. On message integrity in cryptographic protocols, *IEEE Symposium on Research on Security and Privacy*, Oakland, CA, May 1992, pp. 85–104.

SGS93   S.G. Stubblebine and V.D. Gligor. Protecting the integrity of privacy-enhanced electronic mail with DES-based authentication codes, *PSRG Workshop on Network and Distributed Systems Security*, San Diego, CA, February 1993.

SH81   Sallie Henry and Dennis Kafura. Software structure metrics based on information flow. *IEEE Transactions on SoftwareEngineering*, 7(5):510–518, September 1981.

SM88   S. Miyaguchi, A. Shiraishi, and A. Shimizu. Fast data encryption algorithm Feal-8, *Review of Electrical Communications Laboratories*, Vol 36 #4, 1988, pp. 433–437.

SMB89   S.M. Bellovin. Security Problems in the TCP/IP protocol suite. *ACM Computer Communications Review*, 19 (2) pp.32–48, April 1989.

SMB90   S.M. Bellovin and M. Merrit. Limitations of the Kerberos authentication system, *Computer Communications Review*, Vol 20 #5, October 1990, pp. 119–132.

SMB92a   S.M. Bellovin and M. Merrit. Encrypted key exchange: password-based protocols secure against dictionary attacks, *Proceedings of the IEEE Computer Society Symposium on Research in Security and Privacy*, Oakland, CA, May 1992, pp. 72–84.

SMB92b   S.M. Bellovin. There be dragons, *UNIX Security Symposium III*, Baltimore, MD, September 1992, pp. 1–16.

SMB93   S.M. Bellovin and M. Merrit. Augmented encrypted key exchange, *Proceedings of the First ACM Conference on Computer and Communications Security*, November 1993, pp. 244–250.

SMB94   S.M. Bellovin and W. Cheswick. Network firewalls. *IEEE Communications Magazine*, September 1994.

SS91   S. Snapp et al. A system for distributed intrusion detection. *Proceedings, COMPCON Spring '91*, 1991.

SW83   S. Wiesner, Conjugate coding, *Sigact News*, Vol 15, No. 1, 1983, pp. 78–88; original manuscript written circa 1970.

TE85   T. ElGamal. A public key cryptosystem and a signature scheme based on discrete logarithms, *IEEE Transactions on Information Theory*, Vol 31, 1985, pp. 469–472.

TFL90   T.F. Lunt, D.E. Denning, R.R. Schell, M. Heckman, and W.R. Shockley. The SeaView security model. *IEEE Transactions on Software Engineering*, 16 (6) pp. 593–607, 1990.

TM76   T. J. McCabe. A complexity measure. *IEEE Transactions on Software Engineering*, 2(4) pp. 308–320, December 1976.

TM97   T. Markham. Internet security protocol. *Dr. Dobb's Journal*, June 1997.

UF87   U. Fiege, A. Fiat, and A. Shamir. Zero knowledge proofs of identity, *Proceedings of the ACM Symposium on the Theory of Computing*, ACM Press, New York, 1987, pp. 210–217.

VP96   Vir V. Phoha, Rajesh C. Phoha, and Marvin Rosenstein. Control issues in network security. *Annual Review of Communications* 1996 vol. 49 pp. 617–622.

VP98   Vir V. Phoha and Aaron W. Lingbeck. Denial-of-service attacks on the Internet. *Annual Review of Communications* 1998, vol. 52 pp. 691–693.

VP00   Vir V. Phoha. Internet vulnerabilities: exploitation of BIND and named vulnerabilities involving buffer overflows. *Annual Review of Communications* 2000 vol. 53 pp. 696–699.

VV	V. Varadharajan. A security reference model for a distributed object system and its application, *Proceedings, 15th National Computer Security Conference*, 1992.
WD76a	W. Diffie and M.E Hellman. A critique of the proposed Data Encryption Standard, *Communications of the ACM*, vol 19 #3, 1976, pp. 164–165.
WD76b	W. Diffie and M.E. Hellman. New directions in cryptography, *IEEE Transactions on Information Theory*, Vol 22 #6, 1976, pp. 644–654.
WD77	W. Diffie and M.E. Hellman. Exhaustive cryptanalysis of the NBS Data Encryption Standard, *Computer*, Vol 10 #6, 1977, pp. 74–84.
WD79	W. Diffie and M.E. Hellman. Privacy and authentication: an introduction to cryptography, *Proceedings of the IEEE*, Vol 67 #3, March 1979, pp. 397–427.
WD88	W. Diffie. The first ten years of public-key cryptography, *Proceedings of the IEEE*, Vol 7 #5, May 1988, pp. 560–577.
WF95	W. Ford. Advances in public-key certificate standards. *ACM SIGSAC Review*, July 1995.
WH81	Warren A. Harrison and Kenneth I. Magel. A complexity measure based on nesting level. *SIGPLAN Notices*, 16(3), pp. 63–74, 1981.
WVE85	Wim van Eck. Electromagnetic radiation from video display units: an eavesdropping risk? *Computers & Security* 4, 1985, pp 269–286. Elsevier Science Publishers B.V. North-Holland.
YD86	Y. Desmedt and A.M. Odlyzko. A chosen text attack on the RSA cryptosystem and some discrete logarithm schemes, *Advances in Cryptology—CRYPTO '85 Proceedings*, Vol 218 of Lecture Notes in Computer Science, Springer-Verlag, Berlin, 1986, pp. 516–521.

TECHNICAL REPORTS

ADB84	A.D. Birrell. *Secure Communication Using Remote Procedure Calls*, CSL-TR 84–2, Xerox Corporation, Palo Alto Research Center, September 1984.
AS81	A. Shamir. *On the Generation of Cryptographically Strong Pseudo-Random Sequences*, Department of Applied Mathematics, The Weizmann Institute of Science, Rehovot, Israel, 1981
BSK93	B.S. Kaliski and S.A.Burton. *Layman's Guide to a Subset of ASN.1, BER and DER*, Technical Note, revised November 1, 1993.
CF85	Cohen, Fred, *Computer Viruses*, Ph.D. Dissertation, University of Southern California, 1985.
DEB73a	D.E. Bell and L.J. LaPadula. *Secure Computer Systems: Mathematical Foundations*, Report ESD-TR-73–275, MITRE Corp., Bedford, MA, 1973.

DEB73b   D.E. Bell, and L.J. LaPadula. *Secure Computer Systems: A Mathematical Model,* Report MTR-2547, MITRE Corp., Bedford, MA, 1973.

DEB74a   D.E. Bell and L.J. LaPadula. *Secure Computer Systems: Mathematical Foundations and Model,* M74–244, MITRE Corp., Bedford, MA, October 1974.

DEB74b   D.E. Bell and L.J. LaPadula. *Secure Computer Systems:* A Refinement of the Mathematical Model, Report ESD-TR-73–278, MITRE Corp., Bedford, MA, 1974.

DEB76   D.E. Bell and L.J. LaPadula. *Secure Computer Systems: Unified Exposition and Multics Interpretation,* Report ESD-TR-75–306, MITRE Corp., Bedford, MA, 1976

ECMAa   European Computer Manufacturers Association. *Commercially-Oriented Functionality Class for Security Evaluation* (COFC). Technical Report ECMA 205, December 1993.

ECMAb   European Computer Manufacturers Association. *Secure Information Processing Versus the Concept of Product Evaluation.* Technical Report ECMA TR/64, December 1993.

EHS88   E.H. Spafford. *The Internet Worm Program: An Analysis,* Purdue Technical Report CSC-TR-823, Purdue University, November 1988.

ES91   Eugene H. Spafford, *The Internet Worm Incident,* Purdue Technical Report CSD-TR-933, West Lafayette, IN 47907–2004, 1991. Also available from citeseer.nj.nec.com/spafford91internet.html.

HE92   H. Eberle. *A High-Speed DES Implementation for Network Applications,* Digital Systems Research Center, Technical Report #90, Palo Alto, CA, September 1992.

ISP97   DoD 5200.1-R, *Information Security Program* January 1997. (Appendix F: *Equivalent Foreign Security Classifications:* contains equivalent security classifications of many countries). Also available from http://www.fas.org/irp/doddir/dod/5200-1r/appendix_f.htm.

KJB77   K.J. Biba. *Integrity Considerations for Secure Computer Systems,* ESD-TR-76–372, USAF Electronic Systems Division, Bedford, MA, April 1977.

MG76   M. Gasser. *A Random Word Generator for Pronounceable Passwords,* Mitre Corp, Bedford, MA, Report MTR-3006, November 1976.

MOR79   M.O. Rabin. *Digitized Signatures and Public Key Function as Intractable as Factorization,* MIT Laboratory for Computer Science, Technical Report 212, January 1979

OG96   The Open Group, *Generic Cryptographic Service API (GCS-API),* 1996.

RP88   R. Perlman. *Network Layer Protocols with Byzantine Robustness,* MIT Laboratory for Computer Science Technical Report #429, October 1988.

SM87   S. Miller, B. Neuman, J. Schiller, and J. Saltzer. *Kerberos Authentication and Authorization System,* Project Athena Technical Plan, Section E.2.1, MIT Project Athena, Cambridge, MA, December 1987.

SM88   S. Miller, B. Neumann, J. Schiller, and J. Saltzer. *Kerberos Authentication and Authorization System. Section E.2.1, Project Athena Technical Plan*, MIT Project Athena, Cambridge, MA. 27 October 1988.

WEB ARTICLES

CPS   *Certification Practices Statement,* verisign, 1996.
http://www.verisign.com/repository/cps

CS96   C. Semeria. *Internet Firewalls and Security.* 3ComCorp., 1996.
http://www.3com.com

GB94   G. Brassard. *A Bibliography of Quantum Cryptography.*
http://www.cs.mcgill.ca/~crepeau/CRYPTO/Biblio-QC.html

INDEX

A

A1 3, 11, 12, 15, 35, 53

A5 3

Abstract Syntax Notation 1 3

access 3, 4, 5, 6, 7, 8, 9, 11, 12, 13, 15, 16, 21, 22, 34, 27, 30, 33, 34, 35, 37, 40, 41, 43, 46, 47, 51, 52, 53, 56, 58, 61, 62, 64, 70, 79, 79, 80, 83, 84, 86, 88, 90, 91, 95, 99, 100, 102, 103, 106, 111, 112, 114, 115, 117, 118, 119, 120, 121, 123, 124, 125, 126, 130, 132, 133, 138, 140, 142

access control 3, 4, 154, 156, 158, 11, 12, 21, 22 30, 35, 40, 56, 79, 81, 83, 84, 88, 91, 102, 103, 111, 115, 120, 121, 126

access control list 4, 151

access control mechanism 4, 56, 81, 84

access control set 4

access level 4

access list 4

access mode 4

access period 4

access profile 4

access type 4, 142

accessible space 4

accountability 4, 28, 30, 43, 62, 63

accounting legend code 4, 43, 151

accounting number 4

accreditation 4, 16, 17, 120, 154

accreditation package 4, 17

accrediting authority 4, 37, 38

accuracy 5, 62

ACL 5

active 5, 26, 32, 95, 99, 141

active attack 5

active threat 5, 99, 141

add-on security 5

address mask 5, 90, 125

administrative security 5

address resolution 5, 7, 111, 114, 234

Address Resolution Protocol 5, 7, 111, 114, 151, 234

Advanced Encryption Standard 6, 51, 66, 114, 151

Advanced Research Project Agency 6, 7, 152

adversary 6, 26, 46, 62, 70, 103, 108

advisory 6, 12, 158, 233

AES 6, 51, 114, 151

AFIWC 6, 151

Air Force Information Warfare Center 6, 151

ALC 5

alert 6, 27, 51

alternative COMSEC custodian 6

American National Standards Institute 6, 151

American Standard Code for Information Interchange 6

ankle-biter 7

anomaly detection model 7

anonymous electronic cash 7

ANSI 7, 46, 151

antijam 7, 151

antispoof 7

H

hacker 57, 58, 70, 118, 123

hacking 57

hacking run 57

handprint system 57

handshaking procedures 57

hard copy key 57

hardwired key 57

hash 15, 38, 57, 58, 84, 85, 115, 117, 118, 121, 133, 161

hashing 58

hash total 58

hashword 58

header 8, 47, 54, 58, 70, 84, 99, 120, 141

high-risk environment 58

high-threat environment 58

high water mark 58

hoax virus 58

honey pot 52, 58

hop 54, 58, 124

host 5, 7, 9, 11, 13, 16, 23, 27, 30, 37, 42, 47, 52, 55, 58, 66, 68, 80, 85, 87, 90 100, 102, 103, 114, 124, 129, 131, 134

human safety 59, 63

I

IA 61

IAB 61, 67, 69, 156

IANA 61, 67, 156

ICMP 61, 67, 102, 123, 156

IDEA 61, 64, 104, 156

identification 12, 17, 61, 63, 75, 77, 101, 102, 113, 123, 131, 134, 134, 156, 156, 157, 160

identity token 61

identity validation 61

IDIOT 61, 156

IEEE 46, 48, 61, 156

IEEE 1363 standard for public-key cryptography 61

IESG 61, 68, 156

IETF 61, 67, 69, 122, 156

IFCC 61

IGP 61, 64, 96, 115, 156

IKE 61, 156

IMAP vulnerability 61

imitative communications deception 26, 62, 84

impersonation 62, 85

implant 62

implementation 3, 23, 29, 31, 33, 54, 62, 69, 79, 83, 96, 100, 119, 123, 131, 140

import 62

inadvertent disclosure 62

Ina Jo 62

incident 27, 28, 52, 54, 62, 107, 152, 153

incomplete parameter checking 62

indicator 62, 80, 85, 126, 151, 158

individual accountability 30, 62

inference channel 62

information assurance 7, 61, 62, 79, 112, 139, 156

information assurance red team 62, 112

information environment 62

information flow chart 62

information label 62

information level 63

information operations 6, 25, 63, 70, 156

information system 3, 6, 12, 25, 27, 28, 38, 58, 61, 63, 70, 71, 80, 89, 91, 111, 115, 119, 126, 127, 129, 151, 154, 156, 158, 159, 161

information system security 28, 63, 71, 91, 129, 151, 155, 156, 158, 159, 161

information system security equipment modification 63, 28

information system security manager 63, 71, 157

information system security officer 63, 71, 91, 157

information system security product 63, 155

Information Technology Security Evaluation Criteria 63, 71

S